THE McCARTNEY FILE

*A Comprehensive Guide
to his Life and Career*

Compiled by Bill Harry

First published in Great Britain in 1986 by
Virgin Books Ltd, 328 Kensal Road, London W10 5XJ

ISBN 0 86369 157 9

Printed and bound in Great Britain by Richard Clay Ltd
(The Chaucer Press), Suffolk

Typeset by Keyline Graphics, London NW6

Cover and design by Sue Walliker and Ursula Shaw

Cover photos courtesy of
Camera Press, Pictorial Press,
Tom Hanley and Rex Features

Many thanks to EMI and the various press officers for the range of publicity
photographs and album sleeves spanning Paul's career, including the sleeves and
photographs on pages 6/16/18/19/20/22/37/54/78/93/111/117/118/138/139/141/
142/143/145/153/159/160/173/176/179/183/184/185/188. To Tony Riley of Motown
for the Stevie Wonder pic; to 20th Century Fox for 'Give My Regards To Broad
Street'; to Versa Manos of Arista for the Twiggy (p.170) and Jonathan Rowlands
for the Twiggy (p18); to the *Mersey Beat* archives for the early Dick Matthews
photos; to Philip Hall of Stiff Records for the Tracey Ullman's; to Polydor for the
Star Club sleeve; to Virgin Records for the Julian Lennon, Phil Collins, Rupert pics;
to President Records for the Denny Laine pic; to See For Miles for the 'Off The
Beatles Track' cover; to WEA for the Elaine Paige pic; to Paul, Linda, Stephen
Shrimpton and all at MPL; to Bernard Docherty at Rogers & Cowan; to Kathy
Gardner at EMI; to all the Beatle fanzines, particularly the *McCartney Observer,
Club Sandwich, Instant Karma* and *Beatlefan*. Special thanks to Jane Charteris,
Sue Walliker and John Brown at Virgin Books, to Hanson White Publishing for
the Mike McCartney 'Mike Macs White And Blacks' and to Mike McCartney (who
will be famous).
Also thanks to John Halsall at London Features International for the pictures
on pages 12, 25, 29 (Johnny Carson), 34 (John Conteh), 50, 54, 55, 59, 74, 85, 88,
100, 112, 113 and 137.

To the memory of Jim McCartney

Introduction

When journalist Philip Norman came to see me some years ago, he was in a dilemma. He intended writing a biography of the Beatles but had been unable to arrange an interview with a single ex-member. He was considering dropping the project, but I suggested that he interview instead a number of people who had known them well during their early career and gave him dozens of contacts in both Liverpool and Hamburg, many of whom had never been interviewed before regarding their association with the Beatles.

The result was the most detailed and thoroughly researched biography since Hunter Davies' authorised version in 1968. However, although I knew that Philip would be writing with the benefit of hindsight I'd overlooked the fact that, since he hadn't been present at any of the events described in the book, he'd also lack insight. This was most evident in several suppositions he made which almost immediately became treated as fact by writers who used Norman's book for their own research. His assertion that as soon as Brian Epstein laid eyes on John Lennon at the Cavern he fell in love with him is totally inaccurate, for instance.

During the course of Philip's researches, John Lennon died. The book then took on an additional impediment: bias. An author naturally filters his impressions and puts something of himself into his work – but Philip's interpretation of the Beatles story became biased against Paul McCartney. As with so many projects completed after John's death, John was cast as the hero, Paul as the villain.

During the first half of the eighties, I have been called upon a number of times to defend Paul on the radio and in the press because he has been under constant attack in books, newspapers and magazines. For example, the West End play *Lennon* is unfair to Paul, and each new interpretation of the Beatles story attempts to elevate John's participation and reduce Paul's. There have also been a stream of newspaper articles that have presented Paul as mean and mealy-mouthed, by former relatives and associates, such as Angela Williams, Denny Laine and Jo Jo Laine. Add to this the obsession the press seems to have for details of his bank balance whilst ignoring his musical talent and you have single-minded interest in the L.S.Ds rather than the Do-Ray-Mes!

This continual 'knock-Paul' syndrome of the past five years has obviously influenced the critics, which is no doubt why his *Give My Regards to Broad Street* received such a critical bashing. Yet during these years I have had the opportunity of discussing Paul with dozens of fellow artists – and the opinion of his peers is that he is one of the greatest songwriters of the century and a person whose contribution to popular music is inestimable – they range from Kenny Lynch to Barry Manilow, from Wee Willie Harris to Kim Wilde, from Tracey Ullman to Suzi Quatro.

You, the reader, can make up your own mind about Paul. This book merely presents hundreds of facts in a mini-encyclopedia form – but they are facts which contain many stories, taking Paul from his childhood to today. I hope that the cross-referencing within the book and the small subject index at the back will help you to find your way around.

Bill Harry
London 1986

THE McCARTNEY FILE

ABBEY ROAD (1) Album issued in 1969, on 26 September in Britain and on 1 October in America. The tracks written by Paul were: 'Maxwell's Silver Hammer', 'Oh Darling', 'You Never Give Me Your Money', 'She Came In Through The Bathroom Window', 'Golden Slumbers', 'Carry That Weight', 'The End' and 'Her Majesty'.

The photograph on the album sleeve, showing the Beatles walking across the zebra crossing outside Abbey Road Studios, has become one of the most famous rock music images. It has been copied on dozens of other album covers, and tens of thousands of tourists have had photographs taken of themselves striding over the crossing. The idea for the sleeve was Paul's, and the detailed sketch that he made for photographer Iain Macmillan before the picture session is reproduced in Brian Southall's book *Abbey Road* (see *Abbey Road (2)*).

Apart from being imitated and iconised by fans, the *Abbey Road* picture was to assume enormous significance for adherents of the 'Paul Is Dead' (cf) theory, who avidly analysed the cover for so-called 'clues' to support it — and found a liberal sprinkling of them! Most important was the fact that Paul is barefoot in the photograph, which was said to be a Mafia/Grecian (take your pick) sign of death. A Michigan journalist, Fred LaBour, reviewing the album, claimed that the group was leaving a cemetery and that John was dressed as a minister, Ringo as an undertaker and George as a grave-

digger, and pointed out that Paul was out of step with the others, which apparently meant that it was in fact either his corpse, or, more popularly, a substitute who'd had plastic surgery. Proof positive of the imposter theory was the fact that 'Paul' is holding a cigarette in his *right hand* (Macca is left-handed). The reality, of course, was very different, as two quotes from some of those involved demonstrate.

Photographer Iain Macmillan: "Paul turned up in his Oxfam suit and sandals and because it was a hot day he decided to do some shots with the sandals on and some with sandals off. Paul checked all the pictures with a magnifying glass. I don't think the other three were particularly bothered. He chose the nearest shot with the legs stretched in almost uniform style and it was pure coincidence that it happened to be the one with his sandals off. I got the job through John but it was Paul's idea and I was given ten minutes around lunchtime to do it. They came out of the studios, where they were recording, to do it and I managed to take six shots in all."

Paul himself, to DJ Paul Gambaccini: "I just turned up at the photo session. It was a really nice hot day and I think I wore sandals. I only had to walk around the corner to the crossing because I lived pretty nearby. I had me sandals off and on for the session. Of course, when it comes out and people start looking at it and they say: 'Why has he got no shoes on? He's never done that before.' Okay, you've

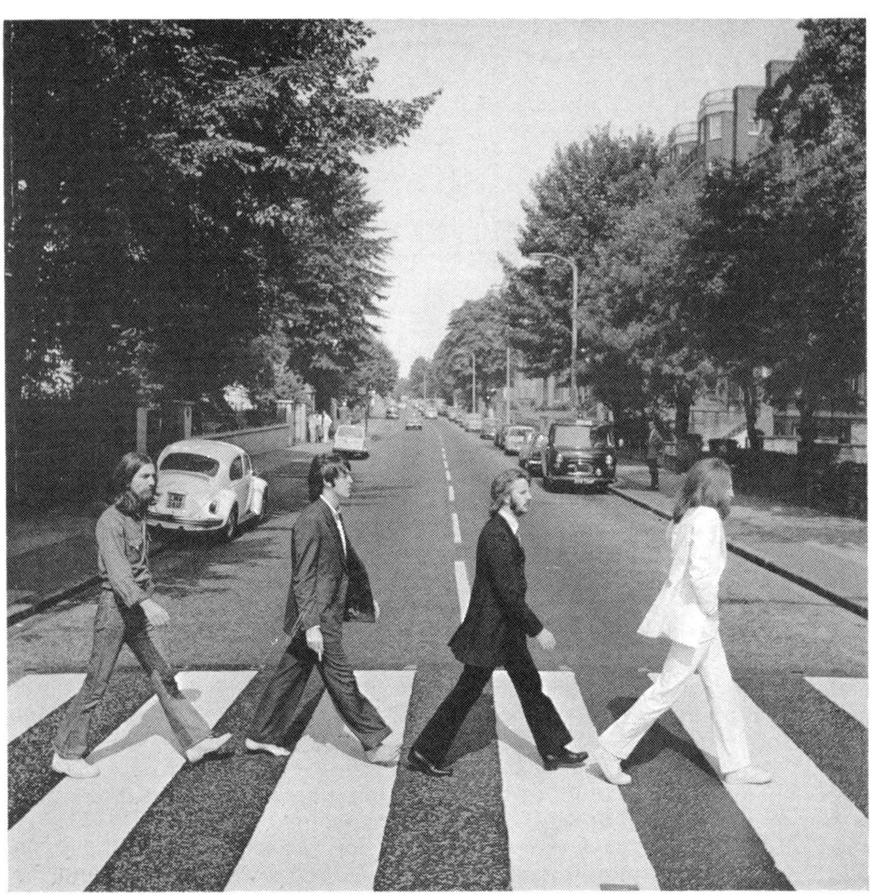

Barefoot and out of step: proof that this was a stand-in for Paul?

never seen me do it before but in actual fact it's just me with me shoes off. Turns out to be some old Mafia sign of death or something."

But 'Paul Is Dead' fanatics were not deterred: in the course of their investigations they also discovered that the registration number (281F) of the Volkswagen car in the photo indicated the age Paul would have been *IF* he had lived, and that the cracked Abbey Road street sign on the back cover was a mystical omen of the split in the group following Paul's 'death'! (See also *Beatles National Lampoon; Campbell, William; Gibbs Russ* and *Shears, Billy*).

ABBEY ROAD (2) Book by EMI Records executive Brian Southall, first published in Britain in 1982 by Patrick Stephens Ltd. In January 1982, Paul wrote a small introduction for it in which he mentioned the nostalgia he felt whenever he used the Abbey Road Studio and how he met Sir Malcolm Sargent and Sir Donald Wolfit on the steps outside. Apart from the portrait illustrating the introduction and the photographs of the Beatles, there are more photographs of Paul in the book than of any other artist.

They include Paul and Linda walking across the famous zebra crossing with their pony Jet; Paul with George Martin (cf) and Norman Smith; Paul drinking a glass of milk; Paul in various disguises for the 'Coming Up' video sessions; giving George Martin a guitar lesson; two further photographs from the 'Coming Up' sessions; two pictures of Paul with boxer John Conteh (cf) and Eamonn Andrews (cf) when the surprise was sprung for Conteh's *This Is Your Life;* Linda and Jet outside Abbey Road; Wings in Scotland with the Campbeltown Pipe Band; four photographs of the Rockestra (cf) sessions; Paul and Linda in the Studio's reception area; Paul and Linda at Vera Samwell's retirement party; Linda with Steve Harley and Denny Laine (cf) at the Studio's 50th Anniversary party.

In a chapter entitled 'Yesterday — McCartney Remembers', Paul reminisces about his time at Abbey Road from 1962 until the present day, and talks about how the Beatles changed the strict formality which existed in the studios at the time, the long hours they spent at recording sessions, the wide range of instruments they could use there and the constant crowds which used to gather outside.

ABRAMS, STEVE In 1967 Steve Abrams was a PhD student at Oxford. The young American was eager to study the effects of marijuana on people to determine whether it was harmless. As it was illegal, he couldn't carry out his research without permission from the Home Office, who referred him to the Chief Constable of Oxford, who refused his request. Steve, nevertheless, went to Chichester to report on the Rolling Stones drug bust trial for *International Times.* When Judge Black sentenced Keith Richards to a year in prison with £500 costs and Mick Jagger to three months with £100 costs, there was a certain amount of sympathy from the public and the national press, both of which felt that the Stones had been unfairly treated. An appeal was lodged and Steve decided to galvanise public opinion even further. Within a matter of hours of the Chichester verdict being given he put into operation an idea he'd had for some time — a full-page advertisement in *The Times* newspaper bearing the signatures of a number of respected people who had an enlightened attitude towards marijuana. He discussed the idea with Miles (of *International Times* and the Indica Gallery) and mentioned the difficulty of obtaining the necessary finance. Miles

approached Paul McCartney and talked him into putting up the money. As it turned out, the bill was paid from the Beatles' advertising account.

The advertisement appeared in *The Times* on 24 July 1967 and began:

The signatories to this petition suggest to the Home Secretary that he implement a five-point programme of cannabis law reform:

1. The Government should permit and encourage research into all aspects of cannabis use, including its medical applications.
2. Allowing the smoking of cannabis on private premises should no longer constitute an offence.
3. Cannabis should be taken off the dangerous drugs list and controlled, rather than prohibited, by a new *ad hoc* instrument.
4. Possession of cannabis should either be legally permitted or at most considered a misdemeanour punishable by a fine of not more than £10 for a first offence and not more than £25 for any subsequent offence.
5. All persons now imprisoned for possession of cannabis or for allowing cannabis to be smoked on private premises should have their sentences commuted.

There were sixty-four signatures within the advertisement in support of the proposal. They included Brian Epstein, John Lennon, Paul McCartney, Ringo Starr, George Harrison, George Melly, David Hockney, David Bailey, David Dimbleby, Kenneth Tynan, Jonathan Miller, R D Laing, painters John Piper and Patrick Procktor, publishers Anthony Blond and Tom Maschler, and Tom Driberg, the MP.

AFTER A FASHION 1983 single by Midge Ure of Ultravox and Mick Karn of Japan. Linda had shown interest in photographing Japan, and Mick invited her to take photographs of the recording session. Linda was to say: "I haven't done anything like this for years. It makes me feel a little nervous. Normally I take pictures out of doors, in natural light. It's only about the fifth time I've ever worked in a studio. Usually my photography is more in the style of Cartier-Bresson, a matter of clicking at the right moment."

Linda began work at 7am and did a number of test shots with Polaroid. After two hours of preparation Linda was ready to take the shots. When the session was over, a buffet lunch – with champagne – was laid on, during which a message arrived: "Enjoy yourselves, all the breast (sic) – after a fashion. Love Paul, and the gang." Paul had left for work two hours earlier than Linda that morning: he was filming *Give My Regards to Broad Street* (cf).

AGAIN AND AGAIN AND AGAIN Song composed by Denny Laine (cf) for the *Back to the Egg* (cf) album. Wings (cf) also performed it on their British tour in 1979, with Denny as lead vocalist.

ALBENTOSA, JAMES Schoolboy from Kent who had been returning from school with his mother and sister in March 1983, when they noticed Paul filming a scene from *Give My Regards to Broad Street* at Teston Locks on the River Medway. The eight-year-old boy struck up a conversation with Paul and told him that he was going to sing 'Oh For The Wings Of A Dove' at his school concert. "He wished me good luck and then started singing the song himself," said James.

ALEXANDER, SIMON A clairvoyant who, in 1980, predicted that Paul and Linda would split up and that Wings (cf) would disband during the course of the year – the former prediction has not yet come true, the latter did the following year.

ALFRED THE GREAT British-made film starring David Hemmings. Paul and Linda attended the première in London's West End on 11 August 1969.

THE ALGARVE Region of Southern Portugal popular with holiday-makers. In his book *The Beatles: Authorised Biography*, Hunter Davies related how Paul, Linda and Heather arrived unexpectedly at his house there. It was December 1968 and the middle of the night; Hunter woke up to hear someone shouting his name very loudly and demanding to be let in. Earlier that evening, back in London, Paul had decided impulsively that he wanted to take up Hunter's open invitation to visit him, and so chartered a jet to fly him, his new girlfriend and her daughter out to Faro, the nearest airport. They stayed about ten days with the Davies', who, as Hunter recalls, were a little bemused, as when they had left England earlier that year (Hunter was on a year's sabbatical after completing *The Beatles)* Paul had been engaged to Jane Asher (cf).

ALL MY LOVING Paul thought up this number while he was shaving one day. He has said: "I wrote 'All My Loving' like a piece of poetry and then, I think, I put a song to it later." The song first appeared on the *With the Beatles* album in November 1963 and was the title track of an EP of the same name in February 1964. It has appeared on many albums, including the American *Meet the Beatles, The Beatles 1962-1966* compilation in 1973, the live *The Beatles at the Hollywood Bowl* in 1977, *The Beatles Collection* in 1978 and the mammoth World Records' *The Beatles Box* and *The Beatles Ballads* in 1980.

The number was also featured in the film *A Hard Day's Night,* and on numerous TV shows including *Sunday Night at the London Palladium, The Ed Sullivan Show* and *With the Beatles.*

It has been recorded by almost a hundred different artists including the Trends, Count Basie, the Chipmunks, Herb Alpert and the George Martin Orchestra.

ALL STAND TOGETHER Song which brought George Martin and Paul together again in the recording studios. The number, penned for a short film about Rupert Bear (cf), was produced by George in his Air Studios on 31 October and 3 November 1980. Paul was backed by the King's Singers and the St Paul's Boys Choir. 'All Stand Together' was eventually released in Britain on Parlophone R6086 on 12 November 1984 and got to No.3 in the charts. The flipside was a humming version of the song, credited to Paul McCartney and the Finchley Frogettes.

ALPIN, KENNY Classmate of Paul's at the Liverpool Institute. Paul once used him as a scapegoat. He'd drawn a rather vulgar sketch of a naked woman for the amusement of his classmates, and had put it in his shirt pocket and forgotten about it. His mother discovered it there before washing the shirt and the embarrassed Paul told her that Kenny Alpin was the artistic culprit. His conscience got the better of him and two days later he confessed.

AMERICAN TOP TEN ROCK IDOLS Poll conducted by the US television programme *American Top Ten* in 1982. On the special edition, the results of viewers' votes were compiled and Elvis Presley came top, Paul came second, and John Lennon third. The full title of the category was: 'The Top Ten Male Performers of the Rock Era'.

AMERICAN MUSIC AWARDS Awards show that was broadcast on American TV on 27 January 1986. Paul had been given the 'Award of Merit'. Satellite transmission beamed him in from London's Hippodrome club where he was presented with the award by Phil Collins (cf). In his acceptance speech Paul thanked a number of people, including "Julian's dad, John." This, of course, was a reference to young Julian Lennon who was in Hollywood participating in the American section of the show.

AMERICAN VIDEO AWARDS Annual event which is the promotional video equivalent of the Oscars. When the awards took place in Los Angeles on 6 April 1983, Paul received a 'Hall of Fame' award. This special tribute was given for his 'outstanding achievement in video'. The award for the Best Soul Video went to 'Ebony and Ivory' and both awards were accepted on Paul's behalf by John Weaver, a producer at Keefco, the company which made 'Ebony And Ivory' and which was established by pop video director Keith McMillan.

AMERSHAM BOYS' HOME Situated in Montserrat (cf), the West Indian island where Paul recorded *Tug of War* (cf), the home is a foster care centre for boys. When Paul was presented with the Ampex Golden Reel Award for the album, he donated the thousand dollar payment that came with it to the boys' home.

AND I LOVE HER Jane Asher was the inspiration for this ballad by Paul, although John gave him a hand with the lyrics. It first appeared on *A Hard Day's Night* in August 1964, followed by the American Capitol EP 'Four By The Beatles'. It next appeared on *The Beatles 1962-1966* in 1978; *The Beatles Ballads* and *The Beatles Rarities* in 1980; and *Reel Music* and *20 Greatest Hits* in 1982. One of the most popular of the Beatle love ballads, it has been recorded by over 300 different artists, covering a range of styles and moods, including Ray Davies, Julie London, Smokey Robinson, Georgie Fame and Connie Francis.

AND THE SUN WILL SHINE Paul Jones single, penned by Robin, Barry and Maurice Gibb and produced by Peter Asher, Jane's brother (cf). The number was issued in Britain on Columbia DB 8379 in March 1968. Paul played drums on the track.

ANDREWS, EAMONN Former Irish boxer who won the Irish Junior Middleweight title. He worked in an insurance office in his native Dublin for a time before moving to London to present the BBC's *Sports Report*. In 1951 he became host of *What's My Line*, a popular television show, before moving in 1964 to Independent Television to host *The Eamonn Andrews Show*, Britain's first late-night chat show. He and his wife Grainne have three children: Emma, Fergal and Niamh

In the sixties he took over as host of Thames Television's series *This Is Your Life*, one of Britain's most popular TV shows, which still has a weekly audience estimated at 20 million. Among the many guests he has spotlighted are Arthur Dooley, George Martin (cf) and John Conteh (cf).

Andrews relates how Conteh came to appear on *This Is Your Life* in his book, *Surprise Of Your Life,* published by Everest Books in 1978. The book sports a backcover colour shot of Andrews with Linda and Paul, which is also reproduced inside in black and white. There is also a photograph of Conteh sitting at a piano with Paul, being surprised by Andrews and his famous 'red' book.

Conteh was twenty-two at the time and had won the World Light Heavyweight Championship title thirty-six days previously. Paul had featured him on his *Band on the Run* (cf) cover and had attended the Championship fight after sending John a telegram reading: "You made me number one. Now you be number one." Because of this, Andrews decided that Paul and Linda could help him to spring the surprise on the new champion. On Wednesday, 6 November 1974, Paul and Linda lured the unsuspecting Conteh to Abbey Road Studios on the pretext that Linda wanted to take some photographs of him and Paul together. Andrews hid behind an acoustic screen; when John was settled at the piano with Paul, he jumped out with his 'red' book and photographer Stan Allen snapped away. Conteh was then driven to the television studios for the programme and a live link was kept open with Abbey Road to enable Paul and Linda to pay their own tribute on the show.

ANNIE Smash hit American musical. Based on the famous 'Little Orphan Annie' comic strip, it was a major stage success on Broadway and in London's West End. *Annie* was also turned into a multi-million dollar musical with Albert Finney starring. Paul purchased the music publishing rights via his MPL (cf) company and took his family to see the musical in both New York and London. He and Linda took thirty-five friends with them to the London première at the Victoria Palace Theatre in May 1978. Paul even bought full-page advertisements in the *Sunday Times* and the *New York Times* to congratulate *Annie's* success.

ANOTHER DAY Paul's first solo single, to which John Lennon reputedly referred in his song 'How Do You Sleep'. The songwriting was credited to Paul and Linda, which caused a slight panic at ATV Music who had spent millions purchasing Northern Songs in a deal that included rights to new material from Paul and John. In a *Rolling Stone* interview with Paul Gambaccini (cf), Paul was to say: "Lew Grade suddenly saw his songwriting concession, which he'd just paid an awful lot of money for, virtually to get hold of John and I, he suddenly saw that I was claiming that I was writing half my stuff with Linda, and that if I was writing half of it she was entitled to a pure half of it, no matter whether she was a recognised songwriter or not. I didn't think that was important, I thought that whoever I worked with, no matter what the method of collaboration was, that person, if they did help on the song, should have a portion of the song for helping me. I think at the time their organisation suddenly thought, 'Hello, they're pulling a fast one, they're trying to get some of the money back', whereas in fact, it was the truth'.

ATV Music instigated legal action, although the matter was eventually settled amicably. Paul wrote to Lew Grade and Lew replied: "I can't remember exactly what it said," commented Paul, "but it was a very nice letter. He's actually okay, Lew, he's all right." The action was dropped and Paul agreed to compensate ATV by making a TV spectacular *James Paul McCartney* (cf) for Grade's company.

'Another Day' was released on Apple R5889 in Britain on 19 February 1971, with 'Oh Woman Oh Why' as the flip. Paul had completed the recording the previous month in New York, backed by Dave Spinozza (guitar), Hugh McCracken (guitar) and Denny Seiwell (drums), in addition to the New York Philharmonic Orchestra. The song topped the British charts. In America it was released on 22 February on Apple 1829 and reached the No.5 position. It was also included on the 1978 album *Wings Greatest.*

ARGUS PRESS The company which launched the *Give My Regards to Broad Street* (cf) computer game on their 'Mind Games' label in February 1985. The game was programmed by a Merseyside firm, Concept Software of Crosby, and five people spent two and a half months on the project. The game became available on Commodore 64 and Spectrum 48K. The blurb on the packet reads: "Seven busy characters, ten lost chords, 15 hours, 48 traffic wardens, 95 London tube stations, 125,720 square feet of London, seven million Londoners, 943 action filled screens. The new single is missing and the band have gone home for the weekend – leaving you just 15 hours to recreate the missing tune. Driving around a full scrolling road map of London and knowing their lifestyles you must find each member of the band and get to the studio on time. Remember the musicians only move around on the Underground. To help you in your search your car computer is linked to the London Transport master computer. Watch out for meanies, wardens and Rath. A great car chase and strategy game full of animation and all wrapped up with McCartney's music. Free inside: Large full-colour map of London showing famous landmarks, tube stations and other information to help you play the game. There are fascinating biographies and colour pics of Paul, Linda, Ringo and other stars of the film who feature in the game. Also included is a colour poster showing actual stills from the film."

ARROW THROUGH ME Track from *Back to the Egg* (cf) only issued as a single in America, on Columbia 1-11070 on 13 August 1979. Co-produced by Paul and Chris Thomas, it had 'Old Siam Sir' on the flip. The track was very unusual because of the absence of guitars. Moog synthesizers and brass instruments had been used to provide the backing. The single reached No.29 in the US charts.

ASHER, JANE Jane's five-year romance with Paul was one of the most publicised affairs of the sixties. She was born in London on 5 April 1946.

Her father, Dr Richard Asher, a specialist in psychic disorders, was consultant in blood and mental diseases at Central Middlesex Hospital in Acton. He died tragically of an overdose of barbiturates and alcohol; his body was found on 26 April 1969. Jane's mother was a professor of classical music at Guildhall School of Music and Drama, and had, coincidentally, taught George Martin (cf) to play the oboe.

Jane and Paul first met on 9 May 1963. The Beatles and Brian Epstein were having a snack in the Royal Court Hotel in Sloane Square, where they were staying while rehearsing at the Royal Albert Hall, when Jane approached them. She told them that she had been asked to write an article about the group for the *Radio Times*. They were all charmed by her, but it was George who seemed to engage most of her attention as she joined them on a trip to journalist Chris Hutchin's flat in the Kings Road. During the course of the next few hours Paul began to show his interest in Jane and the others left him to talk to her alone. Later he took her home and arranged to meet her again. The romance became public when they were snapped by a photographer as they left the Prince of Wales Theatre after seeing Paul Simon's play *Never Too Late*.

Jane lived with her parents in a large house in Wimpole Street and Paul was invited to use a spare room whenever he was in London, an offer he often took up between 1963 and 1966. The couple were then always in the public eye. Jane stretched Paul's appreciation of the arts; they went to the theatre and art galleries together, and holidayed in exotic places. She helped Paul select his new car, a midnight blue Aston Martin DB6, and to find the five-storey Victorian house in Cavendish Avenue in St John's Wood, which he moved to in 1966. She then helped him to decorate it, and even had her own key. She also encouraged him to buy a farm in Scotland, suggesting it would be a good idea for them to have a remote retreat to which they could escape from the pressures of being constantly in the

Paul and Jane – a fairytale romance for the media

public eye. (See *High Park Farm*.)

Jane didn't appreciate the constant hounding by the press and resented being regarded merely as Paul's girl-friend – she had her own career as an actress to pursue. Paul, however, didn't like the idea of Jane being too independent; he wanted her to become a housewife, to settle down and look after the kids when they were married. When she went to Bristol to appear with the Old Vic Company, Paul was furious and wrote the song 'I'm Looking Through You'. But he couldn't keep away and went to Bristol to see her. It was while in Bristol that he got the idea for the song 'Eleanor Rigby' (cf). Jane, in fact, was the inspiration for most of his love songs, including 'Here, There and Everywhere' (cf) and 'And I Love Her' (cf). The press kept urging them to announce a wedding date. Jane would say, "I certainly would be most surprised if I married anyone but Paul", while Paul kept denying engagement plans, even publicly, such as on one of the group's *Ready, Steady, Go!* appearances in March 1964.

Despite such denials, the romance continued, Paul and Jane remaining close and often being seen together in their spare time, although their careers were still very separate.

In 1967 Jane left for a three-month tour of America with the Bristol Old Vic Company. In response to the pre-dictably critical clamour from the media, she said, "They [the press] just don't understand about actresses and the theatre. I've become a publicity freak and this I resent. How do I begin to tell you what it means to an actress who is trying to make it on talent alone?" While in America, Jane cele-brated her twenty-first birthday; Paul flew over to the States to see her performance in *Romeo and Juliet* and attended her birthday party in Den-ver, composing 'Magical Mystery Tour on his way back. Eight months later, on Christmas Day, he proposed and gave Jane an emerald and diamond engagement ring. On 1 January 1968 she visited his family and the couple announced that they intended to get married later in the year. In June they attended the wedding of Paul's brother Mike to Angela Fishwick. The next month the romance was over.

In Jane's absences, Paul had always dated other girls, including folk singer Julie Felix (cf), but it was his affair with an American girl who had come to work for Apple, Francie Schwartz (cf), that proved his undoing. Jane came home to the Cavendish Road house unexpectedly one night when a tour had ended early, and found Schwartz in residence. She drove off in a fury, her mother arriving later to collect her belongings. On 20 July 1968, Jane announced on BBC TV's *Dee Time* that the engagement was off. The couple did meet on one or two occasions shortly after the announcement and Jane was to say: "I know it sounds corny, but we still see each other and love each other, but it hasn't worked out. Perhaps we'll be childhood sweethearts and meet again and get married when we're about seventy."

Jane first became an actress when her parents took their three children to a theatrical agency, thinking it would be fun for them to learn to act. There was Peter, who was two years older than Jane, and Clare, who was two years younger. All three children had striking red hair. Jane's first major acting role was as a deaf mute in the film *Mandy* when she was five. She also appeared in *The Quatermass Experiment* as the little girl who approaches the alien on a canal bank. Her stage debut was at the Oxford Playhouse in *Alice in Wonderland* when she was twelve, two years later becoming the youngest actress to play Wendy in the London production of *Peter Pan*. Throughout her teens she appeared in television dramas such as *The Cold Equations,* and in films such as *The Greengage Summer* and Walt Disney's *The Prince and the Pauper*. During the sixties she appeared regularly on stage, in television and films. Her stage roles included the Broadway production of *The Philanthropist* and many apperances with the Bristol Old Vic. Her films included *The Buttercup Chain, The Masque of the Red Death* and *Henry VIII* and she also appeared in television dramas such as *The*

Stone Tapes.

She met cartoonist Gerald Scarfe in the early seventies and the two became lovers. Their daughter Kate was born on 17 April 1974. Jane had appeared in further parts, including a television production of *Romeo and Juliet* and the movie *The Deep End.* After the birth of Kate she curtailed her acting career for a while, but appeared in the stage version of *Whose Life Is It Anyway?* Two more children were born and she and Gerald were eventually married in 1981. She returned to acting in the eighties with many television appearances, such as with Jeremy Irons, in *Brideshead Revisisted,* with James Fox in *Love Is Old, Love Is New,* a drama about a couple obsessed with the sixties which featured a lot of Beatles music, and with Laurence Olivier in John Mortimer's *A Voyage Round My Father.* Other TV appearances included the costume drama *Hawkmoor* and an episode of *Tales of the Unexpected.* She teamed up with James Fox once again for the film *Runners,* and in 1985 with Ian Holm and Coral Browne for *Dreamchild.* Jane has also been busy with her hobbies, ornate cake decoration and fancy dress, and by 1984 had published three books on the subjects.

ASIMOV, ISAAC The world's most prolific science-fiction author, with over two hundred books to his credit. In one of them, the second volume of his autobiography, he describes how he met Paul in December 1974. Paul had been toying with an idea of a sci-fi film using Wings and had worked out a rough outline about a terrestrial pop group being replaced by alien imposters. He asked Asimov if he would write a story that would be suitable for a screenplay based on the

Tracey Ullman – shared a song with Paul on the very first 'Aspel and Company'

idea. Asimov obliged and Paul paid him. However, Paul wasn't too happy with the rough draft and decided not to use it. He then asked Isaac if he could develop the idea from a piece of dialogue that he'd written himself, but the author said "No."

ASPEL AND COMPANY Chat show series from London Weekend Television, first aired in 1984. Paul was a guest on the very first show, broadcast on Saturday, 9 June. He discussed several subjects with host Michael Aspel, including the origin of his 'Picasso's Last Words' song. "I met Dustin Hoffman and he said could you just write them [songs] like that? He threw me a copy of a magazine story on Picasso, the night before his death, and I wrote this song which went on the *Band on the Run* (cf) album." Aspel asked him if he still had an incentive to write songs these days. Paul answered: "It's just that I like it. I like to sit down with a piano and guitar and just try to write a song." Discussing inspiration, he said. "I just kind of make it up. 'Michelle' – I've never met her. I make it up, that's how I write. George Harrison couldn't understand that." He discussed his children: "When I ask them what they think of my music and they tell me they like it, I think it's because they want to stay up late." He also commented: "At home I'm not famous, I'm just Dad," citing as an example an incident when one of his children turned round to him in Scotland and said, "Are you Paul McCartney?"

Paul then plugged a contest in which viewers were invited to send in a painting of Buddy Holly (cf) to tie in with his 1984 Buddy Holly Week. He then sang Holly's 'That'll Be The Day' with Tracey Ullman (also a guest) (cf) and Michael Aspel.

ASSO Boxer dog owned by Peter Eckhorn, manager of Hamburg's Top Ten Club. Nicknamed 'the hound from Hell', he was a fierce animal who attacked musicians as they attempted to traverse a narrow passageway from the main street to the club interior. Apart from biting Paul McCartney, the beast also sank its teeth into Alex Harvey and Dave Berry. Asso died from a heart attack while pursuing yet another musician!

ATLANTIS Single by Donovan (cf), produced by Mickie Most and issued on 22 November 1968 on Pye 7NI7660. Paul played tambourine and also provided backing vocals on the track.

ATTENTION Number penned by Paul for Ringo's *Stop and Smell the Roses* album. Paul provides some backing vocals and plays bass guitar and piano.

THE BABY Nickname which the Exis (Existentialists) gave to Paul during the Beatles first trip to Hamburg. The 'Exis' were the students who attended their gigs and who included Astrid Kirchherr. They called George 'The Beautiful One' and John 'The Sidie Man.'

BABY FACE Paul recorded this number during his trip to New Orleans in 1975. He was backed by Wings and the Tuxedo Brass Band and the recording session was filmed for *The Sound of One Hand Clapping,* one of Paul's film projects that has never been released.

BABY'S REQUEST The last track on the *Band on the Run* album (cf). The number was also issued as the flipside of the August 1979 single 'Getting Closer' (cf). 'Baby's Request', a two-and-a-half minute track, was one of the songs used in the 'Back to the Egg' (cf) promotional video. It has been said that Paul originally wrote the number for an MOR act called the Mills Brothers to record.

BABY, YOU'RE A RICH MAN Song issued as the flipside of 'All You Need Is Love' and which had a similar genesis to 'A Day In The Life' (cf). Two separate songs, one by John, one by Paul, were fused together. The number penned by John had been called 'One Of The Beautiful People' and the song by Paul, 'Baby, You're A Rich Man'. It was said that the numbers had been merged to provide a song for the *Yellow Submarine* film, but was then rushed out as the 'B' side to a single. The song is, in fact, heard only in part in *Yellow Submarine*.

BACK IN THE USSR Paul originally wrote this song for a television documentary about Twiggy (cf) which didn't come off. It was a fusion of Beach Boys style with a little of Chuck Berry's 'Back In The USA' thrown in. As Twiggy didn't use the number, it was used to open *The Beatles* white album. Paul handled the lead guitar honours on the track while John and George played bass. The number also appears on *The Beatles 1967-1970* album, the 1980 *Rock and Roll Music* compilation and on the *Beatles Box* set.

Twiggy – 'Back In The USSR' was written for her proposed TV documentary

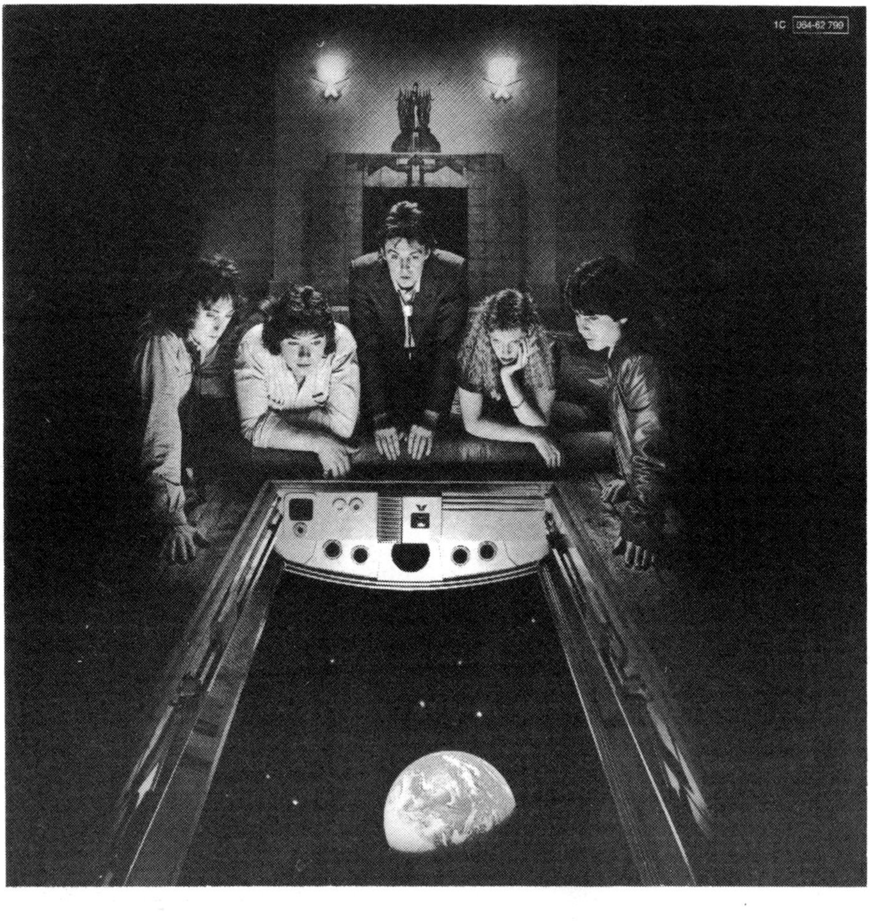

'Back to the Egg' album cover – one of many designed by Hipgnosis

THE BACK SEAT OF MY CAR A track from *Ram* which was issued as a single on Apple R5914 on 13 August 1971 with the credit 'Paul And Linda McCartney'. 'Heart Of The Country' was the flip. The record failed to make as much impact as Paul's previous single 'Another day' (cf), issued earlier that year, only reaching No.39 in the British charts, and thus not even registering in a number of the music papers, which only carried a Top 30 chart at the time. It wasn't released at all in America.

BACK TO THE EGG Album produced during 1978 and 1979 by Paul and Chris Thomas at several locations, including the Spirit of Ranachan Studio (see *Rude Studios)* in Scotland, Lympne Castle in Kent and The Replica Studio (cf) and EMI Studios in London. Engineer on the sessions was Phil McDonald, assisted by Mark Vigars. It was released in 1979, in Britain on Parlophone/MPL PCTC 257 on 8 June and in America on Columbia FC 36057 on 24 May, the first Wings album to be issued on that label. *Back to the Egg* reached No.4 in Britain and No.8 in America.

A special half-hour promotional video was made to accompany the album. The album cover featured a fantasy scene, designed by Hipgnosis (cf) and depicting Wings in a small living-room peering at a space in the floor through which the planet Earth could be seen hovering. The album featured two tracks from the supergroup Rockestra: 'Rockestra Theme' and 'So Glad To See You Here'. The other tracks were: Side one; 'Reception', 'Getting Closer', 'We're Open Tonight', 'Spin It On', 'Again And Again And Again', 'Old Siam Sir', and 'Arrow Through Me'; Side Two; 'To You'; 'After The Ball', 'Million Miles', 'Winter Rose', 'Love Awake', 'The Broadcast', and 'Baby's Request'.

BACKWARDS TRAVELLER/CUFF LINK Track featured on *London Town* (cf). It was also used as the flipside of the 'With A Little Luck' (cf) single, issued a week prior to the album on 23 March 1978. Paul plays drums on the track.

BAILEY, DAVID Britain's best-known contemporary photographer. Bailey was one of the varied group of talented people who came to the fore as part of the 'Swinging London' scene in the sixties. He reviewed Linda's work when her book *Photographs* was published in 1982 and commented: "If Linda would stop taking snaps of Paul, she could take more real photos, ones that are worth taking. Who wants to see a picture of someone's bloke in the bath? The fact that he's a famous face doesn't make it a picture. If Linda wants to be really good she'll have to work at it all the time. There's no such thing as a good part-time photographer. She's no technician but her more formalised pictures show she has got the talent. You can tell her photos are women's photographs – there's a certain softness in the approach. Why are the best photographers men? Well, it's a tough job and physically exhausting. I'm enjoying her new book – it's much better than the first one. Now all she's got to do is buy a large tripod and look through it, concentrating on taking photographs, not family snaps."

Bailey could be said to be guilty of the same thing, as he often used photographs of his then wife, model Marie Helvin, as the dominant feature in his books, particularly in *Trouble and Strife*.

BAKER, CHERYL Blonde singer with the British hit band Bucks Fizz (named after a concoction of champagne and orange juice). In December 1983 on her way to a recording session, she was caught in a traffic jam. Paul happened to be in the car next to hers and they began to chat. Paul asked for her autograph and she arrived late for her session!

BAKER, CELIA Clothes designer who, together with Tony Walker, made and designed the costumes for Wings first major tour. The only stipulation they were given was that both Paul and Linda wanted the costumes to be in the same colours as those featured on the *Venus and Mars* album sleeve: red, yellow, black and white. Celia and Tony had three weeks in which to complete the entire project.

THE BALLAD OF JAMES PAUL McCARTNEY Track written and recorded by David Peel and featured on his album *Bring Back the Beatles*, issued in America on Orange 004 in 1977.

BALLAD OF PAUL Record by Mystery Tour with 'Ballad Of Paul (Follow The Bouncing Ball)' on the flip. A novelty disc issued on MGM 14097 in 1969.

BAND ON THE RUN Issued in 1973, in Britain on Apple PAS 10007 on 30 November and in America on Apple SO 3415 on 5 December, this was the first to top the charts on both sides of the Atlantic and the first Wings LP to go platinum. There were initial difficulties when Paul set off to record the album in Nigeria. Five days before they were due to leave Henry McCul-

A host of celebrities trapped by a searchlight

lough (cf) resigned from the band and then three hours before the plane was due to take off Denny Seiwell (cf) abruptly announced his departure. Paul, Linda and Denny Laine (cf) nonetheless flew out to Lagos and recorded tracks in two studios there – the EMI studios and Ginger Baker's ARC Studios. There was some bad feeling when Nigerian musicians (see *Ransome-Kuti, Fela)* suggested that Paul was trying to capitalise on African music, but Paul had no intention of 'ripping off' the local style. In fact, on their return to London they had percussion added to the 'Bluebird' track at AIR Studios by Remi Kabaka who, by coincidence, had been born in Lagos – but he was the only African musician on the album. Faced with the last-minute defection of two of his musicians, Paul improvised by playing several instruments himself, including guitar, bass drums and synthesisers. Orchestral backings were added at AIR Studios by Tony Visconti, who also did some arrangements. The album was produced by Paul with the help of engineer George Emerick.

The tracks on the album are: 'Band On The Run', 'Jet', 'Bluebird', 'Mrs Vandebilt', 'Let Me Roll It', 'Mamunia', 'No Words', 'Picasso's Last Words' and 'Nineteen Hundred And Eighty Five'. Rumour has it that the title track was inspired by a remark George Harrison made about the problems at Apple: "If we ever get out of here."

'Picasso's Last Words' (see *Aspel and Company)* was inspired by the Spanish painter's last words from his deathbed: "Drink to me, drink to my health, you know I can't drink alone." It has also been suggested that Paul took a slightly satirical dig at John Lennon on the 'Let Me Roll It' track. Paul cowrote 'No Words' with Denny Laine and composed the rest of the material himself.

The album spawned three hit singles. 'Helen Wheels' (cf) had been included on the American album but not the British one and was a chart single in the UK. 'Jet' and 'Band On The Run' became hit singles in both Britain and America.

For the *Band on the Run* cover Paul gathered together several celebrities to pose with him, Linda and Denny. The group included James Coburn, MP Clement Freud, chat show host Michael Parkinson, singer Kenny Lynch, horror star Christopher Lee and Liverpool boxing champion John Conteh (cf). All are caught cowering in the beam of a powerful spotlight

BARRY STERN GALLERY Gallery in Sydney, Australia, where an exhibition of Linda's photographs was on display from 23 July to 12 August 1983.

THE BEATLES Double album, released in November 1968 and often called *The White Album* because of its

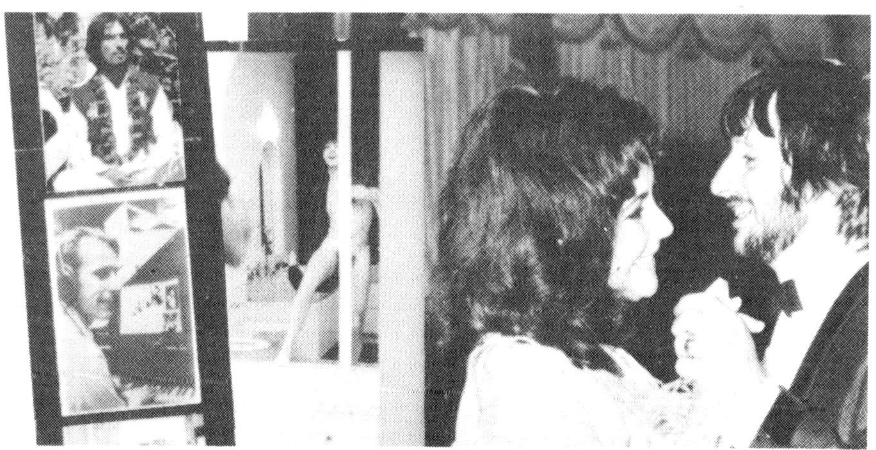

Part of the montage poster included with 'The Beatles' white album, showing Paul's controversial 'nude' pose

The same poster sported this 'nude' of John

plain white cover. It contained several numbers written by Paul. They are: 'Back In The USSR', 'Martha My Dear', 'Blackbird', 'Ob-La-Di, Ob-La-Da', 'Wild Honey Pie', 'Rocky Racoon', 'Why Don't We Do It In The Road', 'Mother Nature's Son', 'Honey Pie', 'I Will' and 'Helter Skelter'. He also co-wrote 'Birthday' with John. Included with the album were four colour shots of the individual Beatles and a large poster with a montage of photographs. A minute photograph of Paul, completely nude, although discreetly posed behind a white column, caused an outcry in the British press at the time, although a larger photograph of John in the nude on the same poster was virtually ignored.

THE BEATLES AT THE BEEB The Beatles performed 88 different songs for BBC radio in the sixties. The numbers on which Paul McCartney sang lead vocals were: 'All My Loving'; 'And I Love Her'; 'Beautiful Dreamer'; 'Besame Mucho'; 'Can't Buy Me Love'; 'Clarabella'; 'Dream Baby'; 'The Hippy Hippy Shake'; 'The Honeymoon Song'; 'I'll Follow The Sun'; 'I'm Gonna Sit Right Down And Cry (Over You)'; 'I Saw Her Standing There'; 'Kansas City'; 'Hey! Hey! Hey!'; 'Long Tall Sally'; 'Love Me Do'; 'Lucille'; 'The Night Before'; 'Ooh! My Soul'; 'PS I Love You'; 'She's A Woman'; 'Sure To Fall (In Love With You)'; 'A Taste Of Honey'; 'That's All Right Mama'; 'Things We Said Today'; 'Till There Was You' and 'Young Blood'.

THE BEATLES BREAK-UP Paul began proceedings to dissolve the Beatles partnership because of advice from his legal representative John Eastman, his brother-in-law, that it would be the only way he could break away from Allen Klein, who had been appointed manager of Apple's affairs over Paul's protests. Paul had orginally wanted Eastman & Eastman, his in-law's family law firm, to represent Apple, but the other members of the group disagreed. Paul, however, felt very strongly about Klein. There were many decisions, apart from financial ones, which upset Paul. Klein, for instance, brought in Phil Spector to remix the *Let It Be* tapes. This interfered with the artistic control the Beatles had over their own product. It was most obvious in Paul's case when Spector completely altered the atmosphere of 'The Long And Winding Road' (cf) by adding lush strings, lots of voices, the usual Phil Spector 'Wall of Sound'. In other words, he was imposing his own particular style over Paul's music without Paul having any say in the matter.

The legal partnership as it stood had originally been set up in April

1967. In 1969 John had privately announced that he would not work with the Beatles again and was annoyed when Paul made a public statement in a newspaper in April 1970 to the effect that the Beatles had ceased to exist as a group. In an interview with *Rolling Stone* magazine in December 1970, John said that Paul's attempts to dominate the group had led to its break-up. He said that all the other members of the Beatles had "got fed up being side men for Paul."

The writ eventually issued by Paul was: "A declaration that the partnership business carried out by the plaintiff and the defendants under the name of 'The Beatles and Co' and constituted by a deed of partnership dated 19 April 1967, and made between the parties hereto ought to be dissolved and that accordingly the same be dissolved."

During the course of the case, Paul was able to point out how Klein had tried to cause discontent and had told him over the phone: "You know why John is angry with you? It is because you came off better than he did on *Let It Be.*" Klein also said to him: "The real trouble is Yoko. She is the one with ambition." Paul said, "I often wonder what John would have said if he had heard that remark."

David Hurst, QC, acting for Paul, said that Allen Klein had instructed his accountants not to give Paul information about the group's finances. "He is a man of bad commercial reputation. Mr McCartney has never either accepted him as manager or trusted him. And on the evidence his attitude has been fully justified." The reasons put forward for the dissolution were: (1) The Beatles had long since ceased to perform together as a group, so the whole purpose of the partnership had gone. (2) In 1969, Mr McCartney's partners, in the teeth of his opposition and in breach of the partnership deal, had appointed Mr Klein's company Abkco Industries Ltd as the partnership's exclusive business managers. (3) Mr McCartney had never been given audited accounts in the four years since the partnership was formed.

BEATLES NATIONAL LAMPOON Special Beatles edition of the American humorous magazine, issued in October 1977, with a cover depicting the Fab Four squashed flat on the Abbey Road zebra crossing by a passing steam roller. Among the features is a satire of the 'Paul Is Dead' (cf) affair, entitled 'He Blew His Mind Out In A Car: The True Story Of Paul McCartney's Death', which relates how, on the morning of 18 January 1967, Paul left a party at Guildford, Surrey. Hours later his body was found in the wreck of the car, having been garrotted, stabbed and shot several times. There is a double-page photograph showing his body on a mortuary slab with a bruise on the temple, knife in the chest and tire marks across his stomach and shins. Such black humour was probably the best response to the absurdities of the 'Paul Is Dead' affair.

BEATLE, PAUL McCARTNEY Magazine published in America in 1964 by SMH Publications. It was part of a series of separate publications on each member of the band.

BEAUTIFUL BOY The John Lennon song featured on the *Double Fantasy* album. When Paul made his selection of favourite records for the *Desert Island Discs* (cf) programme, he chose this song as his favourite and added, "It's very moving."

BE-BOP-A-LULA Major hit single for Gene Vincent in the fifties and the first record which Paul ever bought. (See also *Desert Island Discs*).

BEES IN MY BONNET Book by Angus MacVicar, published in 1983. The author claims that the Mull of Kintyre which Paul refers to in his song (cf) is not the actual rugged Mull itself, but a softer stretch of coast twenty-five miles away. He mentions that a local piper had composed a tune called 'Mull Of Kintyre' long before Paul's number was written.

BEDE GALLERY Situated in Springwell Park, Jarrow, the gallery ran an exhibition of Linda's photographs from 9 February to 6 March 1983.

Old friend Cilla Black: she began her career singing numbers by Paul

BIRTHDAY Song penned jointly by John and Paul at the latter's house in Cavendish Avenue. They had cut short a recording session because they wanted to rush back to Paul's place to watch the movie *The Girl Can't Help It*. Later, they wrote the number. John and Paul sang the song together, with Paul playing piano on the track, although the instrument had been adjusted to sound like an electric harpsichord. The number was included on their white album, *The Beatles*.

BLACK, CILLA Priscilla Maria Veronica White was a typist for a Liverpool cable company at the age of 17, used to work occasionally at the Zodiac coffee club in the evenings (the stories about her being the Cavern cloakroom girl were greatly exaggerated as she only unofficially helped out once or twice) and also sang with some local bands. It was a mistake in the *Mersey Beat* newpaper which christened her Cilla Black. At the age of 20 she signed with Brian Epstein and found fame on the wave of euphoria which swept Britain when Beatlemania was born. Her first single was Paul's composition 'Love Of The Loved', which was issued on Parlophone R5065 on 27 September 1963. It didn't fare too well considering it was a Beatles number and the group were riding a crest of a wave, but it did manage to creep to No.35 in the charts. Cilla's biggest hits came with Bacharach and David numbers such as 'Anyone Who Had A Heart' and 'You're My World', both topping the charts. Her fourth release was another Paul-penned song 'It's For You', issued on Parlophone R5162 on 31 July 1964 reaching No.7 in the British charts. It was issued in America on Capitol 5258 on 27 August, reaching No.79 in the US charts. Her third Paul song was one which he composed for her television series. Entitled 'Step Inside Love', it was issued on Parlophone R5674 on 8 May 1968 and reached No.8 in the British charts. It was issued in America on Bell 726 on 6 May, but made no impact.

On Paul's fortieth birthday, Cilla sent him a telegram which read: "Life begins at 40, what the 'ell 'ave you been doing all these years?"

THE BLACKBOARD JUNGLE Famous fifties' film starring Glenn Ford and Sidney Poitier which featured the Bill Haley number 'Rock Around The Clock'. When Paul was sixteen he went along to see the film with George Harrison, who was only fifteen. To make George look a little bit older and thus ensure his entrance to the cinema, they went into the back garden to get some mud to put on George's upper lip to give the impression of a moustache!

BLACK DYKE MILLS BAND Famous British brass band of international repute, with whom Paul recorded his composition 'Thingumybob', the theme tune of London Weekend Television's comedy series of the same name (cf). On 30 April 1968, a Sunday afternoon, he went to Bradford in Yorkshire to record the single, which he also arranged. The band, conducted by Geoffrey Brand, also produced an instrumental version of 'Yellow Submarine' for the flip, which Paul produced. The single was issued in Britain on Apple 4 on 6 September 1968, but failed to register in the charts. In America, 'Yellow Submarine' became the 'A' side when the disc was issued on Apple 1800 on 26 August 1968. Although the band never recorded for the Apple label again, Paul was to feature them on a Wings album over a decade later, in 1979, when they performed on 'Winter Rose' and 'Love Awake' for *Back to the Egg (cf)*.

BLANKIT'S FIRST SHOW 1985 film short from MPL (cf) in which Linda relates the story of Blankit, son of the Appaloosa pony that she had bought in Texas in the seventies (see *Lucky Spot*). The movie shows Blankit at Parkhurst Stables with his trainer Peter Larrigan and follows the horse on his first show in front of judges. Included on the soundtrack are songs such as 'The Man', 'Sweetest Little Show', 'All You Horse Riders', 'The Other Me' and 'Hey Hey'.

BLUEBIRD Song penned by Paul and included on the 1973 album *Band on the Run* (cf). Paul first perfomed the number with Linda two years previously on a live radio interview in New York. 'Bluebird' was one of the numbers in the repertoire of the 1975/76 world tour and was also included on the *Wings Over America* (cf) album.

BLUE JEANS British teen weekly which ran a McCartney 'Likes And Dislikes' feature in 1980. Paul revealed that 'Lucille' was his favourite song, that he drank rum and coke, enjoyed steak and chips and rated the Marx Brothers' *A Day At The Races* as one of his favourite movies. His film star favourites were Humphrey Bogart, Woody Allen and Jack Lemmon, and his favourite colours were black and dark blue.

BOGEY MUSIC Track on *McCartney II* (cf). The number was written after Paul had been introduced to the popular British children's book *Fungus the Bogeyman,* a most unusual creation by Raymond Briggs. Bogeydom exists in dank, subterranean tunnels where Fungus lives with his wife Mildew and son Mould in a place of filth and slime.

BOIL CRISIS Punk song written by Paul after he'd seen an 'Oil Crisis' headline in a newspaper.

THE BONZO DOG DOO DAH BAND, Highly individual, eccentric group of ex-art students who formed a band in 1965. They can be seen in the film *Magical Mystery Tour* performing at Raymond's Revue Bar, a Soho strip club. They also played at the Beatles celebration party at the end of filming, when they were joined by members of the Beach Boys and Fred Lennon, John's dad. In 1968 the group were having problems recording a single called 'I'm The Urban Spaceman', penned by group member Neil Innes. They approached Paul to produce it for them and he agreed. The saxophonist and group's model maker (they included bizarre models in their stage act) Roger Ruskin Spear told journalist Chris Welch in an interview: "We really needed someone we would all respect to produce us, and Paul was asked if he could come down and help us out. We had met him before when we appeared in a scene in the *Magical Mystery Tour.*" Paul turned up for the session at Chappell's recording studio in Bond Street. He showed the bass player Joel Druckman what to play but "he wouldn't

The Bonzo Dog Doo Dah Band: Paul played ukelele with them

play the bass line on the record. In the end he did play some ukelele. He thrashed at it along with Neil Innes and Viv Stanshall, out in the corridor, and you can hear it plucking in the background." Joel had brought a number of names over from America, one of which was Apollo C. Vermouth, and it was decided that Paul would use it as a pseudonym. Roger told Chris: "Of course, it was cleverly leaked to the press that it was really Paul McCartney. He was only with us for a day but it was extraordinary what he achieved."

The record was issued in Britain in October 1968 and reached No.5 in the charts, but didn't make any great impact when it was issued in the States in December. When the album *Urban Spaceman,* which contained the track, was issued in America in June 1969, Paul's name had replaced the Apollo C. Vermouth credit.

BORED AS BUTTERSCOTCH Track on Mike McCartney's 1972 album *Woman* (cf). The number is credited as being written by Mike McGear, Roger McGough and 'Friend'. The 'Friend' was Paul.

BRAINSBY, TONY British publicist who acted as Paul's personal PR for several years in the seventies.

BRATBY, JOHN Fashionable British artist in the fifties and sixties. Paul spent two hours sitting for Bratby in his studio and three portraits were completed. The paintings were shown at Bratby's West End exhibition at the Zwemmer Gallery, which opened on 7 November 1967, with a £350 price tag on each.

BRITISH ROCK & POP AWARDS Annual event in the British music industry, organised by the *Daily Mirror* newspaper and BBC TV's *Nationwide* programme. Paul was presented by DJ Dave Lee Travis with the Outstanding Music Personality of 1979 Award at a special reception at the Café Royal in London's West End in February, 1980.

BRITTON, GEOFF Drummer and karate specialist, Geoff had been in rock

Wings' members Geoff Britton and Jimmy McCulloch: not the best of friends

bands such as the Wild Angels and was teaching karate in Maidstone when he was informed by one of his pupils, Clifford Davies, former manager of Fleetwood Mac, that Paul was holding auditions in London for a Wings drummer to replace Denny Seiwell (cf). On 26 April 1974 Geoff applied and was given an audition at the Albery Theatre, St Martin's Lane, London. He was put on the short list and attended a further audition at a ballroom in Camden. On 16 May he received confirmation that he'd got the job. Unfortunately, there were frictions within the band and Geoff didn't get on well with either Jimmy McCulloch (cf) or Denny Laine (cf); during recordings in New Orleans the following year he was sacked.

BROADWAY AVENUE Situated in Wallasey, L.45, 'over the water' from Liverpool. The McCartney family lived in No.92 for almost two years in 1942 and 1943. Jim and Mary McCartney had moved into the small house with baby Paul, but decided to move back to Liverpool after Mike McCartney was born, because being near the docks the street suffered some of the worst air raids.

BROLLY, BRIAN Managing Director of MPL Communications Ltd (cf) and Paul's business manager for five years from 1974 to 1978 when he resigned. He gave no public statement as to the reason for his resignation but later became a director of Andrew Lloyd Webber's 'The Really Useful Company'.

BROTHER PAUL Disc inspired by the 'Paul Is Dead' (cf) rumour. Issued in the US on Silver Fox 121 in 1969, it was by Billy Shears and the All Americans and had 'Message To Seymour' as the flip.

BROWN, BRYAN Australian actor whose films include *Breaker Morant, Kim* and *Tai Pan.* Brown has also starred in a number of television epics such as *A Town Like Alice* and *The Thorn Birds* (during the filming of which he met British actress Rachel Ward whom he would later marry). Paul was looking for an Australian actor to portray his manager in *Give My Regards to Broad Street* (cf) and picked Brown, commenting: "I had the idea to take some of the elements from my life and to slightly exaggerate or change the facts wherever necessary. So, Stephen Shrimpton (cf), mild-mannered Australian manager of MPL in London, became Steve Stan-

Bryan Brown

ley, tough, outspoken Aussie with a sarcastic streak."

THE BRUCE McMOUSE SHOW, In 1974 Paul worked out several ideas for movies which he wanted to make with the film arm of his MPL (cf) organisation. One of them was to be a television special called *The Bruce McMouse Show,* a documentary of the 1972 Wings tour of Europe that would use actual film clips intercut with animation relating the adventures of a family of mice (Bruce, his wife, Yvonne, and kids Soily, Swooney and Swat) who lived under the stage.

BRYNNER, YUL The late film actor, best remembered for his roles in *The King and I* and *The Magnificent Seven.* Yul presented Paul with a special Ivor Novello Award (cf) at a luncheon in London on 9 May 1980.

CAFE ON THE LEFT BANK The first number recorded by Wings when they arrived at the Virgin Islands for the *London Town* (cf) album sessions.

CALDWELL, IRIS Attractive blonde sister of the late Liverpool Beat group leader Rory Storm, Iris was one of the Liverpool girls who went out with Paul for a while. The romance lasted for twelve months, and for at least six they were serious enough about each other to be what Northerners would call 'going steady'. Iris trained to be a dancer from the age of fifteen and appeared as a showgirl at holiday camps and on variety shows. I remember her appearing on one of the bills at the Tower Ballroom which featured the Beatles and several other Mersey acts. She was wearing a brief costume which highlighted her slim legs in fishnet stockings and Paul couldn't keep his eyes off her. She was seventeen when Paul dated her and when discussing the period in interviews for publications such as *Beatles Monthly,* she commented: "Epstein was not very pleased that I was going out with Paul and I wasn't allowed to go anywhere with the group in case any of their fans saw me. But every night after they'd appeared at the Cavern, Paul would come round to our house

Paul and John with Rory Storm, Iris Caldwell's brother

– and when they went away to Hamburg he used to write me the most fantastic letters which I wish now that I'd kept because they were very funny letters, talking about all the things that happened to them, and sometimes he'd illustrate them with a little cartoon. In those days they had funny names for people and Paul always used to call me 'Harris' and he signed his letters 'Paul McCoombie'. I can remember one letter he'd sent in which he wrote: "We've been down to London jumping around" and he illustrated it with a little picture of himself jumping around on his bum.

"The first song they recorded together after signing with Epstein, 'Love Me Do', was a song that Paul had written for me – and when the record entered the *New Musical Express* chart at No.27 I was over the moon and going round saying 'Cor', 'Wow', 'Jeez', because a song written for me was in the charts. Then there was another time that Paul was round at our house and he started writing out the words for this song he'd written called 'Please Please Me'. I told him I thought the words sounded terrible.

"I remember once my Mum told him he had no feelings, so he phoned her up one night and said 'Listen to this song I've just written' and sang her 'Yesterday' over the phone. That was when they were appearing at the ABC, Blackpool. After he'd finished the song he said, 'There – and you say I've got no feelings!'

"Paul was very hard to dislike. Even in his teens there was something about him, a sort of charisma that used to strike people when they met him for the first time. And he always knew exactly where he was going, even though people often used to tell them they would never make it.

"We used to travel down to the pictures by bus, and then when they started getting successful he went out and bought a second-hand Ford Classic – and I thought, 'Wow – I'm going out with a feller who's got a car!' That was a big thing because we were all broke and not many people of our age could afford cars in Liverpool.

"The only present Paul ever gave me was a pair of black leather gloves that he brought me back from Hamburg, but he was always sending me letters and postcards.

"When Rory had to go into Broadgreen Hospital in Liverpool to have a cartilage operation, Paul took me into the hospital to see him. There were all these people lying ill in bed, some of them looking so pale that they could have been at death's door – and then when Paul the Beatle walked in they all started to rise from their beds, carrying sticks and crutches, and hobbling down the ward to shake his hand or ask for his autograph!

"I'm quite sure there were many other girls around at that time, but I didn't know about any of them, and I didn't actually know that he was going out with anyone else, if you see what I mean. I used to say to him, 'Why don't you go out with somebody else?' though I never thought that he did, and then when he came back from London once and said that he had met Jane Asher I didn't want to go out with him anymore, though we remained good friends and kept a good relationship."

Alvin Stardust: as Shane Fenton he married Iris Caldwell

Iris married singer Shane Fenton in 1964 and they went on the road as a double act. Shane was to change his name to Alvin Stardust and had the major chart success which had eluded him in the sixties. The couple were divorced several years later and in 1983 Iris remarried.

CALL IT SUICIDE Title of song Paul wrote from Frank Sinatra.

CAMPBELL, WILLIAM During the period of the 'Paul Is Dead' (cf) rumours, London's *Evening News* published a story stating that John, George and Ringo had replaced Paul with a double named William Campbell. According to the *News*, Campbell had undergone plastic surgery to look more like the Beatle he was impersonating. (See also *Gibbs, Russ* and *Shears, Billy.*)

CAN'T BUY ME LOVE Paul wrote this song when the Beatles were in Miami, Florida, on their first American trip during 1964. John gave him a hand, but it was mainly Paul's work, which is why he was upset when critics assumed that the title was refering to 'love for sale'. He commented: "Personally, I think you can put any interpretation you want to anything, but when someone says 'Can't Buy Me Love' is about a prostitute, I draw the line. That's going too far." The number was released as a single in March 1964 and several weeks later, famous jazz singer Ella Fitzgerald issued her version, which reached No.30 in the British charts. Ella's was the most famous version, apart from the Beatles' own, but there have actually been about seventy different versions of the song by artists such as Mary Wells, Brenda Lee, Gerry Mulligan, Johnny Rivers, the Supremes, Chet Atkins and James Last.

CAPITOL RECORDS In 1962 Capitol Records, as the American branch of EMI Records, was offered Beatles product to release. Alan Livingstone, then head of Capitol, made the much quoted statement: "We don't think the Beatles will do anything in this market" and EMI went on to deal with Vee Jay. It rapidly became obvious that the Beatles were hot property and Capitol did a rapid about-turn, even launching a major promotional campaign when the group arrived in America in February 1964.

After the Beatles disbanded, Paul remained with the label until 1979

Capitol Records only just signed the Beatles in time to promote their first American tour

when he joined George Harrison, Ringo Starr and Apple Records in a five million dollar law suit against the company, alleging breach of contract, claiming Capitol had failed to pay them their full royalities. Paul signed with CBS Records in North America and remained with them until rejoining Capitol on 29 October 1985 in a deal negotiated with Bhaskar Menon, the company's Chairman, President and Chief Executive Officer. Commenting on the agreement, he said: "Paul is a very special part of the EMI music family and I am absolutely delighted that we have renewed our longstanding relationship with him. It is particularly gratifying that McCartney now returns home to Capitol Records in North America where we have greatly missed the privilege of representing his recording career since 1979." Paul sent him a telex: "Dear Bhaskar, it's great to be back, knowing we can catch up with old acquaintances and hopefully make many new friends. All the best to the lads and lasses in the field – now let's get on with making hits. Warm personal regards, Paul McCartney."

CAROLINA ON MY MIND Track on James Taylor's debut album for Apple, entitled *James Taylor,* on which Paul played bass guitar.

CARSON, JOHNNY One of America's leading television chat show hosts.

Johnny Carson: he and Paul didn't hit it off

Paul appeared on his programme, *The Tonight Show*, on 23 October 1984. It was Carson's birthday and he brought on a cake with one candle, which he blew out himself. The two didn't seem to hit it off, Paul pointing out that the *Carson Show* had flopped when it was given a series of screenings in Britain. (See also *The Tonight Show*).

CASEY, HOWIE Saxophonist from Liverpool. Howie's own early band, the Seniors, were popular in Liverpool in the late fifties before the Beatles, and were the first Mersey group to travel to Hamburg. Alan Williams, who had booked them into the Kaiser Keller club there, wrote to Howie that he was going to send the Beatles over too. Howie wrote back in protest. According to Alan, in his book *'The Man Who Gave the Beatles Away'*: "I got a quick reply from Howie. I was shocked. He wrote back to the effect: 'Look, man, we've got a great scene going here in Hamburg. Now you want to f--- it up by sending over that bum group, the Beatles. They're no good. We don't want them here and they will be bad for the scene. . .' and so on." Howie spoke to me about the Beatles on that very first trip soon after he returned to Liverpool and commented: "Paul had terrific talent and used to play left-handed guitar. He didn't actually play it, he had the amp turned down low." Howie's group became the first Mersey Beat band to have a record released in Britain, but they never achieved chart success, although the group's singer Freddie Starr became successful as a comedian.

Howie was to team up with Paul in later years, playing on his records and touring with Wings as tenor saxophonist. One of his noted sax solos is to be found on 'Bluebird' from *Band on the Run* (cf). He also appeared on the albums *Wings at the Speed of Sound* (cf) and *Wings Over America* (cf) and singles 'Jet' (cf) and 'Coming Up'.

CATTIA German girl, surname not known, who was one of Paul's girlfriends from the early Hamburg days. When the group returned to Ham-

burg for a concert at the Merck Halle in June 1966, Cattia turned up backstage to visit them, along with several other friends, including Astrid and Gibson Kemp, Bert Kaempfert and Bettina, former barmaid at the Star Club.

CAVENDISH, LESLIE Hair stylist who worked for Vidal Sasoon and cut Paul's hair on a number of occasions in the mid-sixties, including one style in which he cropped it particularly short. Cavendish was one of the passengers on the *Magical Mystery Tour*.

CHARITY BUBBLES 1969 Scaffold (see *McCartney, Mike*) single on which Paul played guitar.

CHILDREN CHILDREN Number from the *London Town* (cf) album which was co-written by Paul and Denny Laine. Originally inspired by a waterfall in Paul's garden, the track was recorded at Abbey Road.

THE CIMARONS A long-established British reggae band who originally formed at a youth club in Harlesden in 1967. They made their debut album in 1973 with *In Time* and became the first reggae band to tour Africa. When Paul had the idea of a reggae band performing pop standards, particularly those from the MPL (cf) catalogue, the Cimarons fitted the bill. Paul's company sponsored the recordings and their first release from the project was a single of Paul's song 'With A Little Luck', issued in Britain on 29 January 1982 on I.M.P IMPS 50, with Buddy Holly's 'Peggy Sue' on the flip. The album 'Reggaebility' was issued on 26 February of the same year on Pickwick SHM 3106. Tracks on the album included the Lennon/ McCartney composition 'Love Me Do' and three of Paul's songs – 'With A Little Luck', 'Mull Of Kintyre' and 'C Moon', and he personally directed the group's video for the 'Big Girls Don't Cry' single. The group's line-up is: Locksley Gichie, guitar; Winston Reid, vocals; Sonny Binns, keyboards; Jah Bunny, drums and percussion; Elroy Bailey, bass.

CLARKE, BRIAN Artist who designed *Tug of War* album cover. Paul and Linda attended an exhibition of his work at a Mayfair Gallery on 14 June 1983, where they met an old friend, Marianne Faithfull.

CLARKE, STANLEY One of the world's most respected bassists. When George Martin (cf) and Paul discussed the recording of the *Tug of War* (cf) album, to be recorded in Montserrat (cf), George suggested that he include some of the world's top musicians on their particular instruments. They include Paddy Maloney of the Chieftains, acknowledged as the best living exponent of the Uilleann pipes, Britain's major clarinetist Jack Brymer, and Stanley Clarke. It was while they were jamming in the studio during the recording of *Tug of War* that Stanley and Paul collaborated on 'Hey Hey', an instrumental which was to be included on *Pipes of Peace* (cf).

CLIFF BENNETT & THE REBEL ROUSERS Group formed in 1961 and led by Cliff Bennett, who was born in Slough. They appeared at the Star Club, Hamburg, and became friendly with many of the Liverpool bands. Their first hit came in 1964 with 'One Way Love', issued on the Parlophone label. But their biggest hit was in 1966 with 'Got To Get You Into My Life' which reached No.6 in the British charts. The number was written and produced by Paul.

CLIFF, EDGAR History teacher at Liverpool Institute (cf) when Paul was a pupil. He got on well with Paul and suggested to him that he would make a good teacher and should seriously consider it as a career.

C MOON The 'B' side of 'Hi, Hi, Hi' (cf). It received much radio exposure when the 'A' side was banned by the BBC. Describing the song, Paul commented: "Remember Sam The Sham and 'Wooly Bully'? Well, there's a line in that that says: 'Let's not be L7' – and at the time everyone was saying 'What's L7 mean?' Well, L7, it was

The Cimarons: reggaefying pop standards from the MPL catalogue

The late Alma Cogan

explained at the time, means a square – put L and 7 together and you get a square. So I thought of the idea of getting a C and a crescent moon together to get the opposite of a square. So 'C Moon' means 'Cool'."

COGAN, ALMA British singer who, for a time, was escorted by Beatles manager Brian Epstein. Tragically, she died in the mid-sixties. It was rumoured that Paul played tambourine on her record 'I Knew Right Away', which was recorded at Abbey Road Studios, but this has since been disproved.

COLD CUTS An album project announced by Paul in 1975. He'd collected a number of studio tracks that had been layed down since 1970, but hadn't been issued on record, and he intended issuing a selection of them on an album to be called *Cold Cuts*. Over the years, other teasing tidbits about the project filtered out as the number of completed but unissued tracks increased. Paul was said to have completed the project in 1980, for release in 1981. It was also said that John's death in December 1980 caused him to postpone his plans. Then Wings disbanded and, as Paul had intended using tracks by Wings members such as Denny Laine (cf), he obviously had to make changes. He had by now amassed enough of his own solo material to more than furnish a complete album but no such work has ever been issued. Numbers which would be eligible for *Cold Cuts* include: 'My Carnival', 'Boil Crisis', 'Cage', 'Mama's Little Girl', 'Hey Diddy', 'Tragedy', 'Did We Meet Somewhere Before' and 'Same Time, Next Year'. (See also *Unreleased Songs*.)

COLD TURKEY FOR KAMPUCHEA Bootleg album of Wings' recordings. The tracks include: 'Got To Get You Into My Life', 'Spin It On', 'No Words', 'Go Now', 'Coming Up', 'Goodnight Tonight', 'Yesterday', 'Mull Of Kintyre', 'Getting Close', 'Every Night', 'Again And Again And Again', 'I've Had Enough', 'No Words', 'Cook Of The House', 'Old Siam Sir', 'Maybe I'm Amazed', 'Fool On The Hill', 'Hot As Sun', 'Twenty Flight Rock', 'Arrow Through Me', 'Band On The Run', 'Rockestra Theme', 'Lucille' and 'Let It Be'.

The bootleg was issued in 1982 and was the first album to contain the complete numbers from the Hammersmith Odeon show.

COLLINS, JOAN British actress whose career received a major boost when she was given a starring role in the American soap opera *Dynasty*. In 1980, when asked to name whom she considered her ten sexiest men, she placed Paul at the top of the list, citing his 'little boy quality' as one of his assets. Her other choices included Prince Andrew and Sean Connery.

COLLINS, PHIL Former vocalist/drummer with Genesis who has carved a highly successful solo career for himself. In 1981 there were rumours in the music business that he would be joining Wings, but one of his spokesmen said: "Phil Collins is doing just fine by himself and with Genesis and doesn't have time to help out any old retired group that needs a bit of attention." (See also *American Music Awards*.)

Phil Collins: rumour once had it that he was joining Wings

THE CONCERTS FOR KAMPUCHEA Double-album released on 3 April 1981 on Atlantic K60153 in Britain, which had been recorded at the series of Hammersmith Odeon concerts from 26-29 December 1979 in aid of the suffering people in Kampuchea. The entire fourth side of the album comprises six tracks, three with Paul and Wings and three with Paul and the Rockestra (cf). The tracks are: 'Got To Get You Into My Life', 'Every Night', 'Coming Up', 'Lucille', 'Let It Be' and 'Rockestra Theme'.

There was also a television special of the concert in which Paul performed, simply called *Concerts for the People of Kampuchea*. Directed by Keith McMillan the 90-minute film was networked on Independent Television in Britain on 4 January 1981.

Paul's Liverpudlian mate, boxer John Conteh

CONTEH, JOHN Famous Liverpool Boxer, born in 1951 in the Toxteth area. His mother was of Irish descent and his father came from Sierra Leone. He was to become one of Britain's most glamorous boxers and was, for a time, the Light Heavyweight Champion of the World. In his biography *I, Conteh,* he describes one of the highlights of his life: the 1964 Civic Reception of the Beatles. A boy in short pants, he was jostling among

the crowds in Lime Street and managed to duck under a policeman's horse in order to get a better view. He later got to know Paul personally, was included on the *Band on the Run* (cf) album cover and had personal greetings from Paul when he was spotlighted on Thames TV's *This Is Your Life*. (See *Andrews, Eamonn.*)

THE COOLER An intriguing film short starring Paul, Linda, Ringo Starr and Barbara Bach. Paul wanted to help Ringo in the promotion of his album *Stop and Smell the Roses* (cf) and arranged for MPL (cf) to make the 11-minute video. The result was described as a surrealist musical and concerned a prison camp of the future patrolled entirely by women, with Barbara as the Camp Commandant

Ringo and Barbara in 'The Cooler'

and Linda as a prison guard. Ringo is an escaped prisoner who is recaptured and thrown into solitary confinement. He has visions. Paul appears as a country music bass player, as a fellow prisoner and as Ringo's father. The video was directed by Kevin Godley and Lol Creme and was the official British Entry in the Short Film category at the Cannes Film Festival on 24 May 1982. It featured three numbers from *Stop and Smell the Roses:* 'Private

Property' and 'Attention', both written by Paul, and 'Sure To Fall' by Carl Perkins (cf), Quinton Claunch and William Cantre.

CORFU Paul, Linda and Heather holidayed in Corfu during June 1969. They rented a villa on the Greek island. As Paul had been working hard in the studios when he and Linda got married the previous March this must have been a kind of belated honeymoon for them. (See *Thumbin' A Ride.*)

CORNELL, LYN Blonde singer from Liverpool who'd lived quite close to Paul. She became a member of the Vernon Girls and married musician Andy White. It was Andy who was hired by George Martin to play drums on 'Love Me Do', although Ringo was also allowed to cut a version of the number. Andy's performance is included on the British and American albums. Lyn was booked for the special all-British edition of the US TV series *Shindig* on which the Beatles appeared, and during rehearsals at the Granville Theatre, Fulham, was able to talk over old times with Paul.

CROSSROADS Popular and second longest-running soap opera on British television. The theme tune was penned by Tony Hatch (who, when he was an A&R man for Pye, went to Liverpool and recorded several bands, including the Undertakers and the Chants). Paul rearranged Hatch's theme tune from *Crossroads,* including it on his 1975 album *Venus and Mars* (cf). The television company later used Paul's version as their theme for a time. Incidentally, the programme has been responsible for a few pop hits. Stephanie De Sykes appeared on the show and sang 'Born With A Smile On My Face', which became a Top Ten hit for her (she later married Stu James, former lead singer with Liverpool band the Mojos). Paul's cousin Kate Robbins (cf) also had a chart hit from *Crossroads,* 'More Than In Love'.

CULBERTSON, ROD The actor who portrayed Paul in the made-for-TV movie *The Birth of the Beatles.*

CUMMINS, JEFF Artist from the Hipgnosis design group who drew the colourful illustration on the sleeve of the special limited-edition 12" single 'Temporary Secretary' issued in Britain in September 1980. The cover showed Paul in knitted v-necked sweater, jeans and sneakers, holding a telephone while balancing a bespectacled secretary on his knee – she is taking shortand. Jeff also designed the inner sleeve of the *Wings Over America* (cf) album.

DAHNER, BERT One of Paul's cousins. He devises crosswords for the Wings Fun Club magazine *Club Sandwich.*

DALGLISH, KENNY Scottish footballer who became a leading striker for Liverpool and then their player/ manager. Paul mentions him by name on the live version of 'Coming Up'.

DALLAS One of the most successful television soap operas of all time. An American series by Lorimer Productions, *Dallas* is a saga of an oil-rich family called the Ewings who live in a sprawling ranch called Southfork, situated on the outskirts of the Texas city. In the eighties, due to the rivalry from another popular American soap opera, *Dynasty,* the producers of *Dallas* began looking for internationally known celebrities to appear in the series. Late in 1984, Paul was offered almost one million pounds to make a series of appearances in the role of a wealthy British landowner, spread over eight episodes at £110,000 each. He declined, saying that he didn't want to be separated from his children. Quite frankly, if Paul wanted to be reduced to appearing in soap operas to make money, the Beatles might as well have appeared in a string of second-rate movies in the sixties, as Elvis did. No, the legend would surely have suffered a severe blow if Paul had actually accepted that *Dallas* role.

DANIEL, JEFFREY American singer, former member of Shalamar. He made his screen debut in *Give My Regards to Broad Street* (cf) and commented: "That's all about Paul's real life versus his unconscious dream life. I play myself in one of the dream sequences." He appeared as the robot dancer prior to the 'Silly Love Song' sequence.

Radio series on the BBC Light Programme. Paul was the show's guest on 6 August 1966. (See also *Frost, David.*)

Jeffrey Daniel: 'Broad Street' gave him his first screen role

DAVIS, META The meter maid who claims to have inspired Paul's song 'Lovely Rita' (cf). She retired after nineteen years as a traffic warden on Wednesday, 4 September 1985, when the media gave her story maximum coverage. She appeared on both BBC and ITV news that evening, pictured walking across the Abbey Road zebra crossing and discussing how she gave Paul his ticket (although she called him Paul 'McCarthy' in the interviews).

In 1967 Mrs Davis, who lives in St John's Wood, was once giving Paul's car a ticket in Garden Road, when he turned up. She comments: "He saw that my name was Meta and he laughed and said 'That would make a nice jingle, I could use that.' We chatted for a few minutes and then he drove off. I didn't think any more of it, but later the song came out and although I knew the record was about me I never bought a copy."

Paul didn't recognise her when, a few years later, she met him in the reception room of the local vet where she'd taken her cat. Paul was there with his dog and Meta says: "We chatted about animals and he didn't recognise me out of uniform and I didn't tell him who I was."

When the record was originally released in Australia it included Meta's name in the lyrics, but this was changed to Rita in other versions.

A DAY IN THE LIFE A John/Paul collaboration, but one in which they each wrote separate parts, John penning the beginning and end of the number and Paul composing the middle section (see also *Baby, You're A*

The psychedelic age: drugs were said to be behind such songs as 'A Day In The Life'

Rich Man). Paul had already written some of the lyrics for another song, but decided to incorporate them into the number that John had been writing. There is a long chord at the end of the song which lasts for forty-two seconds and it has been suggested that it was only intended to be heard by Martha, Paul's dog! John's section was inspired by two separate items: the death in a car crash of Guinness heiress Tara Browne, a friend of the Beatles, and a story that he'd read in the *Daily Mail* concerning holes in the roads in Blackburn. Paul's rather cheery section, according to Steven Norris, a former schoolmate and now Conservative MP for Oxford East, was based on the bus journey they used to take to school together. In a *Daily Mirror* interview in 1985, Norris commented: "Everyone says that 'A Day In The Life' was about drugs, but Paul always claimed it was about catching the bus to school. I agree. It's exactly what we used to do. *Went upstairs and had a smoke, somebody spoke and I went into a dream.* That's just how I remember it. Getting sleepily out of bed, dragging a comb across your head, then going out and catching the bus, upstairs to the top deck like we all did, still not properly awake and having an untipped Woodbine."

In fact, it was only ever John's part of the song that was said to be about drugs. The BBC banned it nonetheless. It has never been clear why they assumed a drug connection – one suggestion was that they thought the holes in the road referred to holes caused by a drug addict's hypodermic needle.

The number, which has a classical 'feel' and was recorded with forty-two musicians from the London Philharmonic Orchestra, first appeared on *Sgt Pepper* and was also included on the *Beatles 1967-1970* compilation.

THE DAZZLERS One of the names, along with Turpentine, which Paul considered for the band he eventually called Wings.

DEAR BOY Song which Paul co-wrote with Linda for *Ram*.

THE DEFEAT OF THE DOG One of two avant-garde films which Paul made in 1966; the other was called *The Next Spring Then*. Paul screened the films for journalist Patrick Skene Catling and they were mentioned in his article which appeared in *Punch* magazine on 23 November 1966. Catling commented: "They were not like ordinary people's home movies. There were over-exposures, double-exposures, blinding orange lights, quick cuts from professional wrestling to a crowded car park to a close-up of a television weather map. There were long still shots of a grey cloudy sky and a wet, grey pavement, jumping Chinese ivory carvings and affectionate slow-motion studies of his sheepdog Martha and his cat. The accompanying music, on a record player and faultlessly synchronised, was by the Modern Jazz Quartet and Bach."

DESERT ISLAND DISCS An immensely popular British radio show conceived by Roy Plomley (cf), who died in 1985, which has run for over forty years. The show's format is deceptively simple: celebrities are asked to imagine being stranded on a desert island and to select the records they would take with them. In between their choices being played, they discuss their lives and give reasons for their record selection. Paul was the first and only ex-Beatle to appear on the show: on Saturday, 30 January 1982, he became the 1,629th castaway. Each castaway selects eight records and also identifies one particular record which they would keep if they were only allowed a single disc. They also have to suggest a luxury item and a book they would want with them on a desert island. Paul's eight selections were: 'Heartbreak Hotel' by Elvis Presley, 'Sweet Little Sixteen' by Chuck Berry, 'Courtly Dances From Gloriana' by the Julian Bream Consort, 'Be-Bop-A-Lula' by Gene Vincent, 'Searchin'' by the Coasters, 'Tutti Frutti' by Little Richard, 'Walking In The Park With Eloise' by the Country Hams and 'Beautiful Boy' by John Lennon. The last became his special selection, his luxury was a guitar and the book he picked was *Linda's Pictures*. The programme is now hosted by Michael Parkinson who also appears on the cover of *Band on the Run (cf)*.

DISNEY TIME British television special which has been shown annually in the UK each December for a great number of years. The show, hosted by British celebrities, features a selection of clips from Disney films, old and new, with a linking narrative from the celebrity. Paul and Linda were the hosts of the December 1973 programme, presenting their own favourite Disney moments.

DOLLY'S CLUB London venue where Paul and Neil Aspinall met Bob Dylan in May 1966.

DONAGHUE, PETER
Former swimming-pool cleaner who moved in with Sharon Holly, ex-wife of Wings' drummer Steve Holly (cf); the couple had a baby son, Jake, in January 1983. Donaghue also fell in love with Jo Jo Laine (cf), ex-wife of Wings' guitarist Denny Laine (cf); *they* had a baby son, Boston, born in August 1983.

DONOVAN A British 'answer to Bob Dylan' in the sixties. Donovan Leitch, a Glaswegian singer/songwriter, enjoyed a successful run of hits. During 1968 Paul made a guest appearance on Donovan's 'Atlantis' single playing tambourine and providing some backing vocals. He'd also dropped into the studio during Donovan's recording of 'Mellow Yellow' and at one point sang the words 'Mellow Yellow'. A fifteen-minute session between the two artists, also from 1968, has been captured for all time on an American bootleg album *No.3 Abbey Road, NW8*. The interlude was taken from a studio warm-up between Donovan and Paul, and in their book, *The End of the Beatles,* authors Castleman and Podrazik mention that the two stars sat down together with acoustic guitars and exchanged songs-in-the-works, with Paul offering 'Blackbird' and 'Heather' and Donovan selecting numbers from what eventually became *HMS Donovan*.

DON'T DIG NO PAKISTANIS Intended to be another of Paul's political statements in song. He initially wrote the lyrics using the tune of 'Get Back' (cf). He recorded it during the *Let It Be* sessions, but it was never released and eventually became 'Get Back' (see also *Give Ireland Back To The Irish.)*

DON'T LET IT BRING YOU DOWN Another song recorded in the Virgin Islands for the *London Town* (cf) album and another Denny Laine/Paul McCartney joint work (see *Children Children*). On the track both musicians play Irish whistles, which are known as flageolets.

DORSEY, TONY Leader of the Wings horn section during the 1975/76 world tour. The trombonist first worked for Paul in New Orleans during the recording of *Venus and Mars*. Paul asked him to lead the horn section for his next tour and Tony chose Steve Howard on trumpet and flugelhorn, Thaddeus Richard on soprano and alto saxophones, clarinet and flute, and Howie Casey (cf) on tenor saxophone. He played trombone in addition to writing the arrangements.

DRAKE'S DRUM Racehorse which Paul bought for £1,200 as a present for his father's 62nd birthday on 6 July 1964. The horse came second on its very first race after the purchase. The most exciting moment occured on 26 March 1966 when both Paul and his father were at Liverpool's famous Aintree racecourse to watch Drake's Drum win the Hylton Plate, coming in at 20-1. Paul was particularly pleased at the pride his father felt, leading the horse into the winner's enclosure. In later years, Paul retired the horse to his farm in Scotland (see *High Park Farm.)*

DRUGS Paul's flirtations with drugs began, as far as anyone can tell, with mild 'uppers' such as purple hearts, in Liverpool. In Hamburg, the boys were known to take similar stimulants, such as Preludin and Captogen, which could be obtained in local chemist's shops without a prescription but which they used to buy from Rosa, the lavatory attendant at the Kaiser Keller and, later on, the Top Ten Club.

Singer Bob Dylan introduced the Beatles to marijuana in 1964 and at the time Paul was quoted as saying: "I'm thinking for the first time, really *thinking.*" However, it was for his use of LSD that Paul first hit the headlines in connection with drugs. LSD or 'acid' is a chemical hallucinogenic and Paul was to admit that he'd taken it in an interview that appeared in *Life* magazine in America on 16 June 1967. This created such a furore that Paul was interviewed on the subject, for a TV news programme broadcast on 19 June. The same day, the *Daily Mirror* also published an interview in which Paul discussed taking LSD. The confession led to Evangelist Billy Graham declaring he would pray for Paul's salvation!

The interview on television went as follows:

Q: Paul, how often have you taken LSD?

Paul: Er, four times.

Q: And where did you get it from?

Paul: Well, you know, I mean, if I was to say where I got it from, you know, it's illegal and everything, it's silly to say that so I'd rather not say it.

Q: Don't you believe that this was a matter which you should have kept private?

Paul: Well, the thing is, you know, that I was asked a question by a newspaper and the decision was whether to tell a lie or tell the truth, you know. I decided to tell him the truth but I didn't really want to say anything because if I'd had my way I wouldn't have told anyone because I'm not trying to spread the word about this but the man from the newspaper is the man from the mass medium. I'll keep it a personal thing if he does too, you know, if he keeps it quiet. But he wanted to spread it so it's his responsibility for spreading it. Not mine.

Q: But you're a public figure and you said it in the first place. You must have known that it would make the newspapers.

Paul: Yes, but to say it, you know, is only to tell the truth. I'm telling the truth. I don't know what everyone is so angry about.

Q: Well, do you think you have encouraged your fans to take drugs?

Paul: I don't think it will make any difference, you know, I don't think my fans are going to take drugs just because I did. But the thing is that's not the point anyway. I was asked whether I had or not and from then on the whole bit about how far it's going to encourage is up to the newspapers and up to you, you know, on television. I mean you're spreading this now at this moment. This is going into all the homes in Britain and I'd rather it didn't you know. But you're asking me the question and if you want me to be honest, I'll be honest.

Q: But as a public figure, surely you've got a responsibility not to say any. . .

Paul: No, it's you who've got the responsibility not to spread this now. You know I'm quite prepared to keep it as a very personal thing if you will too. If you'll shut up about it, I will!

However, it was his association with cannabis which continued to dog him. In August 1972, during the Wings tour of Europe, Paul found himself in trouble when the group appeared in Sweden. As soon as Wings had finished their set at the Scandinavian Hall, Gothenberg, the police stepped in and cut off the PA system. They were waiting to question Paul, Linda and Denny Seiwell and took them to the local police headquarters, together with Paul's secretary Rebecca Hinds. Customs officers had apparently intercepted seven ounces of marijuana which had been sent from London addressed to Paul. A senior police officer commented: "We told them we had found the cannabis in a letter and at first they said they knew nothing about it. But after we had questioned them for about three hours they confessed and told the truth. McCartney, his wife and Seiwell told us they smoked hash every day. They said they were almost addicted to it. They said they had made arrangements to have drugs posted to them each day they played in different countries so they wouldn't have to take any drugs through the customs themselves."

John Morris, the tour operator, said "Paul, Linda and Denny did admit to the Swedish police that they used hash. At first they denied it but the police gave them a rough time and started threatening all sorts of things. The police said they would bar the group from leaving the country unless they confessed."

Gothenburg's public prosecutor, Lennart Angelin, released them after a preliminary fine of £1,000. He said: "They were not arrested since it was obvious that they were going to use the cannabis for themselves and not pass it on."

Paul, Linda and Denny were fined on 12 August 1972. Not too long after the Swedish incident a police constable, Norman McPhee, set off to Paul's two farms in Campbeltown ostensibly to check the security in his and Linda's absence. McPhee had been on a drugs identification course in Glasgow and when he visited High Park (cf), one of Paul's farms, for some reason he checked one of the greenhouses where he said he became suspicious of some plants. He returned to his station, later returning to the farm with six other policemen. A thorough search turned up no further evidence and in December Paul was charged on three counts, including those of possessing cannabis and cultivating cannabis plants. He was asked to appear in court the following year, in March 1973. The hearing took place on 8 March and the Court was told that in September 1972 a crime prevention officer had gone to the farm to check that it was secure. He had noticed some plants in the greenhouse with the tomatoes and had returned to the station to consult a reference book. To the charge of knowingly cultivating the plants, Paul pleaded guilty. To the two other charges of possessing cannabis he pleaded not guilty — and the

charges were dropped. His lawyer told the Court how Paul had received the seeds in the post and, being interested in horticulture, had planted them. The Sheriff, convicting him on the first count, commented: "I take into account that you are a public figure of considerable interest, particularly to young people, and I must deal with you accordingly. The fine will be £100."

Paul said: "I was planning on writing a few songs in jail. You have to be careful. I look on it like Prohibition but you have to recognise the law. I think the law should be changed — make it like the law of homosexuality with consenting adults in private. I don't think cannabis is as dangerous as drink. I'm dead against hard drugs."

The next drugs affair happened in 1975. Wings had begun recording *Venus and Mars* (cf) in America between January and April. They were using the Sea Saint Studios in New Orleans and the Wally Heider Studios in Los Angeles. One night, on their way home, shortly after midnight, from the Wally Heider Studios to Malibu, the trouble began. It was Monday, 3 March and Paul was driving a silver Lincoln Continental with Linda at his side and their three children on the back seat. Driving along Santa Monica Boulevard, Paul failed to stop for a red light and a Highway Patrol motorcyclist flagged him down. The motorcyclist approached their vehicle and said that he smelt a strange substance as he put his head inside the car. He then found a smouldering joint on the floor and discovered a small amount of marijuana, between 16 and 18.5 grammes, in Linda's purse. Linda immediately admitted that the joint had been hers and that Paul had no part in it. They were taken to West Los Angeles police station and Paul was told that he was free to take the children home. Linda was detained for two hours before bail was arranged; in April she was taken to court after being charged with possession. In May, the judge, Brian Cuhan, said that he would be prepared to have the charges dropped if Linda agreed to have six sessions with a psychiatrist. She said she would and the case was dismissed. The judge also agreed that she could have the sessions in London. This arrangement was not unusual, as a Los Angeles police officer commented: "After six months instruction by approved counsellors, first offence drug charges — like that facing Mrs McCartney — are usually dropped."

Paul was later to comment: "The only really unfortunate thing about it is that it starts to get you a reputation as a kind of druggie. It is really only a minor offence. It isn't something we take too seriously, and of course the press image is really far worse. We're not serious drug addicts or anything. The fact is that it's illegal, and if a thing's illegal you're liable to get caught doing it."

A year later, Paul's convictions were to catch up with him. As part of the Wings world tour of 1976, Paul intended to make appearances in Japan. These would be his first performances there for ten years, since the Beatles appeared at the Budo Kan Hall in Tokyo in July 1966. All arrangements had been made and tickets to all the concerts had been sold out in advance, lavish programmes had been printed, but just as Paul and company were due to fly from Australia to Japan, they were told that Paul's visa had been cancelled at the last minute by Japan's Minister of Justice due to Paul's drug convictions in Sweden and Scotland in '72 and '73 respectively.

However, this incident was to prove minor in comparison to their next, horrific experience with Japan. Wings had finally confirmed that they would be allowed to tour the world's second biggest record market and were to appear at eleven concerts in Japan in January 1980. Once again, all the tickets were sold out well in advance. All the main equipment for the tour had been sent to Japan in advance and Paul, Linda and the children had gone to New York for Christmas to visit Linda's family. They set off from the Big Apple on a 14-hour flight to Tokyo with just their personal baggage. As they went through Customs at Narita Airport, they were asked to open their luggage. In the first case opened there was a polythene bag which, when examined, was found to contain almost half a pound of marijuana. Jo Jo Laine was to say: "Linda had left Twenty Thai sticks of grass in her make-up bags. . . Paul took the rap."

The Customs officials called the police and Paul was led away handcuffed. Narcotics officers questioned him and after five hours of interrogation he admitted that he had smoked pot for eleven years and had obtained the grass which had been found in his bag from a friend in America. Linda and the three children were taken to a hotel in Tokyo and the tour was cancelled, disappointing the 100,000 who had been lucky enough to obtain tickets.

Paul was told that he could be in jail for up to twenty days before being charged. He was intially shocked when Albert Marshall, the British Vice-Consul visited him on the first night. Paul believed the situation was a storm in a teacup until Marshall told him otherwise. Paul recapped: "I thought, fantastic, good old consul, he is going to get me out. He just sat down and said, 'Well, it could be eight years, you know.'"

As he was not Japanese, Paul was allowed coffee and bread rather than the usual rice and green tea given to detainees. He had to sleep on a mat on the floor, Japanese style, and was awakened by a guard at 6am each morning. He also had to retire to bed each night at 8pm, was only allowed half an hour of exercise in his cell each day and was denied access to his guitar and writing material. (See also *Japanese Jailbird*.)

In all, Paul was to spend ten days in the Japanese prison. Linda was first able to visit him on the fifth day and told him that she was worried he might be sentenced to three months. She saw him again on the eighth day (she made three visits in all) when she was accompanied by her lawyer brother John, and brought Paul a cheese sandwich, some fruit and science-fiction books. Paul had been allowed a change of clothes and some blankets, but it was a week before he was able to take a bath. He was offered the option of bathing alone or in the communal prison bathhouse. He chose the latter. He commented: "Life in jail isn't so bad. The prison wasn't the rat-infested hole I thought it was going to be. For the first few days I was worrying all the time. For eight days I didn't see any daylight at all. I had to eat seaweed and onion soup for breakfast. I shared a bath with a man who was in for murder and all because I didn't think." He also commented: "At first I thought it was barbaric that they put handcuffs on me twice a day when I went to see the investigators. There seemed to be a different lot each time. I had made a confession on the night I was arrested and apologised for breaking Japanese law but they still wanted to know everything. I had to go through my whole life story, school, father's name, income, even my medal from the Queen. Perhaps they decided to deport me because I was totally frank with them."

Paul was deported, carted off from prison directly to the airport, still in handcuffs and surrounded by twelve policemen. Linda was to say that Paul had been released because of a loophole in the law – since his visa had been taken from him at the airport on arrival he was, in fact, an illegal alien. The Japanese authorities said that they released him because he showed signs of repentance. In fact, he did seem to repent his actions to reporters on his flight back home, via Anchorage, Alaska, and Amsterdam, Holland. On the plane to Alaska he told the press: "I have been a fool. What I did was incredibly dumb. My God, how stupid I have been. I had just come from America and I still had the American attitude that marijuana isn't too bad. I didn't appreciate how strict the Japanese are about it. I was really scared thinking I might be in prison for so long. I've made up my mind. I've been smoking marijuana for more than eleven years, and I'm never going to touch the stuff again."

Despite this declaration, Paul again made the headlines in January 1984, after being busted in Barbados. Paul, Linda, James and Stella had been staying at a luxury nineteenth century villa on the holiday island. On the evening of Saturday the fourteenth, three police cars arrived at the villa and drug squad officers declared that they'd had a 'tip-off' that drugs were on the premises. Paul handed ten grammes of cannabis to them and they discovered another seven in Linda's handbag.

They were then taken to police headquarters in Bridgetown, the capital, where they were questioned for two hours. Their passports, together with £1,000 in cash, were confiscated, then they were released on bail for the sum of £1,400.

The couple appeared at Holetown Magistrate's Court where they were charged with possessing marijuana, to which they both pleaded guilty.

Their Defence Attorney, David Simmonds, told the magistrate: "The male accused is of considerable international standing. He is a very talented and creative person. People who have this talent sometimes need inspiration. I'm instructed that Mr McCartney and his wife obtained the vegetable matter from someone on Holetown Beach. They are not pushers."

The Assistant Police Commissioner, Keith Whittaker, commented: "The law is for everybody on the island – and that includes McCartney. We are treating this as a very serious case. I don't know if he'd be welcome here again." Police Inspector Alan Long also commented: "By their example the McCartney's are encouraging our young people to use drugs." The couple were fined £70.

They then flew back to London – and were stopped by Customs men at Heathrow Airport who discovered more cannabis in a film canister in Linda's luggage. On 24 January, Linda pleaded guilty to possession and was fined £75. The two busts so close together caused a furore in the British press, with many people airing their views on both sides of the marijuana question. Paul's brother Mike, coming to the defence, said: "As kids, Paul and I were taught moderation and toleration by my Dad. Other people could do with the same lesson. The idea that marijuana leads to heroin is rubbish. It's like saying a few drinks makes you an alcoholic."

Denny Laine has made several statements regarding Paul's use of cannabis in some national newspaper articles, claiming that Paul and Linda get through two ounces of cannabis each day, the equivalent of £1,000 worth of marijuana per week. He also claimed that they had once smuggled a small amount through Customs in the hood of baby James's coat.

DUNBAR, GEOFF British animation specialist. He co-wrote a script with Paul for the Rupert Bear (cf) film.

DUNE Spectacular 1984 sci-fi film, based on the Frank Herbert novel. Paul was offered a part in the film, but declined. Sting appeared in the movie as a villain.

DURBAND, DUSTY Sixth-form teacher of English at Liverpool Institute. Paul claimed he was the only teacher he liked and mentioned that he told the boys about books such as *Lady Chatterley's Lover* and Chaucer's *The Miller's Tale*, pointing out that they weren't dirty books but examples of good literature.

EAST GATE FARM 160-acre farm that Paul and Linda bought from Jim Higgs in 1978 for a fee in excess of £100,000. Situated near the village of Peasmarch, near Rye in East Sussex, it is close to the two-bedroom cottage which they first moved into in that area in 1975. In 1982 the couple had the farmhouse demolished and a five-bedroom house built on the site. They also have a swimming pool, stables and a paddock for their horses. Their estate is called Waterfall and is surrounded by a six-foot fence, constructed in a way that makes it very difficult for any intruder to scale. There is also a 65-foot tower. These security measures prompted journalist Chris Hutchins to dub the property 'Paulditz'. Paul on the other hand, maintains that the fence was erected to prevent foxes from getting in to attack his pheasants and peacocks and that the tower enables the family to look over the surrounding countryside.

The cottage found an ideal use in 1983 when it became the setting for Linda's daughter Heather's twenty-first birthday party. More than a hundred local people were invited and a marquee was erected on the grounds. Music was provided by Fun Boy Three and guests included Ringo Starr and Barbara Bach. The main food was vegetarian stew, there was ample red and white wine and the party continued until 5pm.

EASTER, DAVID Bristol-born actor who was twenty-five when he appeared in *Give My Regards to Broad Street* (cf). Following his appearance in Paul's film, he became a regular member of the cast of *Brookside*, the Channel 4 soap opera based in Liverpool.

EAT AT HOME One of the tracks from the 1971 album *Ram* (cf) which was co-penned by Paul and Linda. Wings performed the number during their European tour.

EBONY & IVORY Paul's song about racial equality on which he shared the vocals with Stevie Wonder. The single was issued in Britain on Parlophone R6054 on 29 March 1982 and topped the charts, giving Stevie his first British No. 1. There was also a 12" version of the number. In the US it was issued on Columbia 44-02878 on 16 April 1982 and also went to No. 1. The flipside was a number which Paul co-wrote with Denny Laine called 'Rainclouds'. 'Ebony & Ivory' was inspired by something Paul had heard Spike Milligan say (see *Making Music*).

ECHOES BBC Radio London programme. Paul was interviewed by DJ Stuart Coleman about his music on 17 June 1984. The programme was syndicated in America later in the year.

EDGE, 'CLIFF' Teacher at the Liverpool Institute (cf). Paul reminisced to Chris Welch in an interview: "I remember one day when the guy in the Remo Four brought a guitar — I brought a guitar and George brought his guitar and we went into the History room, Cliff Edge's room. The teacher's name was Mr Edge, see, and we called him 'Cliff'. I remember doing 'Long Tall Sally' and all the old stuff and it was the nearest we ever got to a high school hop."

ELEANOR RIGBY Song issued in 1966, on Parlophone R5493 in Britain on 5 August and in America on Capitol 5715 on 8 August. The No.1 single was a double 'A' side with 'Yellow Submarine'; 'Eleanor Rigby' was also featured on the *Revolver* album, issued in Britain on the same day. A few months later, in December, it resurfaced on *A Collection of Beatles Oldies (But Goldies)* and also appeared on several albums, including *The Beatles 1962-1966* and *The Beatles Box*. It was re-released among a batch of singles to celebrate the group's twentieth anniversary in 1982

From what Paul had said about the song in the sixties, it was assumed that Eleanor Rigby was a figment of his imagination, yet in 1984 stories in the press suggested that Eleanor Rigby had been a real person. This was because a tombstone for Eleanor Rigby had been discovered in the graveyard of St Peter's Church in Liverpool, the same church where Paul and John had first met. Could he have seen the gravestone as a young lad and held the name in his subconscious? Or is it just pure coincidence?

When the *Sun* newspaper ran a story about the song in 1984, it published a photograph of fomer dancehall compère Tom McKenzie posing at the side of the gravestone and commented that Tom was also the Father McKenzie referred to. Yet in Paul's version of the origin of the number, Father McKenzie was also fictitious. Here is what Paul has said at various times to the press: "(It) started off with sitting down at the piano and getting the first line of the melody, and playing around with words. I think it was 'Miss Daisy Hawkins' originally; then it was her picking up the rice in a church after a wedding. That's how nearly all our songs start, with the first line just suggesting itself from books or newspapers.

"At first I thought it was a young Miss Daisy Hawkins, a bit like 'Annabel Lee', but not so sexy; but then I saw I'd said she was picking up the rice in church so she had to be a cleaner; she had missed the wedding, and she was suddenly lonely. In fact she had missed it all – she was the spinster type.

"Jane [Asher] was in a play in Bristol then, and I was walking round the streets waiting for her to finish. I didn't really like 'Daisy Hawkins' – I wanted a name that was more real. The thought just came: "Eleanor Rigby picks up the rice and lives in a dream" – so there she was. The next thing was Father Mackenzie. It was going to be Father McCartney, but then I thought that was a bit of a hang-up for my Dad, being in this lonely song. So we looked through the phone book. That's the beauty of working at random – it does come up perfectly, much better than if you try to think it with your intellect.

"Anyway, there was Father Mackenzie, and he was just as I had imagined him, lonely, darning his socks. We weren't sure if the song was going to go on. In the next verse we thought of a bin man, an old feller going through dustbins; but it got too involved – embarrassing. John and I wondered whether to have Eleanor Rigby and him have a thing going, but we couldn't really see how. When I played it to John, we decided to finish it.

"That was the point anyway. She didn't make it, she never made it with anyone, she didn't even look as if she was going to."

The number has also become one of the most popular Beatles songs to be recorded by other acts with over two hundred recorded versions, including those by Diana Ross & the Supremes, Paul Anka, Frankie Valli, Aretha Franklin, the Four Tops, Johnny Mathis and Vanilla Fudge.

ELLIS, ROBERT One of the photographers used by Paul when Wings were still extant. Ellis took the shots which appeared on the covers of the albums *Red Rose Speedway*, *Wings at the Speed of Sound* (he also took the photo used as a poster and included with the LP) and *Wings Over America*.

ELEVATOR Single by Grapefruit. Despite being discovered by Terry Doran, head of Apple Music, the group's releases were issued by RCA. For their 1968 single 'Elevator', Paul produced a promotional film of the group. He took them to Hyde Park and filmed a three-minute sequence.

EMMETTS GARAGE 4,600-acre estate in Devon which Paul and Linda considered buying in June 1969. The asking price was then £200,000.

EMPIRE BALLROOM Large ballroom situated below ground level in Leicester Square, London, and part of the Moss Empire group. On 8 November 1971 Paul invited one thousand guests to the ballroom to celebrate the release of Wings' first album *Wild Life* (cf). Guests were requested to wear conventional dress and the tone of the affair was similar to that of a typical night at the Empire, with music by the Ray McVay Band, entertainment from a formation dancing team and guests able to buy their own drinks over the bar.

EMPTY HAND Produced by Paul and directed by David Litchfield, this short film was the first project from McCartney Productions, Paul's film company, in 1977. It was a 32-minute documentary featuring the current Wings drummer Geoff Britton (cf), who was a karate expert, at the Amateur Karate Championship where he appeared with the British Amateur Karate Association team.

ENGLISH, JOE It was ironic that drummer Geoff *Britton* (cf) was replaced by an American drummer called Joe *English* in the Wings line-up. Joe was born in Rochester, New York, on 7 February 1949 and became a rock drummer at the age of eighteen when he joined a band called the Jam Factory. For six years the band toured America numerous times supporting acts of the calibre of Jimi Hendrix, Janis Joplin and the Grateful Dead, until they split up in 1973. The demise of the group marked a dark period in Joe's life during which his wife left him, taking their two children with her. He didn't have any gigs and was completely broke. "I was on the bottom," he has said. He managed to get through this bad patch with encouragement from a girlfriend called Dayle and had settled in Georgia where he found regular work as a session musician.

When Geoff Britton left Wings during the *Venus and Mars* (cf) sessions, Tony Dorsey (cf), leader of Paul's horn section, recommended Joe. At the time he was rehearsing with Bonnie Bramlett and intended touring with her, but when he received the offer from Paul he found a replacement for the tour and immediately went to New Orleans to record on *Venus and Mars.*

The album was mixed at the Wally Heider Studio in Los Angeles, and it was on the way there that Paul asked Joe if he'd like to become a member of Wings. He was delighted to accept. He stayed with the band until late in 1977 and quit after completing part of the *London Town* (cf) sessions. He'd also contributed to the albums *Wings at the Speed of Sound* (on which he sang lead vocals on the track 'Must Do Something About That') and *Wings Over America* and had joined the world tour. During Wings' appear-

Joe English, the third Wings drummer

ances at the Omni in Atlanta 18-19 May 1976, Paul introduced Joe from the stage saying he was 'from just down the road in Juliette, Georgia."

When he left the group, Joe stated: "I enjoyed being in Wings and I learned a lot, but I got tired of the months and months sitting in recording studios. I wanted to come home and see if I could make it as Joe English and not off Paul McCartney." He told the American *Beatlefan* that he liked Linda but didn't consider her a good musician or vocalist and that Denny Laine tended to sing off-key. He also commented: "I was continually promised a share of the record royalties, but I never received any," although he qualified the statement by adding that he was very well paid when he was with the band.

After leaving Wings he joined the group Tall Dogs, and later Sea Level.

EPAMINONDAS, ANDROS London-born Greek-Cypriot, Andros gained his experience in the film world with Stanley Kubrick on such films as *A Clockwork Orange, Barry Lyndon* and *The Shining*. He worked for Kubrick for eleven years and has said that he did "everything from scouting locations to organising the money to doing the washing up." Paul made him producer on *Give My Regards to Broad Street* (cf) and was to say: "Andros took a lot of slagging-off during production. People were always coming to me and saying 'that bastard Andros, he's so tight-fisted.' He was the scapegoat because he's little and Greek and he took it all in his stride. What better whipping boy? But I tell you, I look at the budget now and I'm glad to have been involved with him."

ESCORTS, THE A popular Liverpool band who never quite made the major league. They comprised Terry Sylvester (guitar), John Kinrade (guitar), Mike Gregory (bass) and Pete Clarke (drums). Paul took an interest in the band and produced their single 'From Head To Toe' c/w 'Night Time', issued on Columbia DB 8061 on 18 November 1966, but it fared no better than their previous releases. Paul also played tambourine on the 'A' side. Elvis Costello recorded both numbers in the eighties. The group disbanded towards the end of the sixties and Terry and Mike joined the Swinging Blue Jeans for a time, then Terry later became a member of the Hollies. Incidentally, their first Liverpool residency in 1962 arose as a result of a helping hand from Ringo Starr.

EVE, TREVOR British actor who became popular as the private eye Eddie Shoestring in the BBC TV series *Shoestring*. He also appeared with Laurence Olivier in the film *Dracula* and starred in the TV movie *Jamaica Inn*. Trevor played Paul McCartney in the original production of the Willie Rushton play *John, Paul, George, Ringo and Bert* at the Playhouse in Liverpool in 1974.

EVERY NIGHT Track that Paul wrote in Greece in 1969 for his debut solo album *McCartney* (cf), released in 1970. He recorded the number at EMI studios, playing the various instruments himself and double tracking part of the vocal track. He also performed it on the Wings tour of Britain in 1979, and the same year, Phoebe Snow recorded it, giving her a minor hit.

EVERTON Area of Liverpool where Paul's grandparents lived. They moved several times within Everton, from their original home in Fishguard Street where Paul's father was born to Lloyd Street and Salva Street before eventually moving out of the area to Scargreen Avenue in West Derby.

EXECUTIVE Glossy monthly magazine for men which ran a three-page feature on Paul by Mark Steels in the second issue, dated June 1982. The interview began with a discussion of *Tug of War* (cf) and of Paul's teaming with producer George Martin (cf). Paul described how George had contributed to bringing his abilities to the fore on the album. There is also some discussion of how Paul had been trying to get away from 'the Beatles thing' for ten years. He mentions the

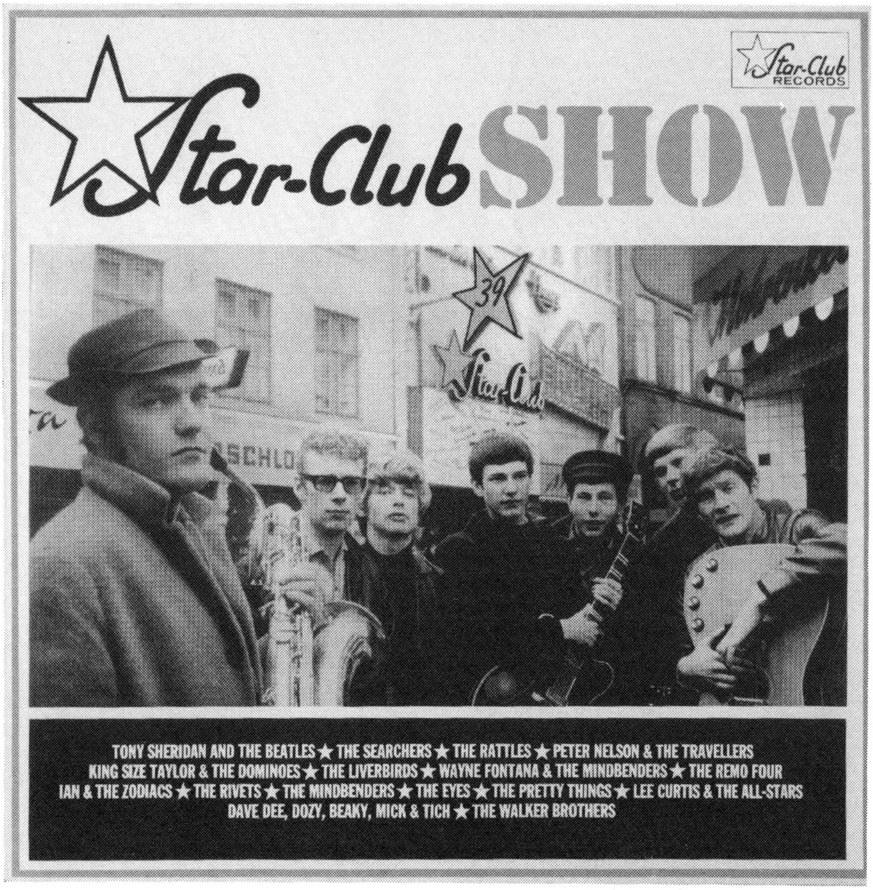
Star-Club RECORDS
Star-Club SHOW
TONY SHERIDAN AND THE BEATLES ★ THE SEARCHERS ★ THE RATTLES ★ PETER NELSON & THE TRAVELLERS
KING SIZE TAYLOR & THE DOMINOES ★ THE LIVERBIRDS ★ WAYNE FONTANA & THE MINDBENDERS ★ THE REMO FOUR
IAN & THE ZODIACS ★ THE RIVETS ★ THE MINDBENDERS ★ THE EYES ★ THE PRETTY THINGS ★ LEE CURTIS & THE ALL-STARS
DAVE DEE, DOZY, BEAKY, MICK & TICH ★ THE WALKER BROTHERS

The 'Star Club Tapes' feature Paul's early rendition of 'Falling In Love Again' (saxophonist Howie Casey (cf) is in the foreground)

fact that he had obtained one of the EMI 4-track machines used on *Sgt Pepper* and had fixed it into his Scottish studio. Discussing *Tug of War*, he once again give credit to Spike Milligan (cf) for the inspiration for the *Ebony & Ivory* track. He discussed a few further tracks from the album and then talked of his relationship with John and how the tribute number 'Here Today' (cf) came about.

THE FACTS ABOUT A POP GROUP: FEATURING WINGS Large format book aimed at the younger reader, published in Britain in 1976 by G Whizzard/Andre Deutsch. The text was written by *Observer* music correspondent Dave Gelly and the photographs were taken by Homer Sykes who accompanied Gelly on the road with the band. Paul contributed a brief introduction. The book was a

The Facts about a Pop Group
Featuring Wings
Introduction by Paul McCartney

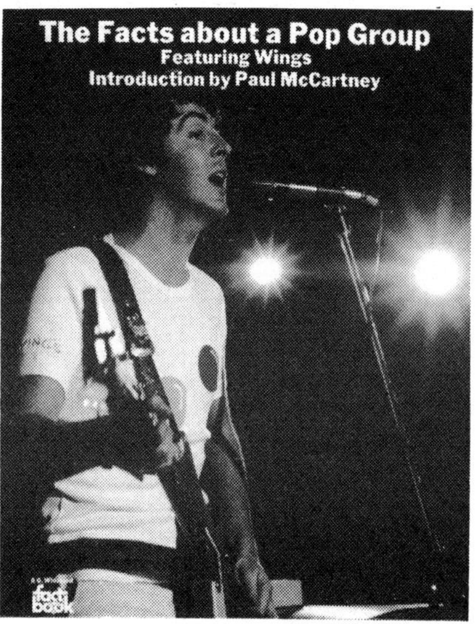

detailed analysis of every aspect of a group's life on the road and began with profiles of each member of Wings, their road crew and sound engineers. There were details of the making of the stage wardrobe; the construction of the stage scenery; the security arrangements at the gigs; stories of fans who had travelled long distances to see the concerts. Ticket touts, bodyguards, the management team, the fan club, travelling by coach, the group's recording, publicity, and even the actual manufacturing of the records are all covered as well.

FALLING IN LOVE AGAIN Song which Paul performed early in his career. The number was originally sung by Marlene Dietrich in the classic German film *The Blue Angel.* Paul sang it at the Star Club, and it can be heard on the Star Club recordings, first issued in June 1977 as a two-album set by Lingasong. (See also *I Saw Her Standing There).*

THE FAMILY WAY British film starring Hayley Mills, John Mills and Hywel Bennett, produced by the Boulting Brothers. Premièred at the Warner Theatre, London, on 18 December 1966, the movie gave Paul his

Hayley Mills in 'The Family Way'

first credit as a solo composer. He had produced twenty-six minutes of music for the film, arranged for him by George Martin (cf). A soundtrack album (Decca SKL 4847) was released on 6 January 1967; two singles from the album were also issued – 'Love In The Open Air' c/w 'Theme From The Family Way' (United Artists UP 1165) on 23 December 1966, and 'Love In The Open Air' c/w 'Bahama Sound' (United Artists UA 50148) on 24 April 1967.

FAMOUS GROUPIES Number written by Paul in Scotland and recorded in

Paul, George and Ringo with Faron

In 1984 Faron tried to auction a pair of Paul's trousers at Sotheby's

the Virgin Islands for *London Town* (cf).

FARON Real name Bill Ruffley. Faron was leader of Liverpool band Faron's Flamingos, who appeared on a number of bills with the Beatles. A popular lead singer, Faron had been nicknamed 'The Panda-Footed Prince of Prance' by local DJ Bob Wooler. While on a visit to Liverpool in the seventies, I was told that Faron had found a pair of old leather trousers in his attic, which he claimed belonged to Paul McCartney, who'd left them behind in a dressing room. The trousers turned up as Lot 214 in Sotheby's 1984 Beatles auction. Paul claimed ownership of the trousers and they were withdrawn. The Sotheby's catalogue entry read: "Paul McCartney's leather trousers, of black leather (altered and worn) with letter of authenticity, © 1960/1. The above were given, in lieu of payment for a meal, to the leader of the group Faron's Flamingos who used to play at the Liverpool Cavern with the Beatles." The value of the trousers had been assessed by Sotheby's at between £600 and £800.

FELIX, JULIE American folk singer based in Britain during the sixties. She appeared regularly on television on

Julie Felix: an unpublicised girlfriend

the *David Frost Show*. Paul arranged for a mutual friend to phone her and fix up a date. They went out together for a time, but the affair was relatively unpublicised.

FELLOWS, GRAHAM Actor who portrayed Paul in the Everyman Theatre, Liverpool, production of the play *Lennon*.

FILMOGRAPHY Paul has always been interested in films and was a regular cinema-goer in his youth. He particularly remembers the time he went to see *The Blackboard Jungle* (cf) with George Harrison. A detailed round-up

'Where Did The Ringo' was Paul's original title suggestion for 'Help!'

'Help!'

'A Hard Day's Night'

of all Paul's film involvements is to be found in 'Paul's Films', a chapter in my book *Beatlemania: An Illustrated Filmography*, published by Virgin Books in 1984. Paul revealed details of eight of his favourite rock movies to journalist Jan Etherington in a feature in the 13 October 1984 issue of the British magazine *TV Times*. The films were *Rock Around the Clock; The Girl Can't Help It; Loving You; A Hard Day's Night; Gimme Shelter; Woodstock; Let the Good Times Roll* and *The Song Remains the Same*. Of *A Hard Day's Night*, he commented: "I hate to say it but when you see the girls in their miniskirts and white floppy hats it does look dated." Of *Let the Good Times Roll*: "Chuck Berry was a main writing influence on John and me – together with Buddy Holly (cf). Of *Gimme Shelter*: ". . . it was made by the Maysles Brothers who made *Beatles in the USA* in 1964, I remember the Maysles well." And of *The Girl Can't Help It*: "I think it was the best rock'n'roll film ever made."

Paul's filmography is:

A Hard Day's Night (1964); *Help!* (1965); *The Next Spring Then* (1966); *The Defeat of the Dog* (1966); *Yellow Submarine* (1966); *The Family Way* (composer, 1967); *Magical Mystery*

'Yellow Submarine'

Tour (1967); *Let It Be* (1969); *Live and Let Die* (composer, 1973); *Empty Hand* (producer, 1974); *Rockshow* (1980); *The Cooler* (1982); *Give My Regards to Broad Street* (1984).

THE FIRST American musical. Paul and Linda saw the show when they were on a visit to New York in November 1981.

FIXING A HOLE Track from *Sgt Pepper* on which Paul sings lead, in addition to playing the harpsichord. Paul was to comment: "This song is just about the hole in the road where the rain gets in; a good old analogy – the hole in your make-up which let's the rain in and stops your mind from going where it will. It's you interfering with things; as when someone walks up to you and says, 'I am the Son of God'. And you say, 'No you're not; I'll crucify you,' and you crucify him. Well that's life, but it is *not* fixing a hole.

"It's about fans too: *See the people standing there/who disagree and never win/and wonder why they don't get in/Silly people, run around/they worry me/and never ask why they don't get in my door.* If they only knew that the best way to get in is not to do that, because obviously anyone who is going to be straight and like a real friend and a real person to us, is going to get in; but they simply stand there and give off, 'we are fans, don't let us in.'

"Sometimes I invite them in, but it starts to be not really the point in a way, because I invited one in, and the next day she was in the *Daily Mirror* with her mother saying we were going to be married. So we tell the fans, 'forget it.'

"If you're a junky sitting in a room *fixing* a hole then that's what it will mean to you, but when I wrote it I meant if there's a crack or the room is uncolourful, then I'll paint it."

THE FLIP WILSON SHOW American TV show hosted by Flip Wilson which presented a promotion film of 'Mary Had A Little Lamb' on 12 October 1972.

FOOL ON THE HILL One of Paul's most haunting ballads, which he included in the *Magical Mystery Tour* film. The number was also featured on the double-EP soundtrack and on *The Beatles 1967-1970*. Wings performed the number on their British tour in 1979. Paul plays piano, flute and recorder on the track, which provided a hit single for Shirley Bassey in the UK and an American chart entry for Sergio Mendez & Brazil 66. The song won a certificate of honour in the 1968/69 Ivor Novello Awards (cf) and there have been over one hundred covers of the song with versions by artists such as Petula Clark, the Four Tops, Aretha Franklin, Lena Horne and Count Basie.

FOR NO ONE Written by Paul, but one of John Lennon's favourite Beatle tracks. The number was included on *Revolver* and *Love Songs*. Cilla Black (cf) recorded the song but didn't achieve chart success with it.

FORTHLIN ROAD Street in Liverpool 18, the Allerton district, a much more middle class and a far pleasanter area than Speke, where the McCartneys had previously lived. The family moved into No. 20 Forthlin Road in 1955 and were to remain there until 1964 when Paul bought Rembrandt (cf) for his father. No. 20 had a nice back garden which overlooked a police training field, and an indoor 'loo', a rarity in those days. It was at Forthlin Road that Mary McCartney discovered she had cancer. (See also *Gaul, Tom.*)

4TH OF JULY Number penned by Paul and Linda McCartney, recorded by John Christie and issued as a single in 1974, in Britain on Polydor 2058-496 on 28 June 1974 and in the States on Capitol 3928 on 1 July. It was produced by David Clarke.

THE FOURMOST, Popular Liverpool band who performed in the same Liverpool halls as the Beatles and were to sign with Brian Epstein and appear on the Beatles Christmas shows in 1963. Their first hit, a Lennon & McCartney number, 'Hello Little Girl' reached No.9 in the British charts and was followed by another Lennon & McCartney song which had been specially written for them, 'I'm In Love', which went to No.17. In 1969, Paul produced their single 'Rosetta', a number which he had found and thought would be suitable for the band. It was issued on CBS 4041 on 21 February but failed to make any impact on the charts. Drummer Dave Lovelady told journalist Spencer Leigh: "Paul liked the way we could mimic instruments with our voices, our 'mouth music', if you like. Brian O'Hara was a trumpet and we were the trombones. We used it on 'Rosetta' and the Beatles did the same thing on 'Lady Madonna'. There were proper instruments on our record as well. I was playing the piano at the session, but Brian O'Hara told me to play it badly. I soon found out why. Paul said, 'Look, I'll do the piano bit', and so he ended up playing on the record."

David Frost

The Fourmost – 'tricked' Paul into playing on their record

FREEZE FRAME Album by Godley and Creme, issued by Polydor on 9 November 1979. Paul made a guest appearance on the album.

FROST, DAVID Television celebrity who first rose to fame in the early sixties with the satirical show *That Was The Week That Was,* Frost became a prominent TV interviewer and hosted several of his own shows on both sides of the Atlantic. Paul first appeared on *The Frost Programme* in Britain on 28 December 1967, during which he discussed the critical reaction to *Magical Mystery Tour.* He told Frost: "People were looking for a plot, but there wasn't one."

At one time Frost had a BBC radio programme, *David Frost at the Phonograph* (cf) on which Paul appeared on 6 August 1966. In June 1968 Paul filmed a one-hour interview in the States with Frost and in October 1968 he introduced his protégé Mary Hopkin on the American TV show *David Frost Presents* (See also *Felix, Julie*).

GAMBACCINI, PAUL American DJ domiciled in Britian. Gambaccini has interviewed Paul on a number of occasions for both press and radio. His series of interviews with Paul for *Rolling Stone* magazine were gathered together in book form for *Paul McCartney: In His Own Words.* He is currently writing another book on Paul. On Sunday, Christmas Eve 1982, he broadcast a programme on Paul on Radio One at four o'clock in the afternoon; this was previewed in the *Radio Times* with the comment: "Paul McCartney is the greatest tunesmith of our time – almost superhumanly so – he is erratic, depending on the discipline he imposes on himself and the degree to which he is willing to work with people who will appreciate his talent."

GAUL, TOM The McCartney's Liverpool neighbour. He moved into 18 Forthlin Road two years before Jim McCartney and his two sons moved in at No. 20. He enjoyed a friendly relationship with Paul and when fans used to gather outside the front door

Paul Gambaccini

of No. 20 he'd let Paul clamber over the backyard fence and rush out the front of his house and into a waiting car. He has said that Paul told him that the essence of some of the lyrics of 'Yesterday' concerned the death of Paul's mother. (See also *Forthlin Road.*)

GENERAL CERTIFICATE OF EDUCATION British educational certificate awarded following the passing of examination in particular subjects. The certificates are in two grades: Ordinary (O' Level) and Advanced (A' Level). Paul took his GCE exams at Liverpool Insitute (cf) and passed in six O' Level subjects, including French, German and Spanish. He had intended to study for a further two years for the A' Level in English Literature in order to pursue a career as a teacher. His career with the Beatles intervened.

GET BACK Number that Paul wrote in Apple Studios during the recording of *Let It Be.* "We were sitting in the studio and we made it up out of thin air," he said, as the number was re-corded shortly after he finished writing it. He was also to comment: "I originally wrote it as a political song: *'Don't dig no Pakistanis taking all the people's jobs, Wilson said to the immigrants, You'd better get back to your Commonwealth homes, Yeah, yeah, yeah, you'd better get back home, Now Enoch said to the folks, Meanwhile back at home, too many Pakistanis, Living in a council flat'.*"

The single was issued in Britain on 11 April 1969 on Apple R5777 with 'Don't Let Me Down' as the flip. It topped the charts in Britain and America and several other countries throughout the world. It was re-released on 6 March 1970 when EMI issued twenty-three Beatles singles at the same time. It reached the No.55 position. The track has also been included on a number of album compilations, including the 1982 *20 Greatest Hits*. There was another version of the song which featured on *Let It Be* (cf) and which has also been used on a number of compilation LPs.

GETTING CLOSER The last British single to be credited to Wings. It was issued as a double 'A' side with 'Baby's Request' (cf) on Parlophone R6027 on 10 August 1979. Both tracks were taken from *Back to the Egg*. The number only managed to reach No.60 in the UK charts. In America 'Getting Closer' was issued on Columbia 3-11020 on 5 June with 'Spin It On' as the flip and reached No.20 in the US charts. Wings included the number as part of their repertoire on their British tour in 1979.

GETTING BETTER A track on *Sgt Pepper* that was penned by Paul with some aid from John on the lyrics of the middle eight. Paul had driven to Primrose Hill in the spring of 1967 to take his dog Martha for a walk. It was a sunny day and Paul recalled a phrase often used by Jimmy Nicol, the drummer who substituted for Ringo during part of their world tour in 1964. Jimmy's phrase was a bit of positive homespun philosophy: "It's getting better." Paul mentioned to John at their next meeting that 'It's Getting

Better' sounded like a good title for a song.

GIBBS, RUSS DJ and programme controller with the Detroit radio station WKNR who, on 12 October 1969, reported that Paul had been dead since 1966 when he was killed in a road accident and had been replaced by a lookalike. He'd received information by telephone from a listener who had told him that the Beatles had been hinting to the world what had happened via clues on their album covers and in the lyrics of their songs. Gibbs began to be inundated with thousands of calls and the 'Paul Is Dead' (cf) rumours swept America like an epidemic. Gibbs pointed out that one of the clues had been on the *Magical Mystery Tour* album sleeve. The stars which compose the word 'Beatles' became a telephone number when studied upside down, he said. He presumed that the number, 537 1438, was in London and called up. The phone was answered by a journalist who didn't know what Gibbs was talking about. When Gibbs tried the number the following week, it had been discontinued.

GIDDY Number penned by Paul for Roger Daltrey's album *One of the Boys* which came out in May 1977.

GIBSON, WAYNE Minor British singer who was in Hamburg in 1961 at the same time as the Beatles. Paul told him that he had a number of original songs which Gibson might be interested in recording. Gibson turned them down saying that the opportunity of his group making records seemed remote. He was, in fact, to record for Decca, Pye and Columbia with his group Wayne Gibson & the Dynamic Sounds and, ironically, was to cut some cover versions of Beatles hits.

GIRALDI, BOB Director of the 'Say Say Say' (cf) promotional video which starred Paul and Michael Jackson (cf). Giraldi commented: "Michael could upstage anybody else but Paul McCartney. There was only one star on that set."

Girl-mad? Michael wrote 'The Girl Is Mine' as a duet for them both, Paul wrote 'Girlfriend' for Michael!

THE GIRL IS MINE Single on which Paul sang a duet with Michael Jackson. Paul was in Los Angeles in May and June 1982 when Jackson was recording his *Thriller* album and joined him on this track, which was produced by Quincy Jones. It was issued in 1982, in America on Epic 34-03288 on 25 October reaching No.2 in the charts, and in Britain on Epic EPC A2729 on 29 October reaching No.4. It was also included as the third track on *Thriller*.

GIRLFRIEND It was not by accident that this track sounded like a Jackson Five number because Paul actually wrote it with Michael Jackson in mind. The number was featured on Wings' *London Town* (cf) album, and was recorded by Michael Jackson the following year for inclusion on his album *Off the Wall*. Jackson then issued it as a single in 1980 when it reached No.30 in the charts.

GIRL'S SCHOOL Song said to have been inspired when Paul noticed some advertisements for pornographic movies in a newspaper. The original title was 'Love School'. The song was issued as a double 'A' side with 'Mull Of Kintyre' (cf) in Britain on Capitol R6018 on 11 November 1977, although it was 'Mull Of Kintyre' which got the credit for making the record the biggest-selling British single of all time, with home sales surpassing the two million mark, a record which lasted until the release of the Band Aid charity single 'Do They Know It's Christmas?' seven years later. In America it was 'Girl's School' which received the major promotion although the single only managed to reach the No.33 position.

GIVE IRELAND BACK TO THE IRISH Song that Paul wrote in reaction to 'Bloody Sunday', the tragedy which took place in Northern Ireland on 3 January 1972, when a number of Catholics were shot dead in a confrontation with British troops. Paul has Irish roots and his mother had been baptised a Catholic, so his sympathies were with the Catholics in this instance. It was also Paul's first major political statement in song and was the first single on which new guitarist Henry McCullough (cf), who was Irish, performed. The single was banned by both the BBC and the IBA, BBC press officer Rodney Collins explaining that it wasn't played on Radio One because it made a political point.

Issued in Britain on Apple R5936 on 25 February 1972, it entered the Top 20 despite the lack of plays, but didn't get higher than No.15. In America, where it was released on Apple 1847 on 28 February, it fared even worse, only reaching No.21 in the charts. Both the British and American releases had an instrumental version on the flip side.

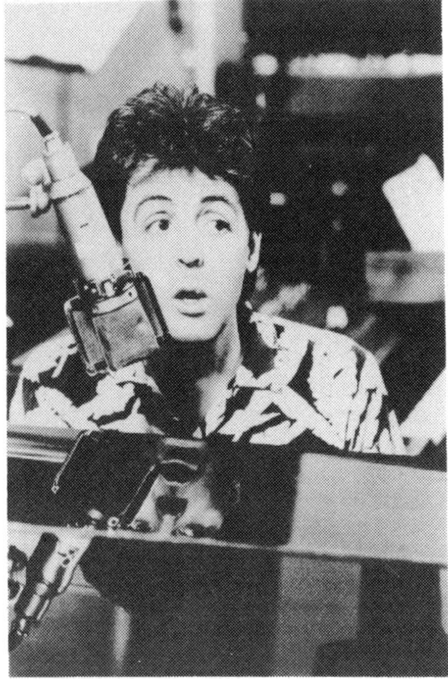

GIVE MY REGARDS TO BROAD STREET

(1)Paul's ambition to produce a major film came to fruition with *Give My Regards to Broad Street,* an original idea of his. He'd initially commissioned playwright Willie Russell to write a script. "It was a nice idea and one it may be possible to resurrect at some point," he has said, "but I felt it wasn't quite right for me at the time." He also had discussions with another playwright, Trevor Nunn, before finally deciding to write the script himself.

The idea for the plot came to him when his chauffeured car was held up in a traffic jam and he jotted down the idea on the spot. He'd remembered a story record producer Chris Thomas had told him about how an assistant had left the master tapes of the Sex Pistol's *Never Mind the Bollocks* on a station platform. He'd been due to take them to the factory and rushed back to the station to find that although the case had been soaked in the rainfall, the tapes were still intact and undamaged.

The film was two years in the planning and pre-production. Shooting eventually began in August 1982, and lasted for twenty-eight weeks. When it opened in 1984, the film was given a number of premières. The American one was held at the Egyptian Theatre, Los Angeles, on 22 October with a special party at the Bistro club. This was followed by a New York première at the Gotham Theatre, with a party

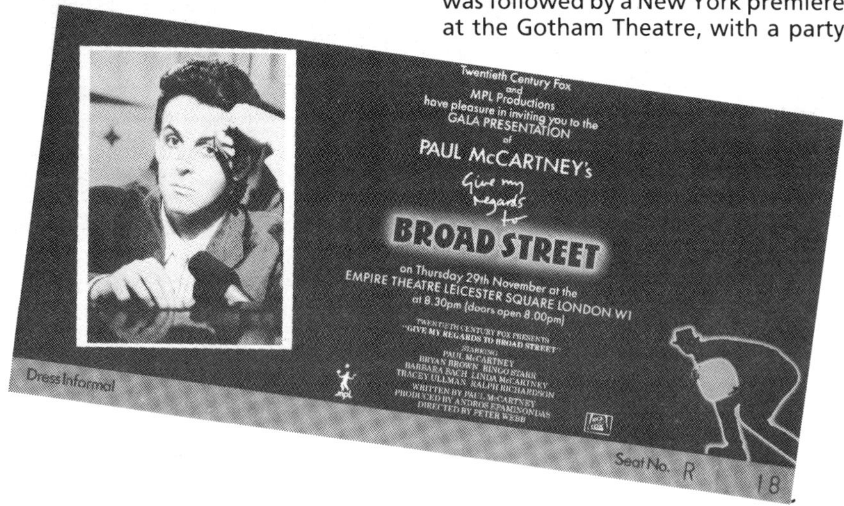

Paul's long-cherished film project was given star-studded premières in Los Angeles . . .

. . . New York, Liverpool and London

at Club A. The Liverpool première took place at the Odeon Cinema on 28 November and Paul was presented with the Freedom of the City at a special ceremony earlier in the day. The London première took place at the Empire, Leicester Square, on 29 November with a pre-première party at the Hippodrome.

Paul promoted the film on dozens of radio and television shows. He'd originally intended using the finances of his MPL (cf) company, but 20th Century Fox stepped in with funding in exchange for worldwide distribution rights. When it opened in 311 cinemas across America, it was savagely panned by the critics and was an initial box office disappointment. The show business magazine *Variety* described it as: "Characterless, bloodless and pointless." Paul commented: "I wanted to make the sort of movie that I like to see. It's an old-fashioned musical, a good night out, nothing heavy. Like most people, I go to the cinema to be entertained, not to see my own problems on the screen."

George Martin (cf) was drafted to work on the arrangements and also to appear as himself. The musicians who appeared included Dave Edmunds, Chris Spedding, John Paul Jones, Eric Stewart, Steve Lukather, Jeff Porcaro, Jody Linscott, Louis Johnson, Dave Gilmour, Dave Mattocks and Herbie Flowers. Songs featured were: 'Good Day Sunshine'; 'Here, There And Everywhere'; 'Wanderlust'; 'No More Lonely Nights'; 'Ballroom Dancing'; 'Silly Love Songs'; 'Not Such A Bad Boy'; 'So Bad'; 'No Values'; 'For No One'; 'Eleanor Rigby'; 'Band On The Run'; 'Zip A Dee Doo Dah'; 'Bless 'Em All'; 'Give My Regards To Broad Street' and 'Sleepy Lagoon'.

Prominent among the cast were Sir Ralph Richardson (cf), Tracey Ullman (cf), Bryan Brown (cf) and the wrestler 'Giant Haystacks'. Director was Peter Webb (cf).

The plot is basically a simple one which begins with Paul sitting in the back of a black limousine on his way to meet his manager Steve (Bryan Brown) for an important meeting. The car is stuck in a long traffic jam and Paul dozes off. He finds himself driving along a country road in his customised Ford, which has its own computer. He receives a call on the car phone from Steve who tells him that the master tapes of his new album have vanished. Harry (Ian Hastings),

The many moods of 'Broad Street': picnics in Victorian dress for 'Eleanor Rigby. . .

. . . and fantasy make-up for the 'Silly Love Songs' sequence

an assitant, hasn't turned up with them. Paul arrives in the boardroom where the sinister banker Rath (John Bennett) makes an appearance. He is seeking to make a takeover bid for Paul's company and will be successful if the tapes are not recovered.

Steve estimates that the missing tapes are worth five or six million pounds and Paul sets off with him to a recording studio, dismissing Steve's fears that Harry may have absconded with the tapes to bootleg them. At the studio Paul tells Ringo Starr and George Martin about the missing tapes and then goes to Elstree Studios where he joins Linda and the band to record the 'Ballroom Dancing' sequence. After a short break in the studio canteen it's off to the make-up room to apply a futuristic look for the 'Silly Love Songs' scene, and then the search for Harry and the missing tapes continues. Paul later fits in some rehearsals in a warehouse before setting off to the BBC for an interview. During a rendition of 'Eleanor Rigby' we are taken back to Victorian times as Paul, Linda, Ringo and Barbara Bach picnic on a river bank. Another scene is Dickensian as Harry is pursued by a giant figure with a bull terrier (shades of Bill Sykes!) and is eventually stabbed by Rath. The visions fade and Paul makes his way to visit the Old Justice, an East End pub where Harry had been spotted the previous evening. He chats to the landlord, Jim, and then drives into central London as the deadline for the takeover nears. Paul comes to Broad Street station and remembers that Harry had mentioned

A comforting peck from Tracey Ullman, who played Sandra in 'Broad Street'

the station when he'd left with the tapes. Paul wanders along the deserted platforms and discovers Harry, who had been accidentally locked inside a hut. Paul is able to return to his office with the tapes in time to beat the deadline of the Rath takover.

Commenting on the 'Ballroom Dancing' sequence, Paul said: "I wanted to do it in either Hammersmith Palais or the Lyceum, but the director said that the reason they don't like doing that in films is that if the lighting man suddenly says 'Take that wall out', it's alright on a set, but you could imagine the manager of the Hammersmith Palais being a bit upset!

"It was great that, we had the band on stage – John Paul Jones on bass, Ringo on drums, Dave Edmunds and Chris Spedding on guitars, Linda and me on piano, so we had that element, which was nice enough anyway. We had the back up guys, who were like the Palais band, then we had the dancers. All the formation dancers, three specialist dancers, then we had another back up of young dancers, who were like the rock'n'roll kids. One of the couples were the people who won our Buddy Holly competition, the guy who had been on the dole in Liverpool until then. So all of these elements, pulling them together, and still trying to have a laugh. I think that works really well in the film."

GIVE MY REGARDS TO BROADSTREET (2) Lavish publication issued by Pavilion Books in 1984 in association

The soundtrack album shot straight to No. 1 in Britain

with MPL Communications to coincide with the release of Paul's film. The text was penned by Andrew Harvey, who was show business editor of the *Daily Express* at the time, and excerpts from the book were serialised in the newspaper. The cover featured the David Dagley photograph that was used in the film's advertising compaign and other photographs were by Linda McCartney, Terry O'Neill, Richard Blandshard and Etienne Bol. There are over 120 colour shots and seventy black-and-white photographs. 'In The Beginning' describes the origin of the film, 'Casting Around' its development, and 'The Story' its plot. In 'The Songs', Paul discusses fourteen tracks used in the film and how he came to write them. 'Private News' is a small section on Paul, Linda and their family life.

GIVE MY REGARDS TO BROAD STREET (3) The album (EL2602781) and compact disc (CDP 2702782) of the film soundtrack were released simultaneously in Britain on 22 October 1984 by EMI Records. The album reached No.1 in the British charts and No.21 in the US. The tracks were: 'No More Lonely Nights'; 'Good Day Sunshine'; 'Corridor Music'; 'Yesterday'; 'Here, There And Everywhere'; 'Wanderlust'; 'Ballroom Dancing'; 'Silly Love Songs'; 'Not Such A Bad Boy'; 'No Values'; 'For No One'; 'Eleanor Rigby'/'Eleanor's Dream'; 'Long And Winding Road'. Paul had originally chosen a shortlist of thirty songs. He commented: "A lot of them were put in for reasons of the plot; we wanted a long one like 'Yesterday', the director wanted that more than me, because I'd sung it a lot of times!" He also said: "We did a special orchestral arrangement that takes new themes based on the *mood* of 'Eleanor Rigby', and we extended it for something like nine minutes without a vocal, which for me is quite a departure. . . The bit we needed the images for was after 'Eleanor Rigby', which was conjured up by the song's mood. So it went to altars and churches, Dickensian characters, carriages, Victorian picnics. I just threw out a lot of images, the director

picked them up and made them into this big anxiety dream."

'Good Day Sunshine', 'Here, There And Everywhere', 'For No One' and 'Eleanor Rigby' all originally appeared on *Revolver*, and 'Eleanor Rigby' (cf) was also a double 'A'-sided single with 'Yellow Submarine'. 'Yesterday' (cf) originally appeared on *Help!* and gave the Beatles their eleventh No.1 in the States when issued as a single. 'The Long And Winding Road' first appeared on *Let It Be*, and Paul also included a new version on *Wings Over America* (cf). 'Silly Love Songs' was Wings' first British No.1 single and also appeared on *Wings at the Speed of Sound* (cf). 'Wanderlust' and 'Ballroom Dancing' originally appeared on Paul's fourth album *Tug of War* (cf); the film version of 'Ballroom Dancing' includes an extra verse which Paul added at the director's request. 'Wanderlust' was also the name of one of the yachts that Wings chartered when they were recording *London Town* (see *Virgin Islands*). 'No More Lonely Nights' (cf) was the first single to be released from the film project and there were several versions of it. 'Not Such A Bad Boy' and 'No Values' were brand new and appeared on the *Broad Street* album for the first time anywhere.

GIVIN' GREASE A RIDE Number which Paul co-wrote with his brother Mike for the 1974 *McGear* album, which Paul also produced. Paul also plays on this track.

GOD BLESS AMERICA A single by Thornton, Fradkin and Unger, issued in America in June 1974. The track was originally recorded in 1971 and was included on the album *Pass on This Side*, issued in July 1974. Wings' drummer Denny Seiwell (cf) had introduced Paul and Linda to Paul Thornton, Leslie Fradkin and Bob Unger and Paul agreed to make a guest appearance on this track. He played bass guitar and also provided backing vocals.

GOLDEN GATE HOTEL When Paul's car broke down in Scotland during a trip to his Campbeltown farm (see *High Park Farm)* the pair booked into the hotel while they waited for a garage to do the repairs.

GOLDEN SLUMBERS English hymn, based on a 400-year-old poem by Thomas Dekker. Paul's stepsister Ruth approached him one day when he was composing on the piano and showed him the sheet music of 'Golden Slumbers', asking if he could read music. He admitted he couldn't, but was intrigued by the number and composed his own lyrics to one of the verses. He then contributed some further additions and the finished song appeared on *Abbey Road* (cf (1)).

GOODMAN GALLERY New York art gallery which presented an exhibition of Linda's photographs from 9-30 September 1982.

GOODNIGHT TONIGHT Wings single issued on Parlophone R6023 on 23 March 1979. There was also a special extended disco version issued on the same day. The number reached No.6 in the British charts. It had been issued in America some days before, on 15 March, on Columbia 3-10939 and reached the No.5 position. The British 12" version was issued on Parlophone 12Y R6023 and the American on Columbia 23-10940. 'Daytime Nightime Suffering' was the flipside on all versions.

GOOD MORNING AMERICA Famous American chat show hosted by Johnny Carson (cf). When Paul appeared on the programme on 23 October 1984, he attracted the biggest studio audience applications ever for the show. He was in the US to promote his film *Give My Regards to Broad Street* (cf (1)). Paul had previously appeared on the programme on 15 May 1968, when the host was Joe Garragiola. On that occasion Paul had discussed the Beatles' plans for setting up their Apple Corps organisation.

GORTIKON, STANLEY Head of the Beatles' American label Capitol Records in 1968 when Paul took him to lunch at London's fashionable Ritz Hotel in Piccadilly. Initially, Paul was told he couldn't enter the restaurant without a tie, but eventually they allowed him to enter wearing a roll-neck sweater.

GOT TO GET YOU INTO MY LIFE Song penned by Paul and featured on *Revolver,* issued on 5 August 1966. On the same day the Cliff Bennett & The Rebel Rousers (cf) single was issued, which Paul had personally produced. American group Earth, Wind and Fire recorded a version for the Robert Stigwood film, *Sgt Pepper's Lonely Hearts Club Band,* and this reached No.4 in the US charts in August 1978, although it only reached No.30 in Britain.

GOTTA SING, GOTTA DANCE Song Paul originally wrote for Twiggy in 1973. The TV special in which she was to sing it was never made, but Paul was able to utilise the number as the highlight of his *James Paul McCartney* (cf) TV spectacular.

GRAFTON BALLROOM Mecca ballroom in West Derby Road, Liverpool. The Beatles made two appearances there in the early sixties. Paul recalled that he entered several talent contests at the Grafton and lost most of them!

GREENHAM COMMON Site of a Cruise missile base in the Berkshire countryside where large groups of women camped out for several months in order to demonstrate their opposition to the weapons. In December 1983, Paul and Linda sent the women some expensive food hampers from London's Fortnum & Mason's, a high-class grocery store in Piccadilly, with the message: "You are doing a great job. Keep it up and don't give in."

GRILLO, OSCAR Film animator who translated Linda's 'Seaside Woman' (cf) into an animated short which won the Palme d'Or at the Cannes Film Festival in 1980. Paul also commissioned him to participate in the animation of a Rupert Bear (cf) cartoon but it was finally done by another artist.

GUILDHALL PORTSMOUTH Venue where the Beatles were due to appear on 12 November 1964 during a British tour. The show was cancelled as Paul was suffering from gastric flu. The booking was rearranged and the Fab Four appeard there a few weeks later on 3 December.

GUINNESS SUPERLATIVES Company which publishes the world's best-selling book, *The Guinness Book of Records.* To celebrate a new edition in 1979 they organised a special promotional reception at London's Les Ambassadeurs Club, announcing that the event was to honour Paul. The date was 24 October and Norris McWhirter, co-founder of the book, presented Paul with a rhodium-plated disc. This unique metal is twice as valuable as platinum and makes a handsome award. It was announced that Paul had been honoured because he was 'The Most Successful Composer And Recording Artist Of All Time' for the following three reasons: 1) he'd written forty-two songs which had sold over a million; 2) he'd been awarded sixty Gold Discs; and 3) he'd sold more records worldwide than anyone else.

HAMBURG Title of article by Paul in the 20 September 1962 issue of Mersey Beat. This report on the Beatles first trip to Hamburg in 1960 was an edited-down version of a letter that Paul had sent me some time previously:

"The first time we went to Hamburg we stayed four and a half months. It's a sort of blown up Blackpool, but with strip clubs instead of waxworks: thousands of strip clubs, bars and pick-up joints, not very picturesque.

"The first time it was pretty rough, but we all had a gear time. The pay wasn't too fab, the digs weren't much good, and we had to play for quite a long time. The club was a small place called the Indra and was owned by the proprietor of the Kaiser Keller, where we also played.

"One night we played at the Top Ten Club and all the customers from the Kaiser Keller came along. Since the Top Ten was a much better club,

we decided to accept the manager's offer and play there. Naturally, the manager of the Kaiser Keller didn't like it. One night prior to leaving his place, we accidentally singed a bit of cord on an old stone wall in the corridor, and he had the police on us. He'd told them that we'd tried to burn his place down, so they said: 'Leave please, thanks very much, but we don't want you to burn our German houses.' Funny, really, because we couldn't have burnt the place if we had gallons of petrol – it was made of stone.

"There was an article on the group in a German magazine. I didn't understand the article, but there was a large photograph of us in the middle page. In the same article there was a photograph of a South African negro pushing the jungle down. I still don't quite know what he has to do with us, but I suppose it has some significance."

HAMILTON, ALAN Author of *Paul McCartney,* the book in the 'Profiles' series of children's books, issued by Hamish Hamilton in 1983. A journalist with the Times newspaper, Hamilton also penned another book in the series: *Queen Elizabeth II.*

HAMILTON GALLERY Situated in Mayfair, London. MPL staged Linda's first London exhibition here, which contained shots from her book *Photographs.* At the show, which ran from 25 September to 15 October 1982, prints were available at prices ranging from £184 to £560.

HAMMERSMITH ODEON Major London concert venue which presented the Beatles Christmas Concerts. Paul and Wings appeared there in 1973 on 25-26-27 May. They returned in 1975 to appear on 17 and 18 September. The venue was used for the 1979 Concerts For Kampuchea (cf) in which several leading musicians joined Wings in a 'Rockestra' (cf) encore.

HANDS ACROSS THE WATER: WINGS TOUR USA Lush photo-record of the Wings American tour between May and June 1976. Published in April 1978 by Paper Tiger in Britain and by Reed Books in America. Produced by Paul's company MPL Communications Ltd, it has graphics by George Hardie, a small introduction written by Paul and a massive portfolio of almost 200 photographs by Aubrey Powell. Pictures were taken almost every hour of the tour in an attempt to capture the complete essence of life on the road. The architecture of the cities they pass, the traffic on the roads, the vista of the landscapes en route, the hotel bedrooms, concert hall corridors, multi-seated arenas are all explored. And, of course, the people: directors, designers, security men, plane pilots, limo drivers, cops, fans, merchandisers, all with faces that tell their own stories. The whole behind-the-scenes life of Paul, Linda and Wings is contained in the book: the family tableaux, the rehearsals and finally, the on-stage fun.

Altogether a marvellous tour souvenir which, in a way, is also a historical document.

HANDS OF LOVE Track on *Red Rose Speedway* (cf), with Linda helping Paul on the vocals.

A HANNEY & CO Name of former Cotton Brokers & Merchants, a firm in Chapel Street, Liverpool, where Jim McCartney (cf), Paul's father, first began work as a sample boy at the age of fourteen. Jim originally earned six shillings a week and by the age of twenty-eight had progressed to the position of Cotton Salesman earning £250 per annum.

HAPPY DAYS Name of yacht hired by Paul and Ringo when they took Jane Asher and Maureen Cox on a holiday in the Virgin Islands in 1964. While he was on the yacht, Paul penned the number 'Things We Said Today', which was featured in *A Hard Day's Night*.

THE HARD ROCK CAFE, Fashionable American style venue in London's Park Lane. On 18 March 1973, Paul and Wings played a one-hour set at the Hard Rock before two hundred guests. The occasion was a charity show to raise money for Release, the London-based organisation that helps victims of drug abuse. At the time, Paul had been convicted of possessing cannabis only ten days previously.

HARRISON, NOEL Singer son of actor Rex Harrison. Noel had a major hit with 'Windmills Of Your Mind' and it was reported that Paul had written a song for him, although I can find no actual evidence of his recording a McCartney original.

HAVE YOU GOT PROBLEMS Paul co-wrote this number with his brother Mike for the 1974 *McGear* album.

HEART OF THE COUNTRY Track from *Ram* (cf) that was issued in Britain as a single with 'Back Seat Of My Car' (cf), but it made little impact, only managing to reach No.39 in the charts. The number was featured on the *James Paul McCartney* (cf) TV special.

HEART THAT YOU BROKE Number which Wings recorded during their sessions in Nashville in 1974.

HEATH, DUNCAN A London-based theatrical agent. Paul signed with him in 1984, having enjoyed his acting stint in *Give My Regards to Broad Street* (cf (1)). Heath is on the look-out for further movie properties for Paul to appear in and commented: "I've worked with Jack Nicholson, Ryan O'Neil, Ralph Richardson – and McCartney's right up there with them. He's absolutely superb."

HEATHER Unreleased song dedicated to his stepdaughter (see *McCartney, Heather*) which Paul wrote and recorded in 1968. (See also *Cold Cuts* and *Unreleased Songs*.)

HEAVEN CAN WAIT Oscar-winning movie directed by and starring Warren Beatty. Paul composed a song specially for the film's soundtrack entitled 'Haven't We Met Somewhere Before?' The number wasn't used then, but re-emerged as the first number in the film *Rock and Roll High School*.

HELEN WHEELS The nickname Paul gave to his Land Rover, which provides the inspiration to a song about his trip from Scotland to London in the vehicle. The single was issued in 1973, in Britain on Apple R5993 on 26 October and in America on Apple 1869 on 12 November. The number went to No.12 in Britain and No.10 in the States. 'Country Dreamer' was the flip. 'Helen Wheels' was included on the American album of *Band on the Run,* but not the British version. (Hell On Wheels! – get it?)

HER MAJESTY Closing track on *Abbey Road* (cf (1)), and the shortest Beatles track on record at twenty-three seconds in length. Paul composed the number in tribute to Queen Elizabeth II and copies of the album were sent to Buckingham Palace. Paul played acoustic guitar and sang solo on the number.

HERE TODAY A ballad, featured on the April 1982 *Tug of War* album, that Paul wrote as his tribute to John Lennon. On it, Paul sings and plays acoustic guitar. Backing is provided by Jack Rothstein and Bernard Patridge on violins, Ian Jewel on viola and Keith Harvey on cello. Paul was to comment: "One of the feelings you always have when someone close to you dies like that is that you wish you could have seen him the day before to square everything up and make sure he knew how much you really cared. The song is about saying to John: 'Do we really have to keep this sort of thing up?' But we never got around to doing it. I guess we never felt any urgency about it. We were behaving like we were going to live forever. . . I was kind of crying when I wrote it."

HERE, THERE AND EVERYWHERE One of Paul's favourite songs: "This one was pretty much mine, written sitting by John's pool. Often I would wait half an hour while he would do something – like get up. So I was sitting there tootling around in E on the guitar." It was included on *Revolver* in 1966 and on *Love Songs* in 1967. Paul re-recorded the number for *Give My Regards to Broad Street.*

HERRE, JOTTE Dutch band who recorded Paul's 'Penina'. It was issued in Holland in 1970 on Philips 369 002PF.

HEUBERS, ERIKA AND BETTINA Mother and daughter who have spent a number of years in a legal battle with Paul. It concerns Erika's claim that Paul is the father of her daughter.

Erika worked in a Hamburg club and said that as a result of an affair with Paul she became pregnant. She also claimed that Paul encouraged her to have an abortion. Paul said that he didn't remember her or any affair they were reputed to have had in 1961.

Erika sued him in 1966 and although Paul didn't admit paternity, he paid up, commenting at a later date: "It was 1966 and we were due to do a European tour. I was told that if the maintenance question wasn't setled we couldn't go to Germany. I wasn't going to sign a crazy document like this, so I didn't. Then we were actually on the plane leaving for the tour when they put the paper under my face and said if I didn't sign, the whole tour was off. They said the agreement would deny I was the father and it was a small amount anyway. I've actually seen a letter from Brian Epstein saying it would be cheaper to sign than not go to Germany where we could make a lot of money."

Paul paid up £2,700 which would be the equivalent of £10,000 today, and claimed that he was virtually tricked into paying for Erika's support until Bettina was 18. When Bettina came of age her mother instigated the current action.

From 1981 the publicity began to plague Paul because everyone acted as if the case against him had been proven – regular newspaper coverage about Bettina kept referring to her as 'Beatle Girl' and similar phrases. Paul has commented: "What I object to most is the effect on my children. It's not fair to them. Why should they suffer? She [Bettina] was on the cover of *Time* magazine in 1983 and there was a picture of her holding one of my record covers with the comment, 'Dad says. . . ' Not even *alleged* father. My kids had to read that. You have to put it down to life being tough at the top."

The case was first heard at the District Court, Schoeneberg, Berlin on 22 February 1983, and Paul appointed a German lawyer, Dr Klaus Wachs, to represent him. The Heubers were asking for maintenance of 1,500 marks per month (approximately £375) and an official declaration from Paul that he was the father. Under German law, if it were proven that Bettina was Paul's daughter, she would be entitled to inherit ten per cent of any money he might leave. This would only be enforcable in Germany – but all German royalities could be frozen.

Paul had agreed to have blood and tissue samples taken and his first blood test was in February 1983. A blood test proves paternity with ninety per cent certainty. It identifies proteins and enzymes in the child which must be present in the mother's or father's blood. In March 1983, he was ordered to pay the £180 a month interim maintenance by the German court who rejected the evidence of the blood test, which had indicated that Paul was not the father.

Paul said: "It seems the girl's blood contains something that is not in mine or the mother's, so it must come from the third person and he is the real father."

In April 1983, the German court finally awarded full maintenance. Paul commented: "One thing I think is very unfair is that the judge is a woman and is pregnant herself. But I'm not going to ask for a different judge, I just want to get the whole thing settled."

In June 1983, stories began to appear in the press with headlines such as 'Beatle Girl Strips To Raise Cash'. Bettina was then twenty and had posed naked for the sexy magazine *High Society*. There were eight pages of her wearing only leather gloves and carrying a glass guitar. It was disclosed that she received £600 for the session and said she was forced to do it because Paul refused to pay the maintenance that had been awarded by the court in April. She'd worked as a kindergarten teacher until then and had hoped to start a new job in September. Her mother, now 39, commented: "The pictures are very tasteful. . . she did the session because she is broke and Paul hasn't paid her any maintenance money yet." In fact it seemed rather naive of her to accept only £600 when the pictures were syndicated throughout the world and must have generated tens of thousands of pounds in reproduction fees.

By the time Bettina was twenty-two and settled in Berlin as a hairdresser, she had lost two cases concerning her claim and Paul had had a further blood test which once again indicated that he was not her father. As Bettina had lost the case, she was liable to pay Paul's legal costs of £60,000. Dr Wachs advised Paul that he pay the money, commenting: "I advised Paul, and he agreed, for psychological reasons he should by no means enforce his right for costs. It was my opinion that if he did, this would give Miss Heubers another cause to make bad publicity for him."

However, after Paul had made the generous gesture, Bettina announced that she would bring another paternity case against him, saying: "I think it is very odd that Paul paid these costs for us and this will be prominently brought forward in our new case."

HEY JUDE This was the Beatles' longest single at seven minutes fifteen seconds and their first to be issued on the Apple label. It was released simultaneously in Britain and America on 26 August 1968, in the UK on Apple R522 and in the US on Apple 2276. It went to No.1 on both sides of the Atlantic and in at least ten other countries around the world. The single was re-released in 1982 as part of the batch of Beatles records celebrating their twentieth anniversary. It was featured on *The Beatles 1967-1970*, and a *Hey Jude* album was issued in the States in 1970 and in Britain in 1979. The song has also been included on the *Beatles Ballads* and *The Beatles Box* in 1980.

Regarded as one of their major

Julian Lennon, the inspiration for 'Hey Jude'

classics, it has been recorded by hundreds of different artists, covering a wide musical spectrum, including Chet Atkins, Count Basie, Petula Clark, Bing Crosby, the Everly Brothers, Ella Fitzgerald, Stan Kenton, Joe Loss and His Orchestra, Wilson Pickett, Elvis Presley and Dionne Warwick. The only version apart from the Beatles' to reach the charts was Pickett's. 'Hey Jude' received the American award for being 'The Most Performed Pop Song' in 1968, 1969 and 1970.

Discussing the origin of the song, Paul says: "It was going to be 'Hey Jules' but it changed. I happened to be driving out to see Cynthia Lennon. I think it was just after John and she had broken up, and I was quite mates with Julian. He's a nice kid, Julian. And I was going out in me car just vaguely singing this song. I started to sing *Hey Jules, don't make it bad,* and then I changed it to *Hey Jude,* you know, the way you do. It was just a name. It was just like 'Hey Luke' or 'Hey Max' or 'Hey Abe' but 'Hey Jude' was better.

"To one feller 'Hey Jude' meant Jew, 'Juden Raus' – 'Jews Get Out'. At the time we had the Apple shop, I went in one night and put whitewash on all windows and rubbed out 'Hey Jude' as a big ad. I thought it was a great thing, nothing happening in the shop, let's use the window as a big advertising thing for the record. So I did this 'Hey Jude' right across the window and some feller from a little Jewish delicatessen rang up the office the next day. He said 'If my sons vere vif me, I'd send von of them around to kill you. You are doing this terrible thing wif the Jewish name. What you vant? Juden Raus, you trying to start the whole Nazi thing again?'"

HI HI HI Single issued by Wings in Britain on Apple R5973 on 1 December 1972. Paul co-wrote the number with Linda, and they also jointly composed the 'B' side 'C Moon' (cf). BBC Radios One and Two banned 'Hi Hi Hi', declaring the lyrics were sexually suggestive. Most disc jockeys played 'C Moon' instead and the single reached No.3 in the British charts despite the ban. It was issued in the States on Apple 1857 on 4 December and

reached No.10 in the charts. 'Hi Hi Hi' was included on *Wings Greatest* and a 'live' version of it was featured on the triple album *Wings Over America*. It was also featured in the UK version of the *James Paul McCartney* (cf) TV special in the repertoires of the 1972 European, the 1973 British and the 1975-76 world tours.

HIGH LIFE British Airways' in-flight magazine for passengers. In the June 1984 issue, Alexander Walker, film critic of London's *The Standard*, interviewed Paul, mainly about the filming of *Give My Regards to Broad Street*.

HIGH PARK FARM At the height of their romance, Jane Asher recommended to Paul that he invest in a farm which they could use as a retreat. In June 1966 they went to view High Park Farm in Scotland. Farmer's wife Janet Brown commented: "Our farm has been up for sale for a while now but what a surprise my husband and I had when we saw the famous pair – Paul told me that it had always been his ambition to own a farm in Scotland." Paul purchased the farm and Jane helped him to furnish it. The farm comprised 183 acres near Machrihanish, the nearest town being Campbeltown. The affair with Jane over, Paul continued to enjoy relaxing at the faraway retreat, which was greeted with equal enthusiasm by Linda when the couple were married.

The area was too bleak and hilly for cows, so Paul bought sheep, almost two hundred of them. However, he couldn't bear the thought of killing them and rarely sent any to market, allowing them to breed. For some time Paul sheared the sheep himself with hand shears, sending the wool to the Wool Marketing Board. The couple also grow lots of vegetables on the farm and stable horses such as Drake's Drum (cf), Honor and Cinnamon, along with ponies Coconut, Cookie and Sugarfoot. Paul took to the farming life and Linda once bought him a tractor as a Christmas present. (See also *Vegetarianism.*)

HIPGNOSIS London-based design firm made up of designers who specialise in music-related work and have been responsible for hundreds of critically acclaimed album sleeves. Aubrey Powell (nicknamed 'Po') and Storm Thorgerson covered the Wings 1976 tour of the US and put together the book *Hands Across the Water* (cf). Storm and Gordon House designed the sleeve of *Band on the Run.* The company won *Music Week's* Album Cover of the Year Award in 1975 for *Venus and Mars* (cf). The photograph of Wings used in the centrefold of the sleeve was taken by Aubrey Powell, and the graphics for the cover and inner sleeve were supplied by George Hardie. Other covers designed by the company include *Wings at the Speed of Sound* (cf), *Wings Over America* (cf), *Thrillington* (cf), *Back to the Egg* (cf) and *Tug of War* (cf). They also assisted Paul with the design and finished artwork for the *London Town* (cf) and *Wings Greatest* (cf) albums.

HOG HILL Name of windmill which Paul bought in 1982, in Icklesham, quite close to his house in Peasmarsh, East Sussex (see *East Gate Farm.)*

HOLLY, BUDDY The legendary rock-'n'roll artist who was a seminal influence on the Beatles. The group played several of his numbers on their early gigs and recorded his 'Words of Love' and 'Crying Waiting Hoping'. Although George Harrison was quoted as saying that the name Beatles was inspired by the motorcycle gang 'the Beetles' led by Lee Marvin in *The Wild Ones*, it is generally acknowledged that the group chose the title when seeking a similar name to that of Holly's backing group the Crickets. Stuart Sutcliffe is said to have thought of the name, John Lennon replacing one of the 'e's' with an 'a'. (Incidentally, *The Wild Ones* was banned in Britain for more than a decade after it was made, therefore the Beatles could not have seen it before choosing a name).

Tragically, Buddy Holly died in an air crash in 1959.

Paul launched the very first 'Buddy Holly Week' in 1976, the year in which he acquired the Buddy Holly catalogue of songs. It was to become an annual event, and Paul chose to stage it in September, the anniversary month of Holly's birth on 7 September 1936. The first week was launched on what would have been Buddy's 40th birthday. The first special guest of honour at the launch was Norman Petty, Buddy's manager and mentor, who presented Paul with a pair of Buddy's cufflinks in recognition of his work in keeping Buddy's name alive. There was also a Buddy Holly disco and a special luncheon.

In 1977 the 'Buddy Holly Week' was held at the Gaumont, Kilburn, in north west London, where Buddy Holly and the Crickets had played in 1958. Paul flew in the Crickets for the event.

The week in 1978 saw Paul organise the British première of the feature film *The Buddy Holly Story*, which was followed by a star-studded party at the West End nightspot Peppermint Park.

Guest of honour at the 1979 event was Buddy's widow Maria Elena, who commented: "Paul told me that Buddy had more influence on his early songwriting than any other singer. Paul was very gracious, and I appreciated what he had to say." Paul again flew in the Crickets to appear at the Hammersmith Odeon, alongside Bob Montgomery (Buddy's first musical partner), Don Everly, Albert Lee and Paul and Linda. The event was filmed by MPL (cf).

The 1980 'Buddy Holly Week' was celebrated by a fan fair at the Clarendon Hotel in Hammersmith, with rare records, memorabilia and photos on display. Capital Radio broadcast an hour-long dramatised biography of Buddy, *The Day the Music Died,* to commemorate the occasion.

The Electric Cinema in Portobello Road, London, was the setting for the 1981 week, with *The Buddy Holly Story* being screened each night, alongside support films, a different one each night, such as *Don't Knock the Rock* and *Shake Rattle and Roll.* There were also commercial advertisements from the period and old Pathé Pictorial newsreels. As with all events associated with the 'Buddy Holly

Week', fans were not charged a penny, Paul's aim being simply to keep Buddy's name and music alive.

The highlight of the 1982 week was a 'Buddy Holly Rock'n'Roll Championship' dance competition. Heats had been held in halls throughout the country and the grand finale took place at the Lyceum, London, on 7 September. The three winning couples (Les and Tanneh Prendergast from Liverpool, Kevin and Pippa Ford

Promotion for 1984's Buddy Holly Week

and Trevor Luff and Helen Shore) were flown, at Paul's expense, for a holiday at Buddy's birthplace in Lubbock, Texas, and were met at Dallas Airport by Maria Elena Holly Diaz.

Lubbock itself hosted the 'Buddy Holly Week' in 1983. A special 'Holly Hop' was held, as well as 'Look Alike Contests' and other events.

In 1984 Paul launched a competition to find the best amateur portrait drawing or sketch of Buddy. Hundreds of artists competed and the first prize was £1,000. Judges were Paul, Humphrey Ocean and David Oxtoby and the top 100 entries were exhibited at the Hamilton Gallery, Carlos Place, London, from 8-14 September.

In 1985 Paul teamed up with BBC 2's *Arena* to produce a 65-minute film to mark the tenth anniversary of the 'Buddy Holly Week'. This was screened on Thursday, 12 September and contained rare footage of Buddy and his contemporaries – Elvis Presley, Chuck Berry and Jerry Lee Lewis. Among those interviewed on the programme were Buddy's brothers Travis and Larry; guitarist Sonny Curtis, an early collaborator; Jerry Allison, drummer with the Crickets and Buddy's best friend; Ben Hall, a Lubbock disc jockey; Joe Mauldin, the Crickets bass player; Vi Petty, Norman Petty's widow; Bob Thiele, head of A&R at Coral Records; Murray Deutch, head of Southern Music; Don and Phil Everly; Keith Richards; Maria Elena Holly Diaz and Paul. Paul commented: "It's hard to believe it's nearly a quarter of a century since his death, but the great thing about Buddy Holly – the great thing about rock'n'roll – is that it's timeless. Some people say that rock'n'roll died with Buddy Holly. I say, 'Rock'n'Roll dead? That'll be the day!'"

The documentary also contained the following archive material:

1 The earliest known concert footage of Elvis Presley, filmed in autumn 1955 in Lubbock Civic Auditorium by Lubbock DJ Ben Hall. In addition to Elvis' performance, the film features backstage glimpses of Johnny Cash, Carl Perkins (cf), Elvis fooling around with his band members, and the nineteen-year-old Buddy Holly.

2 Footage of Chuck Berry, Jerry Lee Lewis, Frankie Lymon & the Teenagers and Screamin' Jay Hawkins on an Alan Freed package tour of America, in the spring of 1985. The film was shot by a fourteen-year-old fan, Tom Cederberg, from his seat in the audience.

3 Buddy Holly and the Crickets on tour in Hawaii, Australia and Britain. This film was shot by Norman Petty, Buddy Holly's Manager and producer between January and March 1958. In addition to shots of the group in Cambridge and Salisbury, the Crickets are also shown onstage at an undetermined British venue. This film had been in Petty's possession since 1958 and had nev-

er been seen before publicly.

4 The world première of the Beatles first ever recording, Buddy Holly's 'That'll Be The Day'. Recorded in Liverpool in 1958 when the group was known as the Quarrymen, the record had been in the hands of a collector for many years and was only recently purchased by Paul.

5 The first showing of the entire, reprocessed home movies made by James Allison, brother of Cricket drummer Jerry Allison. It is the last footage of Buddy alive and was taken in Lubbock in the summer of 1958. Holly and the Crickets are shown riding on their brand new motorcycles and re-enacting scenes

Paul and his protégée Mary Hopkin – she was not happy at Apple

from James Dean's *Rebel Without a Cause.*

6 Buddy Holly and the Crickets on stage in Detroit, Michigan.

HOLLY, STEVE Drummer who replaced Joe English (cf) in Wings in 1978 on the recommendation of Denny Laine (cf). Steve had previously worked with artists such as Elton John and Kiki Dee. (See also *Donaghue, Peter).*

HOLLY DAYS Tribute album to Buddy Holly made by Paul and Denny Laine at Paul's Rude Studios in Scotland. Denny sang lead vocals, Paul produced, played guitar and drums, and provided backing vocals with Linda. The album was issued in 1977, in Britain on EMI 781 (LP) on 6 May and in America on Capitol ST 11588 (LP) on 19 May. Tracks were: 'Heartbeat'; 'Moondreams'; 'Rave On'; 'I'm Gonna Love You Too'; 'Fool's Paradise'; 'Lonesome Tears'; 'It's So Easy'; 'Listen To Me'; 'Look At Me'; 'Take Your Time'; and 'I'm Looking For Someone To Love'.

THE HONORARY CONSUL 1984 film starring Michael Caine and Richard Gere, based on the Graham Greene novel of the same name. The movie was directed by John McKenzie, director of the 'Take It Away' video, and Paul was commissioned to compose the title music. A single, 'Paul McCartney's Theme From The Honorary Consul', by guitarist John Williams was issued on Island Records (IS 155) on 19 December 1983. The film was called *Beyond the Limit* in America.

HOPKIN, MARY A young, blonde folk singer from Pontardawe in Wales who came to the attention of Paul when Twiggy (cf) called him after spotting Mary on the popular TV talent show *Opportunity Knocks,* on which she appeared three times. Paul contacted her and signed her to Apple, deciding to produce her first single himself. He chose the song 'Those Were The Days', a number he had liked for several years and had once suggested that the Moody Blues record. It was among the first of the Apple releases and sold five million copies worldwide. Using the same instrumental backing, Mary also sang the number in Italian, French, Spanish and German. The hits on the Continent led to Paul recording her singing two more numbers in Italian, 'Quelli Erano Giorni' and 'Lontano Dagli Occhi', and another song in French 'Prince En Avignon'. 'Those Were The Days' hit the No.1 spot in Britain and No.2 in America. Paul participated in her early promotion and turned up with Linda at Mary's first press reception at London's Post Office Tower, where Donovan (cf) performed. Jimi Hendrix was also a guest. Mary's second Apple single 'Goodbye' was written and produced by Paul and reached No.2 in Britain and No.13 in America. Paul also produced her album *Postcard* which contained three songs by Donovan on which Paul played guitar.

Dissatisfied with the managers offered to her by Apple, Mary chose her sister Carol to be her manager. Within a year her relations with Apple became strained, and her Apple material was produced initially by Mickie Most and later by Tony Visconti, whom she later married. She left Apple in 1972.

HOPKINS, ADRIAN Liverpool promoter who, in 1977, had booked the group Tangerine Dream on a local gig. On realising that he'd forgotten to pay them their £500 fee, he set off after the group's manager, Andrew Graham Stewart, who'd left the venue a few minutes before in a Land Rover. Adrian caught up with a Land Rover a few minutes later and threw the bundle of money through the open window. It was the wrong one, however, and Paul McCartney found himself with an unexpected lapful of money (which he duly returned!)

HOT AS SUN An instrumental, penned by Paul, that had originally appeared on his 1970 album *McCartney* (cf). Over ten years later Tim Rice added some lyrics to the tune and it was issued as a single by Noosha Fox on Earlobe Records (ELB-S-105) on 24 July 1982. It was also included on the

Elaine Paige: she claimed that Paul wrote 'Hot As Sun' for her

Elaine Paige album of the same title, issued by WEA (K58385) on 2 November 1982. The sleeve notes on Elaine's LP claimed that Paul had written the number specially for her, but he actually wrote it in 1958/59.

HOWARD, MICHELLE According to newspapers, the girl who inspired the song 'Michelle'. Her father, Anthony Howard, who once worked for the Beatles organisation, said: "Michelle was a great friend of the Beatles and they loved her. They wrote a song called 'Michelle' (cf) which was done for her." In January 1981 Michelle hit the headlines in the British press with stories such as 'Drugs Battle of Beatles Michelle' when, aged 23, she was charged with shoplifting and possessing drugs for which she was given a three-week suspended jail sentence. (See also *Aspel and Company*.)

HOWARTH, PHILIP According to journalist Alistair Taylor (not Brian Epstein's former assistant of the same name), Philip Howarth was Paul's first child. Peter Brown's book *The Love You Make* revealed the tale of Paul's illegitimate son, but used false names to protect those involved. He related how Alice Boyle, with the help of her uncle, demanded money from Paul because she was pregnant. According to Brown, Paul paid her £3,000 if she agreed to keep silent on the matter and to understand that the payment was not an admission that Paul was responsible. The boy, Mark Paul Doyle, was born in Liverpool in 1963. In 1983 when the story was revealed in the British press, Alistair Taylor contributed an article entitled 'Secret McCartney Son Spurns Riches' to the *Sun* newspaper on 28 January. He said that Paul's son was called Philip

Howarth, and had been unemployed but was now working in Crosby, near Liverpool. The teenager, when told that he was Paul's son, declared that he didn't want any money. He refused to discuss the matter with the press, but his grandmother, Mrs Vi Cochrane, told of her daughter Anita's love affair with Paul. "They would go out together regularly, although it was not really serious. Then one day she confessed she was pregnant by Paul. It was a bombshell to the family." She added: "Anita just wants to forget the whole business and so does Philip. He is adamant he doesn't want any of Paul McCartney's money." At the time of the revelation, Anita was married with two other children and her husband Christopher commented: "We want to forget the past."

HUGHES, GEOFF Former Liverpool car salesman who worked in Renshaw Street, near the *Mersey Beat* offices. He became an actor following his appearance in the stage musical *Maggie May*, and continued with small parts in films such as *The Virgin Soldiers*. It was Geoff who dubbed the voice of Paul for the *Yellow Submarine* film. His biggest role was Eddie Yates, the good-hearted lodger in *Coronation Street,* which he gave up in December 1984.

HUYSDENS, OKKIE Dutch musician who took the part of Paul on the hit single 'Stars On 45', a segued record featuring several Beatles hits, sung Beatles-style.

I AM YOUR SINGER Song penned by Paul and Linda which was featured on the *Wild Life* album and performed on Wings' European tour of 1972. Paul and Linda performed the number on a New York radio station in 1971 and dedicated the song to their respective fathers.

I FEEL LIKE BUDDY HOLLY 1984 single by Alvin Stardust, penned by Mike Batt, in which Paul is mentioned by name. Alvin had changed his name from Shane Fenton and had for a time been married to Iris Caldwell (cf), an old flame of Paul's.

I LIE AROUND Number penned by Paul and sung by Denny Laine which was issued as the flipside of 'Live And Let Die' in 1973. It was the only single by Wings on which Paul didn't sing lead vocals.

I LOST MY LITTLE GIRL Song Paul wrote in 1962 which was eventually recorded by the Beatles but was never released. (See also *Cold Cuts* and *Unreleased Songs.*)

I SAW HER STANDING THERE A song penned by Paul in the pre-Epstein days which the Beatles used to perform at their local Liverpool gigs. It first appeared as the initial track on the *Please Please Me* album in Britain, then on the 'The Beatles (No.1)' EP. In the States it was included on *Introducing the Beatles* and *Meet the Beatles.* The number also surfaced on *Rock and Roll Music.* The group had performed it as part of their repertoire during their Star Club season in Hamburg and this raw version is to be found on *The Beatles Live at the Star Club* tapes (see also *Falling In Love Again).* Within weeks of *Please Please Me* being released, Duffy Power issued a single of the number, but it failed to make an impact on the charts. A version by John Lennon and Elton John is to be found on the flipside of Elton's 1975 single 'Philadelphia Freedom'. John had appeared on stage with Elton at Madison Square Garden in 1974 and this number was recorded at the concert. John had announced it as ". . . a song written by an old fiancé of mine called Paul."

I SURVIVE Adam Faith album issued by Warner Bros on 6 August 1974. Paul played synthesiser on the tracks 'Change', 'Never Say Goodbye' and 'Goodbye'. He and Linda also provided backing vocals on the track 'Star Song'.

I WANNA BE YOUR MAN Song mainly written by Paul, with a little help from John. The number hadn't actually been completed when Andrew Loog Oldham bumped into John and Paul one day and asked if they had a number suitable for the Rolling Stones to record. The two of them went to the studios and completed the number in about ten minutes. It proved to be a hit for the Stones and, many years later, a minor hit for the Revillos in 1978. The Beatles version was included on *With the Beatles* in Britain and *Meet the Beatles* in the States.

IF YOU'VE GOT TROUBLE Number which Paul composed and sang lead vocals on when it was recorded in late 1965 for *Rubber Soul*. It was not included on the final selection and remains unreleased. (See also *Cold Cuts* and *Unreleased Songs*.)

I'LL FOLLOW THE SUN Song penned by Paul which was included on the *Beatles for Sale* album and EP, the American *Beatles '65* album and the 1977 *Love Songs*.

IN HIS OWN WRITE John Lennon's first book, published by Jonathan Cape in 1964. Paul provides a humorous introduction in which he recounts his initial meeting with a fat schoolboy who was drunk. This was a reference to his meeting with John Lennon at Woolton Village fête. Paul says: "We were twelve then." (John and

Paul in fact met when they were sixteen and fifteen respectively). This was the first of many introductions that Paul was to write as a favour to friends who had books published.

I'M CARRYING A track from *London Town* (cf), one of the numbers recorded in the Virgin Islands (cf). An unusual instrument, a sort of souped up synthesiser, called a 'gizmo' is featured. This was invented by Kevin Godley and Lol Creme, former members of 10cc. The number was used as the flipside of the 'London Town' single.

I'M DOWN Number by Paul which the Beatles recorded in May 1965 and included as the 'B' side of 'Help!' It was also included on the *Rock and Roll Music* and *Rarities*. The group performed the song on their *Ed Sullivan* television appearance in September 1965 and on their 1965 and 1966 world tours when they often closed their concert performances with it.

I'M LOOKING THROUGH YOU One of many songs inspired by Jane Asher (cf) – but not in such a loving frame of mind as most of the others. Paul was angry with her because she had gone to Bristol to appear in a play. He was to comment: "My whole existence for so long centred around a bachelor life: I didn't treat women as most people do. I've always had a lot around, even when I've had a steady girl. My life generally has always been very lazy and not normal. I knew I was selfish. It caused a few rows. Jane went off to Bristol to act. I said, 'OK then, leave, I'll find someone else.' It was shattering to be without her. That was when I wrote 'I'm Looking Through You' – for Jane." The number first surfaced on the 1965 *Rubber Soul* album and has also been featured on the 1978 *The Beatles Collection* and the 1980 *The Beatles Box*. There was an interesting version of the number sung by Vincent Price to the accompaniment of spectral figures in a spoof horror edition of *The Muppet Show*.

INTERNATIONAL MUSIC ACHIEVE-MENT AWARD Prestigious award from the Songwriter's Hall of Fame in America. Paul was the recipient in 1981.

IVOR NOVELLO AWARDS Named after the Welsh composer Ivor Novello, who died in 1951, the Awards are an annual event organised by the British Academy of Songwriters, Composers and Authors.

The Beatles were the recipients of a number of collective Ivor Novello Awards during the sixties. Paul has so

Collective and individual winners of many Ivor Novello Awards

far received six personally: in 1967, for his composition 'Love In The Open Air', featured in the film *The Family Way* (cf) which was voted Best Instrumental Theme; in 1977, for 'Mull Of Kintyre', the Best Selling A-side of that year; in 1979, a Special Award for Outstanding Services to Music; in 1981, for 'Ebony & Ivory' (cf), voted the International Hit of the Year; and in 1984, for 'We All Stand Together', voted the Best Film Theme or Song of that year (George Martin accepted this on Paul's behalf, as Paul couldn't attend the ceremony due to Linda having tonsilitis).

I'VE HAD ENOUGH Song recorded in the Virgin Islands for *London Town* (cf). It was issued as a single on Parlo-

phone R6020 on 16 June 1978 in Britain, but didn't chart. In America it was released on 12 June on Capitol 4594 and reached No.25 in the charts. 'Deliver Your Children' was the flip.

I'VE JUST SEEN A FACE Song that Paul composed for the *Help!* movie and which he sings solo on the soundtrack recording. It was also included on the American release of *Rubber Soul*. Paul performed it on the Wings world tour of 1975/76, which meant that it was one of the tracks on *Wings Over America*.

IVORY IMPACT Double album by American pianist Roger Williams, produced by Paul's brother-in-law John Eastman in 1983 and containing several numbers written by Paul.

JACKSON, MICHAEL Born in August 1958 into a musical family in Gary, Indiana, Michael by the age of five had teamed up with his brothers in their group the Jackson Five. They signed to Detroit's Motown Records and began their climb to fame. They changed their name to the Jacksons in 1976 when they signed to Epic Records.

Paul had met Michael on a couple of occasions, the first at a party held aboard the *Queen Mary*, the second at a party in Beverly Hills. While they were chatting, Paul told him he'd written a song which he considered would be exactly right for him and promised to contact him when he'd polished it up. Unfortunately, he lost the number for a time and didn't call Michael. When he found it again he included it on *London Town* (cf), calling it 'Girlfriend'. When Michael began work on his first solo album for Epic, Quincy Jones brought the number to his attention, saying it would be ideal for him to record. At one time the album was going to be called *Girlfriend,* but became *Off the Wall.* The album sold seven million copies and launched Michael into solo superstardom. 'Girlfriend' became the fifth single issued from the album in Britain and reached No.30 in the charts.

Michael then wrote a number for his next album, *Thriller,* called 'The

Jackson put paid to future joint ventures when he outbid Paul for ownership of Northern Songs

Girl Is Mine'. He thought it would make a suitable duet for him and Paul, and they recorded it in Los Angeles between sessions for Paul's *Tug of War* (cf). *Thriller* was issued in 1982 and became one of the biggest-selling albums of all time. 'This Girl Is Mine' was issued as a single in Britain on Epic EPC A2729 on 29 November 1982 and reached the No.4 position. In the US it was issued on Epic 34-03288 on 3 October 1982 and reached No.2. The song was co-credited to both Michael and Paul as Paul had helped with the finishing touches.

They were to team up again in 1983 when Michael was in Britain. The two of them worked on several numbers in the studios, including 'Say Say Say', (cf) which was issued as a single in October 1983, and 'The Man', which appeared on *Pipes of Peace* (cf).

Ironically, it was Michael Jackson who, in 1985 successfully bought up ATV Music and so became the owner of Northern Songs, which Paul had been trying to buy for several years. Paul teamed up with Yoko Ono in 1981 to make a bid of $21 million for the company, but Michael purchased the catalogue for $34 million.

JAMES PAUL McCARTNEY Hour-long television special made by Sir Lew Grade's company ATV. It was described by the promotional blurb as "... a personal project of Sir Lew Grade, realised through the genius of Paul McCartney and the expertise of producer Gary Smith and director Dwight Hewison." In fact, Paul agreed to do the show in a deal struck to heal the breach caused between him and Sir Lew when Paul co-shared the composing credits with Linda on 'Another Day' (cf). Grade initially believed this was a ruse to cut into the royalties due to his company through its ownership of Lennon and McCartney material. The TV show was filmed in various places: on location in Scotland; in a Liverpool pub, where Gerry Marsden, former leader of Gerry and the Pacemakers, joined Paul and locals in a rousing singalong; and at ATV's Boreham Wood studios in front of a live audience, with Paul and Wings performing 'Big Red Barn', 'The Mess', 'Maybe I'm Amazed' and 'Long Tall Sally'. Paul also performed a medley of 'Bluebird', 'Michelle', 'Heart Of The Country', 'Mary Had A Little Lamb', and 'Yesterday'. Finally, Paul ended the show singing 'Yesterday' to his own acoustic guitar accompaniment. The show's major number was a Busby Berkeley-style musical spectacular, to the tune of 'Gotta Sing, Gotta Dance', a number Paul had originally written for Twiggy (cf). This featured a long-haired moustachioed Paul in a white tail-suit, dancing with a host of showgirls whose costumes and make-up were half male, half female. There were also scenes of Linda taking photographs of Paul, and a clip from the new James Bond movie *Live and Let Die*. Other numbers in the show were 'Little Woman Love', 'Uncle Albert', 'Another Day', 'Oh Woman Oh Why' and 'Hi Hi Hi'.

The programme was first screened in America on 16 April 1973 and in Britain on 7 June of the same year. Paul was to comment: "You could say it's fulfilling an old ambition. Right at the start I fancied myself in a musical comedy. But that was before the Beatles. Don't get me wrong. I'm no Astaire or Gene Kelly and this doesn't mean the start of something big. I don't want to be an all-rounder. I'm sticking to what I am."

The reviews in general were not exactly enthusiastic, *Melody Maker* calling it "overblown and silly."

JAMES, IAN A classmate of Paul's during his Liverpool Institute (cf) days. The two friends virtually taught each other to play guitar, passing tips, playing together. They also used to wander round the visiting fun fairs, trying to pick girls up. They began to look and dress alike, sharing the same hairstyle (like Tony Curtis's, nicknamed the DA, popular at the time) and both wore white sports jackets and drainpipe trousers. Paul said they wore the jackets because of the song 'A White Sports Coat' and described his jacket as having "speckles in it and a flap on the pockets." It was Ian who taught Paul the chords he played to John at their first meeting (see *Vaughan, Ivan* and *Twenty Flight Rock*.)

JAMMING British fan magazine, originally launched by Tony Fletcher and devoted to his favourite group, the Jam. In 1982 a member of the group, Paul Weller, introduced Tony to Paul McCartney and, on the spur of the moment, Tony asked him if he could do an interview. Paul agreed and Tony ran the lengthy piece in the fanzine, which was also distributed on the newstands, boosting its circulation from 5,000 to 15,000. The interview was also bought by the *Daily Mirror* for £5,000 and Tony used the money to prevent his fanzine from folding. It finally ceased publication early in 1986.

JAPANESE JAILBIRD Title of 20,000 word book which Paul penned him-

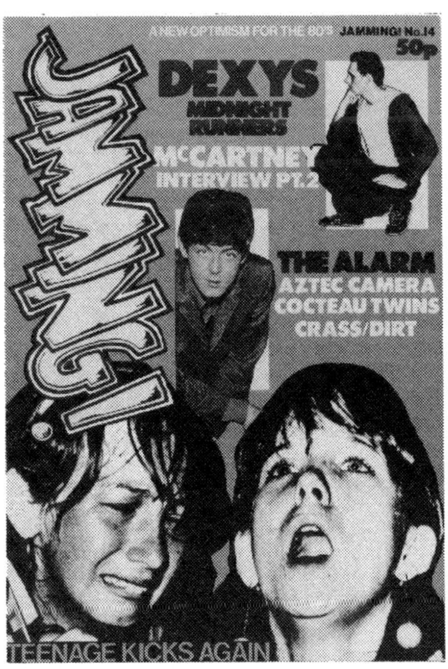

An interview with Paul kept this fanzine solvent

self and completed in 1984. It was based on this thoughts and experiences during the ten days he spent in a jail in Tokyo, Japan, in 1980, when he was arrested at the airport for possession of marijuana (see also *Drugs)*. Paul wrote the book in secret and deposited it in a bank vault. It was a project strictly 'not for publication' (although he did have one copy privately printed for himself). He was to comment: "The mercifully short time I spent in jail cured a block I've experienced as a writer ever since schooldays. It's always been my ambition to write a book."

JAPANESE TEARS (1) When the Wings tour of Japan was cancelled due to Paul's drug bust in 1980 (see *Drugs)*, Denny Laine (cf) decided to write a song about the event, which he called 'Japanese Tears'. The flipside was a number he had recorded in 1978 with Steve Holly (cf) called 'Guess I'm Only Fooling'. The single was issued in 1980, in Britain on Scratch HS 401 on 2 May and in America on 5 May on Arista AS 0511.

JAPANESE TEARS (2) Solo album issued by Denny Laine (cf) following the lack of action on the Wings front in the months following Paul's Japanese drug bust. A number of the tracks had been recorded some time previously, and three of them were actually Wings tracks – 'I Would Only Smile', first recorded in 1973, 'Send Me The Heart', recorded in 1974 and co-written with Paul, and 'Weep For Love', from the 1979 *Back to the Egg* (cf) sessions. The album was issued in Britain on Scratch SCR L 5001 on 5 December 1980, but it was not until 8 August 1983, some time after Wings had officially disbanded, that it was released in America on Takoma TAK 7103. It did not reach the charts in either Britain or the US. Artists appearing on the album, apart from Denny, included Paul and Linda, Howie Casey (cf), Steve Holly (cf), Jo Jo Laine (cf), Henry McCullough (cf) and Denny Seiwell (cf).

JEFFERSON AIRPLANE Major West Coast group of the late sixties. Paul visited them at rehearsals on 4 April 1967 when he was in San Francisco.

JET Although the lyrics of this song mention a lady suffragette, Paul insists the title was inspired by a black Labrador puppy. Paul and Linda were driving in the country one day when they came across a small roadside pet shop. On impulse they bought a little bitch puppy, the runt of the litter. As she grew up, she got into the habit of jumping over the wall of the garden in St John's Wood and would disappear for long periods of time. On one of these walkabouts she got pregnant and some months later gave birth to nine little puppies in the garage. Paul gave names to each of them, including Jet, Brown Megs and Golden Molasses. The song made its bow on *Band on the Run* (cf), and was issued as a single on 18 February 1974, on Apple R5996 in Britain where it went to No.6 in the charts, and on Apple 1871 in America, where it got to No.7. 'Let Me Roll It' was the flip on both sides of the Atlantic, with fellow Liverpudlian Howie Casey (cf) playing sax. A live version of the number was included on *Wings Over America*, recorded during the 1975/76 tour, and the song was also on the *Wings Greatest* compilation. On 4 December 1980 it was issued as the 'B' side of 'Uncle Albert/Admiral Halsey' in America on Columbia Hall of Fame 13-33408.

JOHNS, GLYN A leading British record producer/engineer. Glyn's first association with the Beatles occurred when he acted as an assistant engineer on Jack Good's television special *Around the Beatles*. A few years later Glyn received a phone call from Paul in December 1968, inviting him to work with the Beatles. Paul explained that they were producing their own television show and intended making a documentary and an album from it. The project turned out to be *Let It Be*. The tapes which Glyn recorded, together with George Martin, were later given to Phil Spector to mix. Glyn was to comment: "I cannot bring myself to listen to the Phil Spector version of the album – I heard a few bars of it once, and was totally disgusted, and think it's an absolute load of garbage." (See also *Beatles Break-Up*.)

Paul called Glyn again, this time to work on the *Red Rose Speedway* sessions, but it was said the he felt Paul's work on the album was too slow and he walked out on the sessions.

JONES, JOHN PAUL Leading British bass guitarist and former member of supergroup Led Zeppelin. John appeared on the Rockestra recordings for *Back to the Egg* (cf) and also performed with the Rockestra at the Hammersmith charity concert on 29 December 1979. He appears in some scenes in the film *Give My Regards to Broad Street* (cf (1)), performing during the 'Ballroom Dancing' sequence and at a rehearsal session.

JONES, TREVOR Road manager who oversaw all road managing duties on all the Wings tours. He generally had an average of three other roadies working under his instructions.

JOSEPH WILLIAMS PRIMARY SCHOOL In Naylorsfield Road, Belle Vale, Liverpool 25, the school where both Paul and Mike were moved when Stockton Wood Road became overcrowded. Paul was an apt pupil and came top in most subjects regularly. He did not have any difficulty in passing his 11-Plus examination and gaining entrance to Liverpool Institute (cf).

JUBER, LAURENCE Juber was twenty-five and a session guitarist when he joined Wings (the line-up known as Mark VII) in June 1978, along with drummer Steve Holly (cf). Laurence had worked with artists such as Cleo Laine and had backed Denny Laine (cf) on a television show, performing 'Go Now'. As a result he was invited to audition for Wings. He said, "Paul was one of my earliest influences. I have tremendous respect for him. When I went for the audition I was surprised – I wasn't nervous."

Laurence toured with Wings in 1979, but mainly his time with the group was spent in the recording studios. When the Wings tour of Japan was cancelled, he spent his time making some solo recordings, mainly instrumentals. In 1982 he released five of them on an album called *Standing Time* issued by Breaking Records on BRAK 1 on 9 July. Amongst the tracks was 'Maisie', an instrumental he wrote for *Back to the Egg*, (cf) recorded by Wings but left off the album itself by Paul. On the track, Paul plays bass guitar.

Juber occasionally appears at Beatles conventions in America with his wife Hope, and at one of them he told the American fanzine *Beatlefan* his thoughts about Paul: "He treated me very well. He's a very gentlemanly person, very clever, very demanding and very competitive. He's a good source of information, a brilliant musician and a very nice man, I can't say anything bad about him."

JUNGLE JUICE Band who released a version of Paul's 'Zoo Gang' in Britain one month before Wings issued their own. The record was released on Pye-Bradley BRAD 74071 on 24 May 1974.

JUNIOR'S FARM When Paul and Linda were recording in Nashville in 1974 they stayed at a farm owned by Curly Putnam, also called Junior, and decided to immortalise him on this song. Famed Country musicians Chet Atkins and Floyd Cramer joined Wings on the track. The number was issued in 1974, in Britain on Apple R5999 on 25 October and in the States on Apple 1875 on 4 November. The single reached No.3 in America and No.16 in Britain. The flipside was 'Sally G' a number reputed to have been written in honour of a Country singer whom Paul had met. In 1975 Paul decided to reverse sides, releasing 'Sally G', as the 'A' side with 'Junior's Farm' on the flip, in Britain on Apple R5999 on 7 January and in America on Apple 1875 on 7 February. It only reached No.39 in the US and was the last Paul McCartney and Wings single to be issued by Apple in both Britain and America. 'Junior's Farm' was included on the *Wings Greatest* (cf) compilation.

JUNK Number which Paul originally began to write during a trip to India.

He completed the song in time for *The Beatles* white album sessions, but it wasn't used. The number was recorded again during the *Abbey Road* (cf) sessions but was one of six numbers which were not included on the final selection. It eventually appeared on Paul's solo debut album *McCartney* (cf); he played all the instruments on the number himself, part of which he recorded at his home and part at Morgan studios in London.

KARATE CHAOS A number recorded during Wings' sessions for *Venus and Mars,* and inspired by Geoff Britton, Wings drummer and a karate champion. However, Geoff left the group during the recording sessions for the album and was replaced by Joe English, which is probably why this number was never released.

KENWRIGHT, BILL Now a major West End theatrical producer, Bill attended Liverpool Institute (cf) at the same time as Paul. He commented: "I first knew Paul when we travelled on the same bus to school. He always used to wear a big overcoat with a huge fur collar. We were both keen on acting and on one occasion were both in crowd scenes in a school production of *Saint Joan.*" Bill briefly flirted with a career as a singer before turning to acting; he appeared in the TV soap opera *Coronation Street* before becoming successful as a theatrical producer.

KLOSTERS Swiss ski resort where Paul and Jane Asher spent a short holiday in March 1966.

KLEIN, ALLEN American lawyer brought in to handle Apple Corp affairs and said to be the cause of the Beatles' demise (see *Beatles Break-Up.*)

KNIGHT, IAN Stage designer who specialises in rock shows. Ian designs the complete stage setting for bands, including the scenery, lighting and special effects. His assignments have included shows for the Who, Led Zeppelin and Wings. For the Wings shows he also designed some special back-cloths, one featuring a giant-sized copy of a René Magritte painting to illustrate the number 'C Moon' (cf) and another the David Hockney painting of a chair which was displayed during the number 'Chair'.

KOONING, WILLIAM DE Dutch artist, based in New York. Paul visited him in his studio in February 1981 and Linda took a photograph of them together. The pic was used on the cover of the issue of *Art News* magazine in which Paul discussed De Kooning during an interview.

LADY MADONNA In addition to writing the song, Paul also designed the press advertisements to promote it. The single was issued in Britain on Parlophone R5675 on 15 March 1968 and was the last Beatles single on that label. It was also the last American single to use the Capitol label. The flipside was George Harrison's 'The Inner Light' and while the number topped the charts in Britain it only reached No.2 in *Cashbox* and *Record World* and No.4 in *Billboard.* There is a brass section of four saxophones, with jazzman Ronnie Scott leading Harry Klein, Bill Povey and Bill Jackson. The track was included on a number of compilations, including *The Beatles 1967-1970, Hey Jude* and *The Beatles Box.* A live version of the number is also included on *Wings Over the World* (cf). At the time of the original release, the Beatles mentioned that the arrangement of the number was based on an old song called 'Bad Penny Blues'.

LAINE, DENNY Former member of the Moody Blues who joined Wings in 1971. Paul and Linda first hired drummer Denny Seiwell (cf), who had performed on the *Ram* (cf) album. They then asked Denny Laine, who became the fourth member.

Born Brian Hines in Birmingham on 29 October 1944, he first found fame as a member of the Moody Blues and his vocal rendition of 'Go Now' with the band became a No.1 hit in Britain. After leaving the Moodies he tried a few projects, one of which was the Electric String Band, a group of classi-

Denny Laine: his long friendship with Paul was to turn sour

cally trained violinists and cellists. Brian Epstein booked them to appear at his Saville Theatre, but they weren't a success. In 1967 he made 'Say You Don't Mind', regarded as one of his best recordings, although it wasn't until Colin Blunstone had a hit with it in February 1972 that it was recognised as such. Later Denny joined bands such as Balls, and Ginger Baker's Airforce. When Paul asked him to join Wings he'd already begun working on a solo album, but he dropped everything to go to Scotland to rehearse with Wings and to begin recording the band's debut album *Wild Life* (cf). Denny performed 'Go Now' on the Wings world tour and it's to be found on the triple album *Wings Over America* (cf).

Denny and Paul became close friends, Denny helping in the composition of 'Mull Of Kintyre' (cf). His solo album, *Ahh. . . Laine,* didn't prove to be a big seller, but he continued with further solo ventures. To celebrate the 1976 Buddy Holly Week (see *Holly, Buddy*) Denny issued the Holly number 'It's So Easy' as a single. The following year saw the release of his complete album of Holly numbers called *Holly Days* (cf). Unfortunately Denny's relationship with Paul was soured by the fiasco of the cancelled Japanese tour and Paul's imprisonment in 1980 (see *Drugs*). Denny released a single called 'Japanese Tears' (cf) which pointed a critical finger at Paul. In 1980 Wings disbanded and things began to go seriously wrong for Denny: in 1982 he split up with his wife Jo Jo (cf) and moved to Spain for a time, and in 1983 his company Denny Laine Ltd went bankrupt with debts of £30,000. In 1984 he wrote a series of articles for the *Sun* newspaper which were highly critical of Paul. Entitled 'The Real Paul McCartney' they suggested that Paul was mean and, to a degree, callous. It was ghosted by Dan Slater.

LAINE, JO JO Ex-wife of Denny Laine (cf). Jo Jo first met Denny in Cannes in 1972 when Wings were in the South of France. The couple lived together for a number of years and had two children – a son, Laine, born in Kintyre, then a daughter, Heidi Jo. The couple were married for a brief time but divorced in 1982.

As Denny's 'old lady', Jo Jo spent eight years travelling with him, often in the company of Paul and Linda, and she sold her memoirs to the *Sunday People* in a series published on 17 and 18 April and 1 May 1983. The series was illustrated with some raunchy shots of a bare-breasted Jo Jo, and carried headlines such as 'My Galaxy Of Pop Star Lovers' and 'Lust At First Sight'. The main bulk of the series, however, concerned the private life of Paul and his family. Jo Jo seemed irked that Linda regarded her as a 'groupie' when she first began to go out with Denny – but she admits in the series that she slept around with a host of pop stars, including Rod Stewart, even during the time she was married to Denny. She complains of the spartan conditions when they stayed at Paul's farm in Scotland, yet talks of the plush hotels and champagne life she had as the wife of a Wings member. She intimates that Paul was very mean with Denny, yet talks of the mansion Denny bought in Laleham and how Denny's royalties on one album came to £50,000, and on another £100,000. She admits that Denny was treated like one of the family by the McCartneys, but continually refers to the fact that she personally didn't get on well with Linda. (See also *Donaghue, Peter.*)

LAM *London's Australasian Magazine,* which, on its 100th issue, dated 8 July 1980, presented a cover story on Paul, with a two-page interview by James Kemsley. The twenty-three questions which Kemsley put to Paul began with a mention of the Beatles. Paul said that he did not mind discussing them, pointing out that he had been sensitive about the subject at one time because he'd been trying to establish Wings. He said that there were no Beatle numbers or recordings

Not planning to write his own story

Jo Jo Laine revealed all in a series of highly critical articles

hidden away in vaults, that even numbers such as 'How Do You Do It' had been played on various radio programmes, the Beatles would not get together and and he had re-established a good relationship with John following the earlier rift. He discussed his recent *McCartney II* album and mentioned that he'd liked the *Chorus Line* musical. The Japan bust was discussed and the final question concerned Paul writing his own story: "To write the Paul McCartney story by Paul McCartney, well, that is a much, much bigger ideal that I don't see as a likelihood at the moment."

LAWLEY, SUE Popular British television newcaster. She interviewed Paul for BBC's *Nationwide* TV programme (no longer broadcast) at Abbey Road Studios where he had been completing the recording of *Tug of War* (cf) with George Martin (cf) late in 1981. He mentioned that he was working with different musicians on the album rather than with Wings. Sue asked him if Wings had disbanded, but he said they hadn't, that he was keeping it loose and they could be reformed should the need arise. At that moment he wanted a change and the opportunity to work with other people. She mentioned that he hadn't brought a record out for some time and Paul said that he and George were taking their time and not working to a deadline. Asked if John's death had made him think again about his fame, Paul said he had thought about it, but concluded: "There's nothing you can do." Sue asked if the murder had altered his lifestyle, and he said he'd continue as he was.

LE CIRQUE French restaurant in Manhattan, New York. Paul and Linda dined there with Yoko Ono on 3 April 1982. The three of them discussed plans to regain Northern Songs, which was owned by ATV Music. (See also *Jackson, Michael.*)

Photographer, wife and mother – and the inspiration of many songs, from 'Linda' (1943) to 'The Lovely Linda' (1970)

LEE, PEGGY Celebrated jazz singer, born Norma Engstrom in Jamestown, North Dakota, on 26 May 1920. She had a number of hits in the forties and fifties such as 'Mañana', 'Lover' and 'Fever'. Paul had always admired the blonde-haired singer and was inspired by her 1961 hit 'Til There Was You', a song from *The Music Man* musical, which he performed during early Beatles gigs. When Paul and Linda were invited to Peggy Lee's home for dinner, Paul took along a song he'd written for her as a present. He also produced it as a single, 'Let's Love', which was issued in 1974, in America on Atlantic SD 18108 on 1 October and in Britain on Warner Brothers K50064 on 8 November. The flipside was a shorter version of the same.

LET 'EM IN First track on *Wings at the Speed of Sound* (cf). Also issued in Britain as a single on Parlophone R6015 on 23 July 1976, when it reached the No.2 position. The flipside was 'Beware My Love'. It was included on the *Wings Greatest* (cf) compilation. In America the single was issued on Capitol 4292 on 28 June and reached the No.3 position. It was performed on the 1975/76 Wings tour and a live version can be heard on *Wings Over America* (cf). The doorbell heard at the beginning of the song had been given to Paul as a present by Joe English (cf).

LET IT BE Song that Paul dedicated to his late mother, actually mentioning her by name in the lyric, and on which he took lead vocals. It was released as a single in Britain on Apple R5833 on 6 March 1970 and went to No.1, and in America on Apple 2764 on 11 March 1970 also reaching No.1. The version on the eponymous album (released in May 1970), mixed by Phil Spector, was a contributing factor in the group's eventual split (see *Beatles Break-Up).*

LETTER TO PAUL Novelty disc by Arlen Sanders issued in the US on Faro 616 in 1964 with 'Hopped Up Mustang' on the flip.

LIANE Blonde-haired German barmaid who dated Paul McCartney during the Beatles, season at the Kaiser Keller. Iain Hines mentions her in his reminiscences of the Hamburg scene in the magazine *Fiesta:* "I personally struck up quite a friendship with Paul McCartney. He was at the time going out with a barmaid called Liane, whilst I was going out with her friend Gerda. Every morning at two Paul would arrive from the Kaiser Keller which was closed at that hour, and would listen to our last session. The four of us would go in Gerda's VW to Liane's flat where we would cook hamburgers and listen to Everly Brothers records that Paul had got hold of from seamen who had been to the States."

LIFE MAGAZINE Major American news magazine which, in June 1967, featured an interview with Paul that caused a controversy on both sides of the Atlantic. They asked him whether he used the hallucinogenic drug LSD and he admitted he'd taken it. The story was splashed across the national press in Britain and Paul had to make an appearance on a TV news programme in Britain to explain what he'd meant (see *Drugs).*

LINDA Song written about Linda when she was a little girl in 1943. Songwriter Jack Lawrence was a client of Linda's father, the lawyer Lee Eastman, who mentioned to Lawrence that he'd be willing to accept a song about his daughter in lieu of payment for some legal work he'd done on Lawrence's behalf. Almost twenty years later the number was recorded by Jan and Dean. Paul's publishing company McCartney Productions has now bought the rights to the song.

LINDA'S CALENDARS Every year Linda McCartney (cf) issues special calendars featuring her photographs. The first, in 1981, issued by MPL (cf) was a large publication with six colour shots taken during the making of the 'Coming Up' video. 1982's measured 16½" x 12" and contained a selection of colour pictures reflecting Linda's personal vision of the changing seasons. The 1983 calendar was a 20½" x 14½" production with twelve photographs selected from Linda's book *Photographs*. The 1985 calendar, Linda McCartney's Music Makers, featured twenty-eight colour shots of famous musicians – the Beatles, John Lennon, the Doors, Eric Clapton, Crosby, Stills and Nash, Jefferson Airplane, Jimi Hendrix, the Grateful Dead and B.B.King. Proceeds from sales were donated to Music Therapy, a charity for mentally handicapped children.

LINDA'S PICTURES Excellently produced collection of photographs by Linda McCartney, first published by Alfred Knopf in 1976, and by Ballantine Books in November 1977. It was republished in Britain in 1981 by Pavilion Books. The cover features the same photograph used on the sleeve of the *McCartney* (cf) album. Linda's introduction, adapted from an interview with Patrick Watson, is an outline of her career in photography, beginning with her visit to a Rolling Stones reception in New York (see *McCartney, Linda*) and ending with the revelation that the excitement in taking pictures of rock stars had worn off and she now preferred taking shots of her immediate personal world, particularly her family. This is apparent in the selection of 148 photographs, which begin with the Rolling Stones yacht and culminate in the *McCartney* album cover. The early pictures cover a diverse selection of artists, while the later ones are mainly of Paul and the family. There are photos of Paul in Scotland, Jamaica, Morocco, London and Liverpool: in the studio; making a TV special; diving; and painting a roof. There are also numerous fine pics of the Beatles. Despite her own admission that she hardly knows anything about the technical side of photography, Linda's pictures reveal humour, observation and a love of subject. (See also *Bailey, David*.)

LISTEN TO WHAT THE MAN SAID Wings single recorded in New Orleans in 1975. It was issued in Britain on Capitol R6006 on 16 May 1975, with 'Love In Song' (cf) on the flip, and reached No.6 in the charts. The number was included on *Venus and Mars*

(cf). The same single was issued in the States on Capitol 4091 on 23 May 1985 when it reached No.1. A live version appears on *Wings Over the World*.

LISTEN TO WHAT THE MAN SAYS Two-hour programme broadcast on Radio One on Sunday 22 December 1985, in which Liverpool-born DJ Janice Long interviewed Paul. Excerpts from a number of his records were also played.

A LITTLE BARE This is the title I gave to a *Mersey Beat* article published in September 1962. This was another excerpt from a letter that Paul wrote to me (see also *Hamburg* and *Parisian Rock'n'Roll*). This time it recounted the time the Beatles backed a stripper in a club run by Lord Woodbine. Paul wrote his epistle while the period was still fresh in his memory and referred to the striptease artiste as Janice. Alan Williams, in his 1975 book *The Man Who Gave the Beatles Away*, referred to her as Shirley. Paul's letter went:

"John, George, Stu and I used to play at a Strip Club in Upper Parliament Street, backing Janice the Stripper. At the time we wore little lilac jackets. . . or purple jackets, or something. Well, we played behind Janice and naturally we looked at her. . . the audience looked at her, everybody looked at her, just sort of normal. At the end of the act she would turn round and. . . well, we were all young lads, we'd never seen anything like it before, and we all blushed. . . four blushing red-faced lads.

"Janice brought sheets of music for us to play all her arrangements. She gave us a bit of Beethoven and the Spanish Fire Dance. So in the end we said 'We can't read music, sorry, but instead of the Spanish Fire Dance we can play the Harry Lime Cha-Cha, which we've arranged ourselves, and instead of Beethoven you can have 'Moonglow' or 'September Song' – take your pick. . . and instead of the 'Sabre Dance' we'll give you 'Ramrod'.' So that's what she got. She seemed quite satisfied anyway. . .

The Strip Club wasn't an important chapter in our lives, but it was an interesting one."

LITTLE EDDIE Unrecorded song that Paul wrote. The title was the name of one of his dogs.

LITTLE LAMB DRAGONFLY Track from the 1973 album *Red Rose Speedway*. The song was originally inspired by the death of one of Paul's sheep on his farm.

LITTLE WOMAN LOVE Linda and Paul co-wrote this song. It was issued on the flipside of 'Mary Had A Little Lamb'. Wings performed the number on their British tour in 1983.

THE LIVE AID CONCERT The most spectacular concert in the history of pop music, which took place on 13 July 1985 at Wembley Stadium, London, and John F Kennedy Stadium, Philadelphia, the two venues linked by satellite. Organised by Bob Geldof to raise money for the Ethiopian famine appeal, it was televised throughout the world to over one billion people and raised almost fifty million pounds to help the starving people of Ethiopia. Paul's name was not included in the first bill presented to the press, but Geldof talked him into appearing, arguing that if Paul were to make an appearance he would be able to arrange for the concert to be beamed to more countries than had originally been planned. Paul was the closing act at the Wembley concert and took to the stage shortly after 10 o'clock in the evening. He sang 'Let It Be', but, unfortunately, the sound system was acting up and the vocals of the first half of the song couldn't be heard properly, severely reducing its impact. By the time the mikes were in order, various stars and the entire audience had joined in the big singalong with Paul. This was followed by the rendition of the Band Aid hit 'Feed The World' in which most of the stars appeared on stage and Paul and Pete Townshend hoisted Geldof onto their shoulders in an emotional finale.

LIVE AND LET DIE Song which Paul wrote for the James Bond movie of the same name, starring Roger Moore. This was the eighth Bond movie, and traditionally, a female vocalist had sung the theme song over the title credits. Paul said he would only compose the number if his version, recorded with Wings, was used in the film. The producers agreed, although a version by singer Brenda Arnau was introduced at the end of the film. Paul called on George Martin (cf) to help score and produce the song with the George Martin Orchestra supplementing the Wings track. The film producers then asked Martin to compose a score for the entire film.

'Live And Let Die' was included on the movie soundtrack album, issued in Britain on United Artists UAS 28457 on 6 July 1973 and in the States on United Artists LA 100-G on 2 July 1973. The American album rose to No.17 in the charts, but the British album didn't chart at all. A few days before the soundtrack release, the Wings single had been issued on Apple R5987 on 1 July reaching No.7 in the British charts. In America it had come out on 18 June on Apple 1863 and reached No.2. The number was nominated for an Oscar and George Martin was awarded a Grammy for his arrangement. The flipside of the single was 'I Lie Around', also written by Paul, but sung by Denny Laine.

LIVERPOOL INSTITUTE High school for boys, situated in Mount Street, Liverpool. It was founded in 1825 as a Mechanics Institute, and was officially opened as a school on 15 September 1837. Charles Dickens lectured there in 1844 and famous pupils have included Sir Charles Lamb, Lord Mersey, Sir Henry Enfield and Sir Macalister of Tarbert. In 1890 one half of the school became an Art College and brick walls were built to separate the two buildings internally. The Institute was changed from a fee-paying school to a grammar school in 1944, making it the oldest grammer school in Liverpool. The school motto is *Non Nobis Solum, Sed Toti Mundo Nati*, which means 'Not for ourselves alone but for the good of all the world'.

Paul entered the school when he passed his 11-Plus examination. In the summer of 1957 he took two O'Level exams (see *General Certificate of*

Education) and passed in Spanish, but failed in Latin. He took six further subjects in order to move up into the Sixth Form in 1958. He passed in five and seemed to have a penchant for languages – apart from Spanish, he also has an O'Level in German and French.

The boys nicknamed the school 'the Inny' and their headmaster, J.R.Edwards, 'the Baz'. George Harrison was a year below Paul at the school. Other students included Paul's brother Mike; Neil Aspinall, who became the Beatles road manager; Len Garry, a member of John Lennon's skiffle group, the Quarrymen; Ivan Vaughan (cf), who introduced Paul to John; Peter Sissons, who is now a prominent TV newsreader; Les Chadwick, who was a member of Gerry & the Pacemakers; Colin Manley and Don Andrew, both members of the Remo Four; Bill Kenwright (cf), who became an actor and later a leading theatre impressario; and Stu James, who became a member of the Mojos.

Paul and Mike used to catch the No.86 bus to school and it was during these bus journeys that Paul first got to know George.

It had been anticipated that Paul would enter Teacher's Training College after the Institute, but he took time off to tour Scotland with the Silver Beatles and then went off to Hamburg. He'd had a message from Mr Edwards asking him to visit the Head's office but he wrote back from Hamburg declaring that he'd resigned from the school: "I said: 'Dear Sir, I've got a great job in Germany and I'm earning fifteen pounds.'"

Paul retained a fondness for the school and on Friday 23 November 1979 arranged for Wings to give a special concert for the staff and students of the Liverpool Institute. The concert took place at the Royal Court Theatre (cf), Liverpool.

LIVERPOOL LOU Folk song by Domenic Behan. Paul produced the version by the Scaffold (the group in which his brother appeared), which was issued on Warner Bros in England on K16400 on 24 May 1974 where it entered the Top Ten. No such luck in America,

where it was issued on Warner Bros 8001 on 29 July. The flipside of the disc was a number penned jointly by Paul and Linda called 'Ten Years After On Strawberry Jam'.

LOADER, BRENDER Script girl on *Give My Regards to Broad Street* (cf (1)), nicknamed 'Bunty'. During the filming of the 'Silly Love Songs' sequence, a number of problems occurred and in the ensuing tension, Bunty broke down and cried. Paul started playing the piano to cheer her up with a song he made up on the spot, beginning: *We love Bunty, Bunty's our friend; We love Bunty, we will till the end.*

LONDON TOWN (1) Recordings for this album began at Abbey Road Studios in February 1977. A month was spent recording aboard the yacht *Fair Carol* in the Virgin Islands (cf) in May. Further sessions at Abbey Road and at AIR in London took place in December. By the time of release, Jimmy McCulloch (cf) and Joe English (cf), who both performed on the album, had left the band. There were fourteen numbers on *London Town,* five of which Paul had co-penned with Denny Laine: 'London Town', 'Children Children', 'Deliver Your Children', 'Don't Let It Bring You Down' and 'Morse Moose And The Grey Goose'. The other tracks were: 'Café On The Left Bank', 'I'm Carrying', 'Backwards Traveller'/'Cuff Link', 'Girlfriend', 'I've Had Enough', 'With A Little Luck', 'Name And Address' and 'Famous Groupies'.

London Town was issued on 31 March 1978, in Britain on Parlophone PAS 10012, and in America on Capitol SW 11777; it reached No.4 in the UK charts, and No.2 in the American. The original working title for the album was *Water Wings.*

LONDON TOWN (2) Co-composed by Paul and Denny Laine (cf) during the Wings 1975/76 world tour and the title track of their 1978 album (cf). It was issued as a single the same year on Parlophone R6021 in Britain on 15 September where it had a very poor performance in the charts, managing only to touch the No.60 spot. In Amer-

LONDON TOWN

Half the album was recorded far away in the Virgin Islands

ica it was the last single on Capitol (Capitol 4625), as Paul's future releases were to appear on the Columbia label, and again had a disappointing chart placing at No.39. The flipside was 'I'm Carrying', a number recorded in the Virgin Islands (cf).

THE LONG AND WINDING ROAD Paul's composition from the *Let It Be* sessions on which he sings lead vocal. The number was featured in the film, but Allen Klein gave the tapes of the recording sessions to Phil Spector for remixing. On 'The Long And Winding Road' track Spector included an orchestra with violins, a harp and female choir. Paul was to comment: "I couldn't believe it. I would never have female voices on a Beatles record." In an interview with Paul Gambaccini (cf) in 1973 he remarked: "I'm not struck by the violins and ladies' voices on 'The Long And Winding Road'. I've always put my own strings on. But that's a bit of spilled milk. Nobody minded except me, so I shut up." The number was first featured on *Let It Be* and then on *The Beatles 1967-1970* and the *Love Songs* compilations. Paul performed a new version on the Wings 1975/76 tour, which was included on *Wings Over America (cf)*.

LONG TALL SALLY The first number Paul ever sang on stage. While holidaying at a Butlins camp in Wales, Paul and his younger brother were asked up on stage by a cousin-in-law, who was a Redcoat (official camp steward). The duo sang the Everly Brothers hit 'Bye Bye Love' and then Paul went solo, singing Little Richard's 'Long Tall Sally', a number which he had already practised singing "in one of the classrooms at school" (see *Edge, 'Cliff'*).

LOVE IN SONG Flipside of the 'Listen To What The Man Said' (cf) single and a track on *Venus and Mars* (cf). It has been said that the bass guitar which Paul used on this track was the same one used on Presley's recording of 'Heartbreak Hotel'.

LOVE LETTERS TO THE BEATLES Slim volume of letters from American fans, first published in 1964. Compiler Bill Adler was given permission to make his selection from the hundreds of thousands of letters that had been stored in a New York warehouse. Of the sixty letters which appear in the book, ten were personally addressed to Paul. Writing in large script, betraying an unusually tender age, Shirley of Louisville wrote that she

Little girls confessed their love for Paul

thought Paul was "very sexy and I don't even know what it means"; Jane of New York wanted Paul to ask the policemen to let her through to him and promised not to scratch and bite; eight-year-old Diane from Michigan queried: "My mother wants to know why you came to America"; Amy from Chester confessed she had fainted six times for love of him; Felicia from Florida described herself as happy, fun-loving, swinging, wild and sexy – "I guess you could say I'm just an average teenager". Other Paul fans included Betty from the Bronx,

Margie of Denver, Lucy Walker from Altoona, Isobel of Muncie and Isabelle of Tacoma.

THE LOVELY LINDA Song dedicated to his wife which was the first track on Paul's solo debut album *McCartney* (cf), issued in April 1970.

LOVELY RITA Commenting on his inspiration for this song, Paul has said: "I was bopping about on a piano in Liverpool when someone told me that in America they called parking meter women meter maids. I thought it was great and it got to be 'Rita', meter maid' and then 'Lovely Rita, meter maid, and I was thinking it should be a hate song, but then I thought it would be better to love her and if she was freaky too, like a military man, with a bag on her shoulders. A foot stomper, but nice." In Paul's song, the narrator sees Rita filling in parking tickets and notices that she has an almost military look with her cap and bag. He invites her out to tea, then takes her out to dinner – although Rita ends up paying the bill. He then takes her home, but doesn't quite make it with her as his two sisters are sharing the sofa. (See also *Davis, Meta*.)

Visually, artists interpret Rita as a very sexy woman. In the David Bailey colour photograph in *The Beatles Illustrated Lyrics*, she is a sluttish figure, smoking a cigarette, her cap askew, face heavily made up and her left hand pulling aside her jacket to reveal an ample cleavage. The Robert Rankin illustration in *Behind the Beatles Songs* depicts her clothed only in a hat and black stockings. The number was featured on *Sgt Pepper*. It has also been recorded by several other artists, including Fats Domino and Roy Wood.

LOW PARK FARM Paul bought this farm in 1970 to add to his Scottish acres and to stop trespassers gaining access to the adjacent High Park Farm.

LOW, MR Merseyside journalist, first name unknown, whom Paul wrote to in 1959. The story first came to light in Hunter Davies' *The Beatles: The Authorised Biography*, according to which the Beatles had met a local journalist called Low in a pub and Paul, always conscious of the value of publicity, wrote him a letter about the group, although facts had been altered to make himself seem more colourful. There is no record of whether Mr Low ever replied, nor any details of which paper he worked for, although it seems likely that it was the *Liverpool Echo* or *Liverpool Daily Post,* neither of which would have entertained the idea of writing about an unknown local rock group. Hunter Davies pieced together part of the contents of the letter from scraps of a copy which Paul had made. It read:

"Dear Mr Low, I am sorry about the time I have taken to write to you, but I hope I have not left it too late. Here are some details about the group.

"It consists of four boys: Paul McCartney (guitar), John Lennon (guitar), Stuart Sutcliffe (bass) and George Harrison (another guitar) and is called the. . .

"This line-up may at first seem dull but it must be appreciated that as the boys have above-average instrumental ability they achieve surprisingly varied effects. Their basic beat is off-beat, but this has recently tended to be accompanied by a faint on-beat; thus the overall sound is rather reminiscent of the four in the bar of traditional jazz. This could possibly be put down to the influence of Mr McCartney who led one of the top local jazz bands (Jim Mac's Jazz Band) in the 1920s.

"Modern music is, however, the group's delight, and, as if to prove the point, John and Paul have written over fifty tunes, ballads and faster numbers during the last three years. Some of these tunes are purely instrumental (such as 'Looking Glass', 'Catswalk' and 'Winston's Walk') and others were composed with the modern audience in mind (tunes like 'Thinking Of Linking', 'The One After 909', 'Years Roll Along', and 'Keep Looking That Way').

The group also derive a great deal of pleasure from rearranging old favourites ('Ain't She Sweet', 'You Were Meant For Me', 'Home', 'Moonglow', 'You Are My Sunshine' and others).

"Now for a few details about the boys themselves. John, who leads the group, attends the College of Art, and, as well as being an accomplished guitarist and banjo player, he is an experienced cartoonist. His many interests include painting, the theatre, poetry, and of course, singing. He is nineteen years old and is a founder member of the group.

"Paul is eighteen years old and is reading English Literature at Liverpool University. He, like the other boys, plays more than one instrument – his specialities being the piano and drums, plus of course. . . "

LUCKY SPOT Name of an Appaloosa stallion that Paul and Linda bought in 1976. Wings were touring America and they were in Texas on the way to a gig when Paul and Linda saw the horse grazing by the roadside. They were so struck by the animal that they immediately made enquiries and bought it.

LUNCHBOX & ODD SOX Number recorded for *Venus and Mars* (cf) during the Los Angeles recording sessions in February 1975. It didn't find its way onto that album but was released as a track on the flipside of the 1980 single 'Coming Up'. A second version of 'Coming Up', which had been recorded in Glasgow, had been placed on the flipside and was followed by the 3.47-minute 'Lunchbox & Odd Sox'.

LUTTON, DAVY Drummer who played on the recording session for Linda's 'Seaside Woman' in France in 1972. Paul, Linda, Denny Laine (cf) and Jimmy McCulloch (cf) were also on the session. Lutton later auditioned for the drum spot in Wings, but didn't get it.

McARDLE, ANDREA Young actress who portrayed Little Orphan Annie in the musical *Annie* (cf) at the Alvin Theatre in New York. Paul, Linda, Heather and Stella all went to see the play on 29 April 1977 and went backstage after the show to congratulate Andrea on her peformance.

McCARTNEY (1) There was some internal wrangling at Apple concerning

Paul's first solo album release. Paul had kept a relatively low profile while working on it in his Scottish farm, overdubbing instruments and using a Studer 4-track recorder. With the exception of some vocal help from Linda, it was a one-man album with Paul playing all the instruments: toy xylophone, electric and acoustic guitars, bass, drums mellotron and organ.

Tension between Paul and the other Beatles was already in the air, particularly because of the Allen Klein (cf) affair, and this was unfortunately exacerbated by the release date that Paul wanted for his album. This roughly coincided with the *Let It Be* release and was also close to the release date of Ringo's debut album *Sentimental Journey*. Paul felt that the *Let It Be* project had been around for some time and didn't see why he should alter his plans because of it. Ringo was sent to Paul's St John's Wood house to 'reason' with him. Ringo took two letters along, one from John, the other from George. Paul opened them and vented his anger on Ringo. Ringo was to say later: "I could see the release date of his record had a gigantic emotional significance for him. Whether he was right or wrong to be so emotional, I felt that since he was our friend and since the date was of such immense significance to him, we should let him have his own way."

It was decided that there should be a three-week gap between the release of *McCartney* and *Let It Be* and the release of Ringo's album was brought forward.

McCartney was issued on Apple PCS 7102 on 17 April 1970. It reached No.2 in the British charts and No.1 in the US charts, selling over two million copies.

Not content with showing the world that he was capable of working on a musical project without the other three, Paul was also at pains to put across his viewpoint about the entire Beatles situation as it stood. He prepared his own press release with members of the Apple staff, issuing it in the form of a questionnaire to the Fleet Street papers, radio disc jockeys, and in a limited run on the inner sleeve of the album itself. It read:

Q: Why did you decide to make a solo album?

A: Because I got a Studer 4-track recording machine at home — practised on it (playing all instruments) — liked the results and decided to make it into an album.

Q: Were you influenced by John's adventures with the Plastic Ono Band, and Ringo's solo LP?

A: Sort of, but not really.

Q: Are all the songs by Paul McCartney alone?

A: Yes sir.

Q: Will they be so credited: McCartney?

A: It's a bit daft for them to be Lennon-McCartney-credited, so 'McCartney' it is.

Q: Did you enjoy working as a solo?

A: Very much. I only had me to ask for a decision, and I agreed with me. Remember Linda's on it too, so it's really a double act.

Q: What is Linda's contribution?

A: Strictly speaking she harmonises, but of course it's more than that because she is a shoulder to lean on, a second opinion, and a photographer of renown. More than all this, she believes in me — constantly.

Q: Where was the album recorded?

A: At home, at EMI (No.2 studio) and at Morgan studios (Willesden!)

Q: What is your home equipment (in some detail)?

A: Studer 4-track machine. I only had, however, one mike, and, as Mr Pender, Mr Sweatham and others only managed to take six months or so (slight delay), I worked without VU meters or a mixer, which meant that everything had to be listened to first (for distortion, etc. . .) then recorded. So the answer — Studer, one mike and nerve.

Q: Why did you choose to work in the studios you chose?

A: They were available. EMI is technically good, and Morgan is cosy.

Q: The album was not known about until it was nearly completed. Was this deliberate?

A: Yes, because normally an album is old before it comes out. (aside) Witness 'Get Back'.

Q: Why?

A: I've always wanted to buy a Beatles album like 'people' do and be as surprised as they must be. So this was the next best thing. Linda and I are the only two who will be sick of it by the release date. We love it really.

Q: Are you able to describe the texture or the feel of the theme of the album in a few words?

A: Home, Family, Love.

Q: How long did it take to complete – from when to when?

A: From just before (I think) Xmas, until now. The Lovely Linda was the first thing I recorded at home, and was originally to test the equipment. That was around Xmas.

Q: Assuming all the songs are new to the public, how new are they to you? Are they recent?

A: One was 1959 ('Hot As Sun'), two from India ('Junk', 'Teddy Boy'), and the rest are pretty recent. 'Valentine Day', 'Momma Miss America', and 'OO You' were ad-libbed on the spot.

Q: Which instruments have you played on the album?

A: Bass, drums, acoustic guitar, lead guitar, piano and organ-Mellotron, toy xylophone, bow and arrow.

Q: Have you played all these instruments on earlier recordings?

A: Yes – drums being the one that I wouldn't normally do.

Q: Why did you do all the instruments yourself?

A: I think I'm pretty good.

Q: Will Linda be heard on all future records?

A: Could be; we love singing together, and have plenty of opportunity for practice.

Q: Will Paul and Linda become a John and Yoko?

A: No, they will become Paul and Linda.

Q: Are you pleased with your work?

A: Yes.

Q: Will the other Beatles receive the first copies?

A: Wait and see.

Q: What has recording alone taught you?

A: That to make your own decisions about what you do is easy and playing with yourself is difficult but satisfying.

Q: Who has done the artwork?

A: Linda has taken all the photos, and she and I designed the package.

Q: Is it true that neither Allen Klein nor ABKCO have been nor will be in any way involved with the production, manufacturing, distribution or promotion of this new album?

A: Not if I can help it.

Q: Did you miss the other Beatles and George Martin? Was there a moment eg, when you thought "Wish Ringo was here for this break?"

A: No.

Q: Assuming this is a very big hit album, will you do another?

A: Even if it isn't, I will continue to do what I want – when I want to.

Q: Are you planning a new album or single with the Beatles?

A: No.

Q: Is this album a rest away from the Beatles or the start of a solo career?

A: Time will tell. Being a solo album means it's 'the start of a solo career...' and not being done with the Beatles means it's a rest. So it's both.

Q: Have you any plans for live appearances?

A: No.

Q: Is your break from the Beatles, temporary or permanent, due to personal difference or musical ones?

A: Personal differences, business differences, musical differences, but most of all because I have a better time with my family. Temporary or permanent? I don't know.

Q: Do you forsee a time when Lennon – McCartney becomes an active songwriting partnership again?

A: No.

Q: What do you feel about John's

peace effort? The Plastic Ono Band? Giving back the MBE? Yoko's influence? Yoko?

A: I love John and respect what he does – it doesn't give me any pleasure.

Q: Have you plans to produce any other artists?

A: No.

Q: Were any of the songs on the album originally written with the Beatles in mind?

A: The older ones were. 'Junk' was intended for *Abbey Road*, but something happened 'Teddy Boy' was for *Get Back* but something happened.

Q: Were you pleased with *Abbey Road*? Was it musically restricting?

A: It was a good album. (No.1 for a long time).

Q: What is your relationship with Klein:

A: It isn't – I am not in contact with him, and he does not represent me in any way.

Q: What is your relationship with Apple?

A: It is the office of a company which I part-own with the other three Beatles. I don't go there because I don't like the offices or business, especially when I'm on holiday.

Q: Have you any plans to set up an independent production company?

A: McCartney Productions.

Q: What sort of music has influenced you on this album?

A: Light and loose.

Q: Are you writing more prolifically now? Or less so?

A: About the same. I have a queue waiting to be recorded.

Q: What are your plans now? A holiday? A musical? A movie? Retirement?

A: My only plan is to grow up.

Paul also prepared his own track-by-track commentary on the album.

The Lovely Linda When the Studer 4-track was installed at home, this was the first song I recorded, to test the machine. On the first track was vocal and guitar, second – another acoustic guitar – then overdubbed hand slaps on a book, and finally bass. Written in Scotland, the song is a trailer to the full song which will be recorded in the future.

That Would Be Something This song was written in Scotland in 1969 and recorded at home in London – mixed later at EMI (No.2). I only had one mike, as the mixer and VU meters hadn't arrived (still haven't).
  1. vocal, guitar
  2. tom-tom and cymbal
  3. electric guitar
  4. bass

Valentine Day Recorded at home. Made up as I went along – acoustic guitar first, then drums (maybe drums were first). Anyway – electric guitar and bass were added and the track is all instrumental. Mixed at EMI. This one and 'Momma Miss America' were ad-libbed, with more concern for testing the machine than anything else.

Every Night (Blues). This came from the first two lines, which I've had for a few years. They were added to in 1969 in Greece (Benitses) on holiday. This was recorded at EMI with:
  1. vocal and
  2. acoustic guitar
  3. drums
  4. bass
  5. lead guitar (acoustic)
  6. harmony to the lead guitar
  7. double-tracked vocal in parts
  8. electric guitar (not used)
  9. track.

Hot As Sun A song written in about 1958 or '59 or maybe earlier, when it was one of those songs that you play now and then. The middle was added in Morgan Studio, where the track was recorded recently.
  1. acoustic guitar
  2. electric guitar
  3. drums
  4. rhythm guitar
  5. organ
  6. maracas
  7. bass
  8. bongos.

Glasses Wineglasses played at random and overdubbed on top of each other – the end is a section of a song called 'Suicide' – not yet completed.

Junk Originally written in India, at Maharishi's camp, and completed bit by bit in London. Recorded vocal, two acoustic guitars, and bass at home, and later added to (bass drum, snare with brushes, and small xylophone and harmony) at Morgan.

Man We Was Lonely The chorus (*Man we was lonely*) was written in bed at home, shortly before we finished recording the album. The middle (*I used to ride...*) was done one lunchtime in a great hurry, as we were due to record the song that afternoon. Linda sings harmony on this song, which is our first duet together. The steel-guitar sound is my Telecaster played with a drum peg.

1. guitar
2. voices (two tracks)
3. bass drum
4. bass
5. steel guitar

Oo You The first three tracks were recorded at home as an instrument that might someday become a song. This, like 'Man We Was Lonely', was given lyrics one day after lunch, just before we left for Morgan Studios, where it was finished that afternoon.

Vocals, electric guitar, tambourine, cow bell, and aerosol spray were added at Morgan, and it was mixed there.

On the mix, tape echo was used to move feedback from guitar from one side to another.

Momma Miss America An instrumental recorded completely at home. Made up as I went along — first a sequence of chords, then a melody on top.

Piano, drums, acoustic guitar, electric guitar.

Originally it was two pieces, but they ran into each other by accident and became one.

Teddy Boy Another song started in India, and completed in Scotland and London, gradually. This one was recorded for the *Get Back* film, but later not used.

Recorded partly at home... (guitar, voices and bass)... and finished at Morgan.

Linda and I sing the backing harmonies on the chorus, and occasional oos.

Singalong Junk This was take 1, for the vocal version, which was take 2, and a shorter version.

Guitars and piano and bass, were put on at home, and the rest added at Morgan Studios

The strings are Mellotron, and they were done at the same time as the electric guitar, bass drum, and sizzle cymbal.

Maybe I'm Amazed Written in London, at the piano, with the second verse added slightly later, as if you cared.

Recorded at EMI, No.2 studio
1. piano
2. vocal
3. drums
4. bass
5. and vocal backing
6. and vocal backing
7. solo guitar
8. backing guitars

Linda and I are the vocal backing group. Mixed at EMI.

A movie was made, using Linda's slides and edited to this track.

Kreen-Akrore There was a film on TV about the Kreen-Akrore Indians living in the Brazilian jungle, their lives, and how the white man is trying to change their way of life to his, so the next day, after lunch, I did some drumming. The idea behind it was to get the feeling of their hunt. So later piano, guitar and organ were added to the first section.

The second had a few tracks of voices (Linda and I) and the end had overdubbed breathing, going into organ, and two lead guitars in harmony.

Done at Morgan. Engineer, Robin Black.

The end of the first section has Linda and I doing animal noises (speeded up) and an arrow sound (done live with bow and arrow — the bow broke), then animals stampeding across a guitar case.

There are two drum tracks.

We built a fire in the studio but didn't use it (but used the sound of the twigs breaking).

At the time of release, Langdon Wiiner of *Rolling Stone* wrote: "Its explicit and uniform message is that Paul McCartney, his wife Linda and family have found peace and happiness in a quiet home away from the city, and away from the hassles of the music business." Some years later, Roy Carr and Tony Stewart in *The Beatles Illustrated Record* were to comment: "It was also extremely hastily made, and the very unpretentious qualities which McCartney tried to emphasise were badly misconstrued as ineptitude. Hindsight displays its charms."

Singer Phoebe Snow was to record 'Every Night' (cf), giving her a minor hit in 1979. Generally, most reviewers considered 'Maybe I'm Amazed' (cf)

the outstanding track, although ten years were to elapse before it was issued as a single.

The album cover featured a photograph of a bowl and various cherries on a strip and the gatefold sleeve sported twenty-three of Linda's photographs of the McCartney family life.

McCARTNEY (2) Special 12″ record pressed in white vinyl and sent to radio stations in 1982 to coincide with the release of the 'Ebony & Ivory' single. Apart from 'Ebony & Ivory', two further tracks were included on the promotional disc: 'Ballroom Dancing' and 'The Pound Is Sinking'.

McCARTNEY: THE DEFINITIVE BIOGRAPHY Book penned by rock journalist Chris Salewicz and first published in America in 1986 by St Martin's Press. A well-written account of Paul's life, mainly concentrating on the period up to 1969, with a very brief peek at the subsequent years and a number of pleasing anecdotes.

McCARTNEY, FLORENCE
Paul's fraternal grandmother who was born in the Everton district of Liverpool at 131 Breck Road on 2 June 1874. On 17 May 1896, 21-year-old Florence, neé Clegg, married Joseph McCartney (cf) at Christ Church in Kensington, London. She was known as Florrie and had seven children, two of whom died in early childhood. She died on VE day in 1944.

McCARTNEY, HEATHER Linda's first child, born in Colorado on 31 December 1963. During his early visits to Linda in America, Paul was evidently charmed by Heather, who seems to have brought out his paternal instincts, and in 1969 when he married Linda, he formally adopted Heather. When Wings began touring he asked her whether she'd like to stay at home or join them on the road – she plumped for the travelling life. However, in her early teens Paul allegedly became concerned about the crowd she was mixing with in London to the extent that he decided to move the family, lock, stock and barrel, out to Sussex.

In her late teens, Heather took an interest in photography, getting a job as a darkroom technician and, in 1981, becoming Ilford's Young Printer Of The Year for printing up a photograph she called 'Waterfalls', which was a snap she had taken of Carol and Steve Gadd in Montserrat (cf), when Steve was session drummer on the *Tug of War* recordings. A few years later, in 1984, the press were report-

Paul and Linda, with young James, Stella and Heather

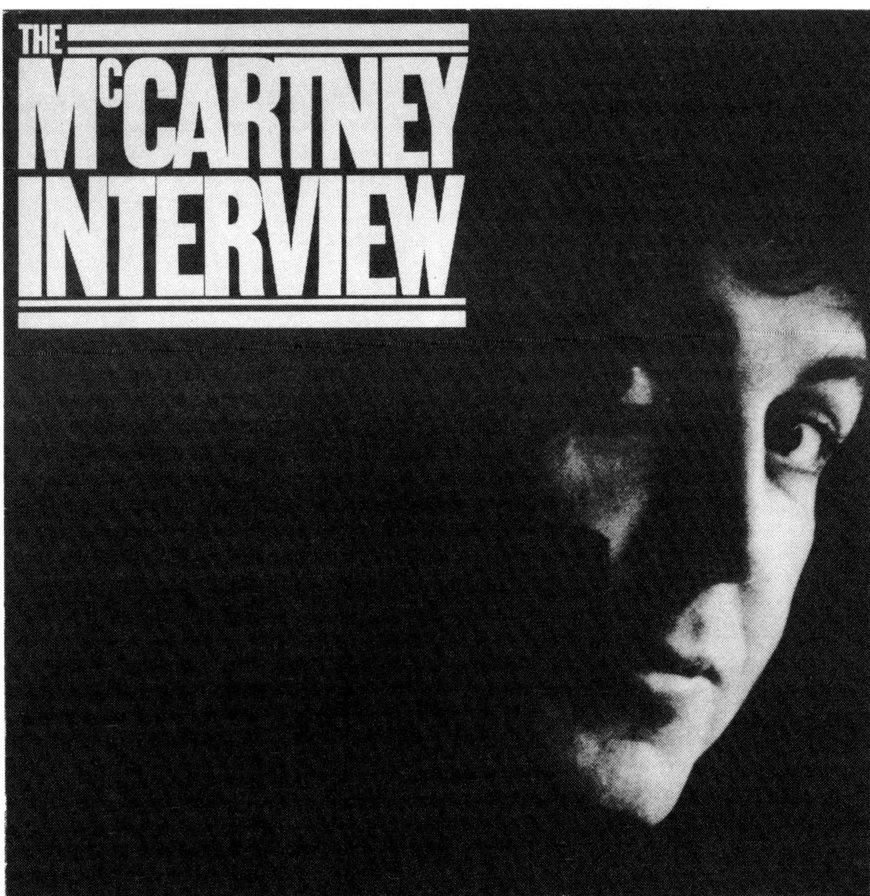

The record of the magazine interview

ing that she'd found a job pulling pints in the Bowler Motel in Sussex near the McCartney home in Peasmarch.

THE McCARTNEY INTERVIEW A unique album which originally saw life as an interview for the American magazine *Musician: Player & Listener.* The publication's managing editor, Vic Garbarini, travelled to London and held an extensive taped interview with Paul at MPL's Soho Square offices. The interview initially appeared in print in 1980, in the August issue of the publication. Paul gave his permission for the tapes to be used on a special two-record promotional set by Columbia in the States to be sent to various radio stations for use by their disc jockeys. It worked so well that Columbia was able to issue an album of the edited interview on Columbia PC 36987 in December of that year in a limited issue of 57,000 copies. The disc was, in fact, nominated for a 1982 Grammy in the 'Best Spoken Word, Documentary, or Drama Recording' category: but this section was won by Orson Welles narrating the sci-fi classic *Donovan's Brain.*

In Britain, EMI issued limited numbers of the album on Parlophone CHAT 1 on 23 February 1981 and deleted it the same day, a gimmick which created an immediate collectors' item.

The sleeve of the British and American releases both carried two photographs of Paul by Linda.

Paul touches on many topics in the interview: his decision to make a solo album (see *McCartney* (1)); Stevie Wonder (cf); his reaction to the critical reviews of *Back to the Egg;* the making of various Beatle albums, including *Sgt Pepper, Abbey Road* (cf(1)), *Rubber Soul* and *The Beatles;* his interest in the bass guitar; Wings' British University tour of 1972 (see *Tours*); the Beatles American visit in February 1964; the break-up of the Beatles (see *The Beatles Break-Up*); British 'New Wave' music and his 'Mary Had A Little Lamb' single. The track-by-track breakdown of subjects covered on the album is as follows:

Side one - *McCartney II;* Negative Criticism Of Beatles and Wings; His influences; *Venus and Mars/Wild Life, Band on the Run;* Musical direction/Ringo/George/'Hey Jude'; *The White Album*/Tension/'Helter Skelter'; *Abbey Road;* Musical background/trumpet, guitar, piano/Learning bass in Hamburg; early Beatles mixes/Motown and Stax influences; The *Sgt Pepper* story/The Beach Boys' *Pet Sounds; Rubber Soul/Revolver;* Fame and success/his and John's reactions; Stage fright during the Beatles and Wings; How Wings started; New Wave/early Beatles; and Creating the Beatles sound/'Love Me Do' and early songs.

Side Two - The Beatles conquest of America; Beatles' haircuts and image; Paying dues in Hamburg and Liverpool/early tours; Weathering pressures/the break-up; Video of 'Coming Up'/reliving the Beatle image; Playing bass; Lennon-McCartney songwriting/dislike of formulas; Beatles imitators; 'I Am The Walrus'/the Black Carnation/*Sgt Pepper* LP cover; New Wave/Bowie, Ferry, Elvis; Getting married/changing perspective/'Waterfalls' and 'Give Ireland Back To The Irish'/'Hi Hi Hi'/banned songs/children's songs/'Mary Had A Little Lamb'.

McCARTNEY, JAMES LOUIS Paul and Linda's first son, born in London on 12 September 1977. His namesakes were Paul's father and Linda's mother.

McCARTNEY, JIM Paul's father, son of Joe and Florence McCartney (cf), born at 8 Fishguard Road, Everton, Liverpool, on 7 July 1902. He had two brothers and three sisters. A bad fall at the age of ten resulted in a broken eardrum, but this didn't prevent him from learning to play the piano by ear. He started work at the age of fourteen as a sample boy at A Hanney & Co, the cotton brokers of Chapel Street, Liverpool, where he received six shillings a week.

At the age of seventeen he began playing ragtime music and his first public appearance with a band was at St Catherine's Hall, Vine Street. Even in those days gimmicks were considered useful in the promotion of bands, so they called themselves the Masked Melody Makers and wore black masks. But when they began to sweat, the dye from the masks ran down their faces, which put paid to that particular idea. Dressed in dinner jackets, they became known as Jim Mac's Band and performed locally for about five years, one of their notable appearances being at a local cinema where the film *The Queen of Sheba* was playing. Their brief was to provide musical background for the silent movie! It was during this period that Jim penned an instrumental number called 'Eloise'.

At the age of twenty-eight he was promoted to the post of salesman and his earnings rocketed up to £250 per year. In 1941, at the age of thirty-nine, he married Mary Mohin (see *McCartney, Mary (1)*) and they moved into furnished rooms in Anfield. The couple were to have two children, Paul and Michael. The cotton exchange was closed during the war years and Jim went to work at Napiers, an engineering firm which produced engines for the Sabre plane. During the evenings he was on call as a voluntary fire-fighter. At the end of the war he found work as an Inspector for Liverpool Corporation's Cleansing Department and later returned to his job at the cotton exchange.

His younger son Michael was to tell journalist George Tremlett in 1963: "We both owe him a lot. He's a very good man, and he's a very stubborn man. . . it would have been easy for him to have gone off with other birds when Mum died, or to have gone out getting drunk every night. But he didn't. He stayed home and looked after us.

*Paul's dad, Jim McCartney: brought up two teenage boys on his own
(from 'Mike Mac's Black and Whites')*

"He's a brilliant salesman with a very fine business brain and he could have gone right to the top in business if he had played the rules like they are now, if he had wanted to kill. He knew that to be a good businessman you have to have that killer streak, and he just wasn't prepared to be like that. And it would have meant neglecting us, and he wasn't prepared to do that either."

In 1964 Paul asked his father to retire. He was then earning £10 a week. Paul also suggested that he move into a nice house 'over the water' and bought Rembrandt (cf), a detached house in Baskervyle Road, Heswall, Cheshire, for £8,750.

On Jim's 62nd birthday, the same year, Paul presented him with a horse called Drake's Drum (cf). Two years later he proudly led the steed into the winner's enclosure at Aintree after it had won the race immediately preceeding the Grand National.

Paul was also to delight his father when he put words to 'Eloise' and recorded the number in Nashville under the title 'Walking In The Park With Eloise' (cf).

Jim was remarried on 24 November 1964 to a widow, Angela Williams (cf).

He died on 18 March 1976 and was cremated at Landican Cemetery, near Heswell.

McCARTNEY, JOE Paul's fraternal grandfather, who died before Paul was born. Joe was born in Everton on 23 November 1866 and lived in the area all his life. He married Florence Clegg (see *McCartney, Florence*) when he was twenty-nine and worked throughout his life as a tobacco cutter at Cope's, a local tobacco firm. A keen amateur musician, his instrument was the big brass double bass which he played in the line-up of two brass bands, one run by Copes, the other by the local branch of the Territorial Army.

McCARTNEY, JOSH First son of Mike and Rowena McCartney (cf) who was born at Arrowe Park Hospital in the Wirral, Merseyside, on 18 August 1983. At the time, the 22-year-old Rowena, a dress designer, was suffer-

ing from a rare disease which causes convulsions during pregnancy. Josh was born nine weeks prematurely and had to be immediately placed in an incubator and life-support machine. He weighed only 2½ lb at birth. Fortunately, he battled for his life and put on weight, causing Mike to comment: "He's absolutely marvellous – a real McFighter."

McCARTNEY, LINDA Linda was born Linda Louise Eastman on 24 September 1942. Her father, Lee V Eastman was an affluent lawyer, who had changed his name from Epstein and collected expensive works of art. Her father's speciality was copyright law in the show business field and he once agreed to undertake legal work for songwriter Jack Lawrence in exchange for a song dedicated to his six-year-old daughter. Lawrence penned 'Linda' (cf) in 1947 and in 1963 it was recorded by Jan & Dean.

Linda's mother, Louise Eastman, was the daughter of a rich Cleveland family, the Linders, who owned major department stores. The family home was in Scarsdale, Westchester County, in upstate New York. They also owned a house in East Hampton and a luxurious flat in Park Avenue.

During her formative years Linda was used to mixing with celebrity guests who were invited to dinner parties at the house, such as William Boyd (Hopalong Cassidy), Hoagy Carmichael and Tommy Dorsey.

Linda, whose star sign is Libra, has commented: "All my teen years were spent with an ear to the radio." She played truant from school to travel to shows at the Paramount Theatre in Brooklyn. "They'd have twenty acts on, twenty-four hours a day. Alan Freed was the MC but sometimes they'd get Fabian or Bobby Darin to MC. I remember seeing Chuck Berry sing 'School Days' for the first time."

She was educated at the exclusive Sarah Lawrence School in Bronxville, near Scarsdale (where Yoko Ono had been a student).

At the age of eighteen, Linda's world fell to pieces when her mother died in a plane crash. Linda had gone to Princeton University to study History and Art. Her mother's death affected her so much that she rushed into marriage with a fellow student, Melvin See. Linda recalls: "My mother died in a plane crash and I got married. It was a mistake." She realised things wouldn't work out: "When he (Melvin) graduated he wanted to go to Africa. I said: 'Look, if I don't get on with you here I'm not going to Africa with you. I won't get on with you there." They'd moved to Tucson, Arizona and Linda had become pregnant. She gave birth to her first daughter Heather on 31 December 1963. See, who was a geophysicist, still hoped that Linda would follow him to Africa but she wrote him a letter telling him she was getting a divorce.

The marriage had only lasted a year, but while she lived in Arizona, Linda had studied Art History at the University of Arizona and had attended a short course on photography given by Hazel Archer at Tucson Art Centre. It was then that she first began taking photographs. She was to say: "Arizona opened up my eyes to the wonder of light and colour."

Linda's break into the professional world of photography had begun when she and Heather moved to New York. Linda was holding down a job as receptionist for *Town & Country* magazine when an invitation to cover a reception for the Rolling Stones on a boat on the Hudson came in — she snapped it up, and found she was the only photographer on board! The photographs established her reputation, she secured an unpaid, but prestigious position as the house photographer at the Fillmore, a popular rock venue which featured major British and American acts, and began to receive commissions to photograph major bands such as the Beach Boys. Today, she has had exhibitions of her photographs in several world capitals and has published two books, *Linda's Pictures* (cf) and *Photographs* (cf).

She photographed the Beatles in 1965 in Austria during the filming of *Help!*, but says that she first met them officially at the Shea Stadium in 1966. She was to recall: "It was John who interested me at the start. He was my Beatle hero. But when I met him the fascination faded fast and I found it was Paul I liked."

In 1967 she came to London to photograph British artists such as the Animals and Traffic. She was taken to the Bag O' Nails club in Kingley Street by Chas Chandler, ex-bass player of the Animals, who introduced her to Paul. They had their first real conversation that night. The following day she visited Apple and was one of the select band of fifteen photographers from around the world who were allowed in on the *Sgt Pepper* recording session.

In May 1969, Paul arrived in New York to promote Apple and gave a number of press conferences. At one of them, Linda slipped him her telephone number and he got in touch and spent a few days with her, meeting and becoming charmed by Heather (see *McCartney, Heather*). He returned to London, then visited Los Angeles a month later and called up Linda with an invitation to join him. They spent a week together before Paul left once again. Linda returned to New York. In November she received an invitation from Paul to join him in London, just five months after he had split up with Jane Asher (cf). "I came over and we lived together for a while, neither of us talked about marriage, we just loved each other and lived together. We liked each other a lot, so being conventional people, one day I thought: 'OK, let's get married, we love each other, let's make it definite.'"

And the occasion did seem to be hastily arranged. Linda, four months pregnant with Mary (see *McCartney, Mary (2)*), went to Marylebone Register Office on 11 March 1969 to book it for the next day at 9.45am. Paul was in the studio recording Jackie Lomax singing 'Thumbin' A Ride' (cf) and, engrossed as he was in his work, forgot to buy a wedding ring. What with the early start the next day, he had to persuade a local jeweller to open his shop after closing time; he bought a plain gold ring for £12.

On the morning of 12 March, determined fans, photographers and journalists, undaunted by the rain, gathered at Paul's Cavendish Road house from six o'clock onwards, hoping to catch a glimpse of the couple. Mike McCartney (cf) was best man, but his train from Liverpool was delayed and he arrived an hour late. He rushed into the Register Office saying "Forgive me, it wasn't my fault. Have you been done?" Fortunately there had been no other weddings booked for that morning, and Paul was able to answer: "No, we've been waiting for you." Linda's daughter Heather was bridesmaid and Peter Brown and Mal Evans were witnesses. None of the Beatles had been invited as Paul had already started litigation to dissolve the group (see *Beatles Break-Up)*. The ceremony was conducted by Registrar Mr E R Sanders, and the marriage was blessed afterwards at the Anglican Church in St John's Wood by the Rev Noel Perry-Gore.

On the couple's return to Cavendish Road, the press were invited in and given champagne while Paul and Linda answered their questions. A rumour had spread that Linda was a rich heiress of the Kodak-Eastman family, but she quickly scotched it, saying that she had nothing to do with them. Paul quipped: "What? I've been done. Where's the money?" Once the press had been satisfied, Paul and Linda went on to the wedding reception proper at the Ritz Hotel, Piccadilly. Later that evening Paul returned to the studios to complete the production of the Jackie Lomax song.

One of the first songs which Paul wrote after the marriage was 'The Lovely Linda' (cf). Paul officially adopted Heather as his daughter and the couple had three more children: Mary, Stella and James Louis.

When Paul formed Wings he wanted Linda to tour with him. There were initially some cruel jibes about her being in the band and she suggested dropping out, but Paul insisted and taught her to play keyboards. She continued to pursue her career as a photographer with some success, and also recorded in her own right, initially using the pseudonym Suzi & the Red Stripes for her record 'Seaside Woman' (cf). She was also involved in two animation films, *The Oriental Nightfish* (cf) and *Seaside Woman* (cf). She had been a keen horsewoman since childhood and today owns twelve horses with Paul.

Paul and Linda have remained close throughout their marriage and have never been apart for longer than the nine days Paul spent in gaol in Japan.

There was originally some hostility towards Linda when she first married Paul and fans looked on her as a pushy American. Over the years fans and the media alike have come to like her, to respect the couple's closeness, and to see her as a talented person in her own right.

McCARTNEY, MARY (1) Paul's mother was born Mary Patricia Mohin on 29 September 1909 at No.2 Third Avenue, Fazakerley, Liverpool. Her mother Mary Theresa Dahner, was a Liverpudlian and her father Owen Mohin an Irishman. The couple had four children – Wilf, Mary, Agnes and Bill. Sadly, Agnes died at the age of two, and was followed by her mother who died giving birth to a fifth child, who also died, in 1919.

Mary was christened a Catholic and became a nurse at Alder Hey hospital at the age of fourteen. She later moved to Walton Hospital, where she was promoted to Nursing Sister at the age of twenty-four. She married Jim McCartney (cf) in 1941 when she was thirty-one and the couple moved to Anfield. When Paul was born at Walton Hospital, Mary gave up her position there to look after him. Her second son Michael was born eighteen months later. She became a health visitor for a while and then a midwife, which meant that she was on call virtually twenty-four hours a day. The family was given accommodation on the various council estates where she was on call to the residents.

Mary was concerned about both her sons making a success in life and was supportive in their schoolwork. She also smoothed out Paul's scouse accent, instilling in him the need to speak in as nice a way as possible. At the age of forty-five she began to suffer from pains in her chest, but dismissed them as being part of the menopause. However, they persisted and were so intense at times that she took bisodal. When she eventually saw a specialist, he diagnosed breast cancer. She underwent an operation, but it was too late – the cancer had spread, the operation exacerbated the condition and she died at the Northern Hospital on 31 October 1956. The 14 year-old Paul, on hearing the news of his mother's death, said: "What are we going to do without her money?" This initial reaction covered up his real grief which set in later; his brother Mike believed the tragedy caused Paul to lose himself in music. In Hunter Davies' *The Authorised Biography,* he said: "It was just after mother's death that it started. It became an obsession. It took over his whole life. You lose a mother – and you find a guitar? I don't know. Perhaps it just came along at that time and became an escape."

Mary was buried at Yew Street Cemetery, Finch Lane, Huyton on 3 November 1956. Both sons were to pay tribute to their mother: Mike by placing her photograph on the cover of his first solo album and Paul by immortalising her in 'Lady Madonna' (cf). Paul's first daughter Mary is also named after his mother.

McCARTNEY, MARY (2) First child of Paul and Linda. She was born at 1.30am on Thursday 29 August 1969, at the Avenue Clinic, St John's Wood, although an earlier announcement had said she was due in December. She weighed 6lbs 8ozs and arrived slightly less than six months after the couple had wed. Two months later Paul and Linda took their new baby up to Scotland with them. It was during this period that the 'Paul Is Dead' (cf) rumours first sprang up in America. In November they took Mary to America to show her to Linda's family.

McCARTNEY, MIKE Paul's brother, Peter Michael McCartney, was born on 7 January 1944 at Walton Hospital, Liverpool, and his first home was in Roach Avenue. He was baptised a Catholic, as was Paul, and joined his brother at their first school, Stock-

wood Road Infants School. When they moved to Ardwick Avenue in Speke, they shared the same bedroom and began to attend Joseph Williams Primary School in Gateacre.

One of the family holidays that Mike recalls is their visit to Butlins Holiday Camp in Filey. One of the Redcoats (official camp stewards) was Mike Robbins, who was married to their cousin Betty. He'd known that the two boys used to sing the Everly Brothers' 'Bye Bye Love' to the family at home (calling themselves the Nurk Twins), and he entered them for a National Talent Contest, organised by the Sunday newspaper the *People*, which was holding heats at the various Butlins camps. He introduced them as the McCartney Brothers. They sang 'Bye Bye Love', then Paul sang a solo version of 'Long Tall Sally' (cf). They weren't eligible for any prizes as they were under-age, but the thirteen-year-old Mike was anyway too nervous to give a confident performance and was literally shaking at his stage debut.

Mike attended Liverpool Institute, but his ambition was to enter Liver-

Mike McGear . . . or McCartney

pool College of Art. Unfortunately, new rules made it mandatory for entrants to have five GCE passes (see *General Certificate of Education)* and Mike was turned down. He was accepted for Birkenhead's Laird School of Art, but was unable to obtain a grant from Liverpool Corporation, so at the age of seventeen, he began his first job at Jackson's the Tailors in Ranelagh Street. The following year he began an apprenticeship at Andrew Bernard, a ladies' hairdresser in the same street. In 1962 he was asked if he'd take part in a sketch at the Merseyside Arts Festival with a post office engineer, John Gorman, and a young teacher, Roger McGough. Mike agreed, but wanted to use a pseudonym. He suggested the name Michael Blank, and he was so credited in the programme. The three decided to stick together as a satirical trio, performing songs and sketches, and called themselves the Scaffold. In 1963 they were asked to appear regularly on Granada Television's weekly magazine programme *Gazette,* so they all gave up their jobs to become professional members of Scaffold. Mike changed his name to Mike McGear as the Beatles were now achieving such incredible success that he didn't want to appear as if he were exploiting his family name. In any event, he was used to pseudonyms as he'd contributed photographs to *Mersey Beat* using the name Francis Michael.

The Scaffold were to prove a tremendous success. In 1968 they were appearing regularly on a BBC satirical show and were also doing live gigs at prestigious venues such as the London Palladium. During the seventies, the Scaffold line-up was regularly supplemented by Neil Innes and Viv Stanshall of the Bonzo Dog Doo Dah Band (cf) and Andy Roberts of the Liverpool Scene, using the collective name Grimms. The Scaffold performed their final live gig on the 'All Fools Show', a charity affair at the Royal Albert Hall on 1 April 1977. There was one further reunion – on Granada Television in 1979 when they teamed up on the programme *What's On* to celebrate the tenth anniversary

of their No.1 hit 'Lily The Pink'.

Mike had married Angela Fishwick in 1968 in a country church ceremony in Caerog, North Wales, with Paul as best man, accompanied by Jane Asher (cf). The marriage produced three daughters, but began to go wrong in the late seventies. The divorce came through in 1979.

After the demise of Scaffold and the collapse of his first marriage, Mike began to write children's books, married Rowena Home (see *McCartney, Rowena)* in 1982 and had a son Josh (cf) in 1983, while occasionally continuing to record. He has also produced various recordings by Liverpool bands.

The Scaffold enjoyed a successful recording career and their first single was produced by George Martin. It was '2 Days Monday', issued on Parlophone R5443 on 6 May 1966. John Burgess was the producer of their second single 'Goodbat Nightman', issued on 2 December of the same year on Parlophone R5548. They had a big chart hit with 'Thank U Very Much', produced by Tony Palmer and issued on Parlophone R5643 on 4 November 1967. This was followed by 'Do You Remember', produced by Norrie Paramor and issued on Parlophone R5679 on 15 March 1968. Their next single '1-2-3' came out on 14 June 1968 on Parlophone R5703. Their biggest success, reaching the No.1 spot in the British charts and proving to be the big hit of the Christmas season, was 'Lily The Pink', issued on 18 October 1968 on Parlophone R5734. Other singles include 'Charity Bubbles'; 'Gin Gan Goolie'; 'All The Way Up'; 'Busdreams'; 'Liverpool Lou' (cf); 'Mummy Won't Be Home For Christmas'; 'Leaving Of Liverpool'; 'Wouldn't It Be Funny If You Didn't Have A Nose?' and 'How Do You Do'.

Paul's first involvement with his younger brother's recording career happened in 1968 when he produced the album *McGough & McGear,* released on Parlophone PCS 7047 on 17 May. He didn't produce the Scaffold's first album *The Scaffold* but did produce their hit single 'Liverpool Lou', as well as Mike's solo album *McGear,* for which he wrote 'What Do We Really

Know?' and 'Leave It' and co-wrote with Mike 'Norton', 'Have You Got Problems?', 'Rainbow Lady', 'Simply Love You' and 'Givin' Grease A Ride'. He also co-wrote 'The Casket' and 'The Man Who Found God On The Moon', this time with Roger McGough.

At Island Records Mike recorded and released the single 'Woman' and an album of the same name in 1972. In 1973 Island issued the group Grimms' eponymous album, followed by a Scaffold album *Fresh Liver* and another Grimms LP *Rockin' Duck*. Mike then signed to Warners who issued *McGear* and *Sold Out* and a number of his singles.

Mike's popularity engendered an American Mike McCartney Fan Club and a fanzine called *Gear Box*. In the eighties he issued the series *Mike Mac's Black & Whites,* a collection of his photographs presented in a handsome range of postcards and posters. He also began to tour American Universities lecturing on his career, Liverpool and the Beatles. In addition to his children's books he has also written his autobiography, *Thank U Very Much: Mike McCartney's Family Album* (called *The Macs* in America).

A teenage Paul on the beach with young cousins Ted and Bett (from 'Mike Mac's Black and Whites')

McCARTNEY, ROWENA Née Home, second wife of Paul's brother Mike. Rowena, a dress designer, was twenty-one when she married the 38 year-old Mike at St Barnabus Church in Penny Lane, Liverpool, on Saturday 29 May 1982. Over six hundred fans gathered outside the church in the morning and waited for Mike to arrive at 2.30pm and Rowena about ten minutes later. Paul was best man, dressed in casual style with grey jacket, blue trousers and white sneakers, and there were five bridesmaids: Mike's three daughters (Benna, 13, Theran, 11, and Abbi, 8) and Rowena's two sisters. The Rev Harrington, who conducted the ceremony, recalled when Paul was a choirboy at the church and commented: "He used to sit up there in the choirbox, making some kind of noise." After the ceremony the wedding party left the church and headed for Hoylake for the reception. Later Mike and Rowena flew to Malta for their honeymoon.

St Barnabus Church, where Mike and Rowena were married

McCARTNEY, RUTH Young Ruth Williams became a member of the McCartney clan at the age of five when on 24 November 1964 her thirty-four year old widowed mother married sixty-two year old Jim McCartney (cf). Ruth became Paul's stepsister, was given the McCartney surname and went to live in Rembrandt (cf), the McCartney home in Hoylake on the Wirral. She recalls that Paul used to refer to her as 'Scabby' because she grazed her knees so often. He once bought her a pet dog, which she called Hamish, after she'd broken her leg in an accident. Jane Asher (cf) was a frequent companion of Paul's in the first three years of Ruth's life at Rembrandt and the young actress taught her to ride a bicycle. At school locally, Ruth came in for a fair amount of bullying from other children, jealous of her connection with the Beatles, and of her meeting the various famous guests who visited Rembrandt, such as Rod Stewart.

At the age of nine she was learning to play the piano and one day was attempting to play 'Golden Slumbers' (cf), a traditional hymn. She wasn't very successful, so Paul helped her out – and as a result he penned his own 'Golden Slumbers', which was included on *Abbey Road* (cf(1)). Ruth also recalls that Paul made up a song about her on the spur of the moment at a birthday party. As a young girl she observed the breakdown of Paul's romance with Jane Asher and the flowering of his relationship with Linda. Ruth, her mother and Jim were guests of Paul and Linda at the Campbeltown farm, where the conditions were very spartan, Ruth recalls.

When she was fifteen, Ruth took an interest in choreography but claims that she didn't get much encouragement from Paul. In all, Ruth spent twelve years in the bosom of the McCartney family, but following stepfather Jim McCartney's death circumstances changed for her and her mother.

For a time Ruth led a dance trio called Talent, but didn't achieve much success. In 1981 she moved to Kings Lynn where she shared a flat with her mother and worked as a salesgirl at the local Debenham's store. But the McCartney name still brought her to the attention of the press. She returned to her love of dancing and in March 1982 entered a 'Claim To Fame' dance competition at the Embassy Club in Mayfair, London, in which she won a heat. Julian Lennon had a sponsorship link with the competition – with the result that their names were romantically linked by the press, although no romance existed.

Eventually, Ruth went to live in Los Angeles where she is pursuing a career in show business (see also *19 Magazine*).

McCARTNEY, STELLA Paul and Linda's second child, born in London on 12 September 1971.

McCARTNEY TODAY American TV special screened by NBC on 18 and 20 June 1982. The 90-minute show was to celebrate Paul's fortieth birthday.

McCARTNEY II Paul's second solo album, issued ten years after his first, in Britain on 16 May 1980 on Parlophone PCTC 258, and in the US on 21 May 1980 on Columbia FC 36511. It reached No.1 in the British charts, and No.3 in the American. As with the first album, Paul composed all the songs and played all the instruments himself. He took six weeks to record the album in 1979, starting in his Sussex farm, completing it at his Scottish farm, and producing and engineering everything himself. The album spawned three hit singles: 'Coming Up', 'Waterfalls' and 'Temporary

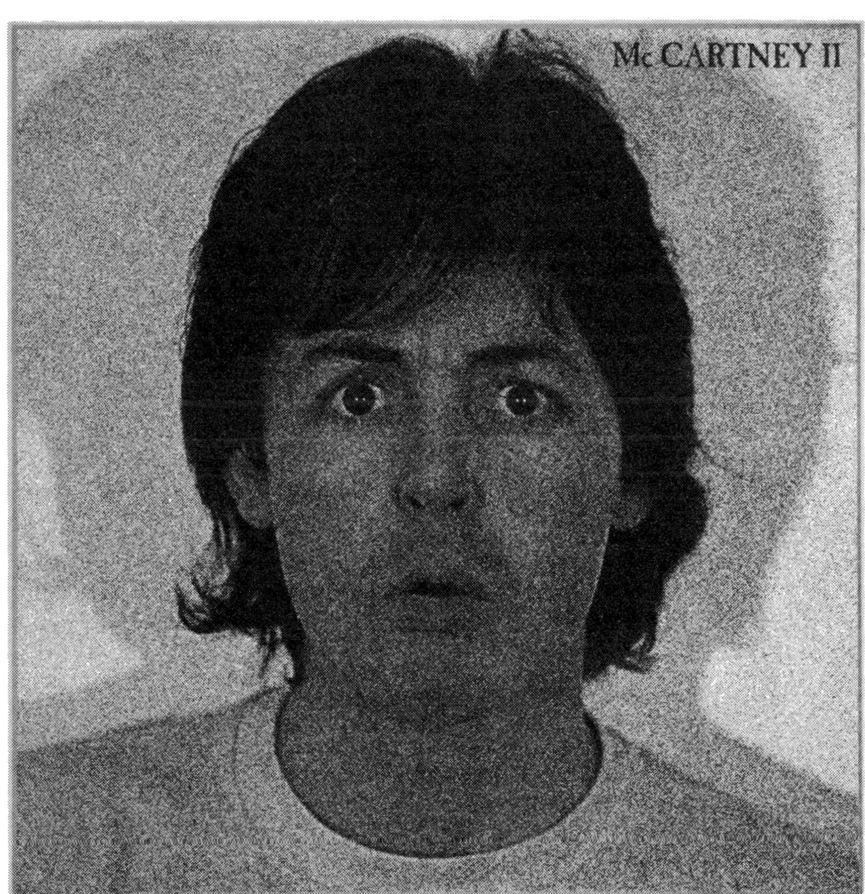

Paul's third solo album spawned three hit singles

Secretary', other tracks being 'On My Way'; 'Nobody Knows'; 'Front Parlour'; 'Summer's Day Song'; 'Frozen Jap'; 'Bogey Music'; 'Darkroom' and 'One Of These Days'.

McCULLOCH, JIMMY Young guitarist who had a brief, but glorious spell with Wings. Jimmy was born in Glasgow on 4 June 1953. At the age of thirteen he joined a band called One In A Million. He was sixteen when he performed on a No.1 record, 'Something In The Air' by Thunderclap Newman. For a short time he was a guitarist in John Mayall's band, following in the footsteps of such musicians as Eric Clapton and Jeff Beck. After the tragic electrocution on stage of Les Harvey (also a Glaswegian), Jimmy replaced him in Stone The Crows. In 1973 he joined the band Blue, managed by Robert Stigwood.

Jimmy had originally met Paul when he first played with Paul, Linda, Denny Laine (cf) and Davy Lutton (cf) in Paris in 1972, backing Linda on the record 'Seaside Woman' (cf). He next met Paul in 1974 when he was hired to play on Mike McCartney's album *McGear*, which Paul was producing. Paul then asked him to join in on some recording sessions with Wings in Nashville in June 1974, and Jimmy became a member of Wings. He recorded on *Venus and Mars*, (cf) *Wings at the Speed of Sound*, (cf) *Wings Over America* (cf), *London Town* (cf) and on the single 'Junior's Farm (cf). He also appeared on tour with the band. Following his appearances on the British gigs, Linda McCartney commented: "Jimmy is great and I think he'll improve a lot, he'll get better and better and really get his own style." He went on the 1975/76 world tour and also on the 1977 tour of America. The American tour had originally been set to begin in either May or June 1976, but Jimmy dislocated his left hand after a concert in Paris and the US trip was postponed.

Two numbers which Jimmy cowrote with Colin Allen, a former member of Stone The Crows, were included in Wings' repertoire. 'Medicine Jar' appears on *Venus and Mars* and *Wings Over America*. Jimmy provided lead vocals for the number and performed it on the world tour. 'Wino Junkie', said to be a nickname for himself, and like 'Medicine Jar' about drugs, was included on the 1976 album *Wings at the Speed of Sound*.

Jimmy drank a lot and was often abrasive and argumentative with people. He argued frequently with Geoff Britton (cf), until the latter left the band. There were even rumours of arguments between him and Paul. Jimmy finally left Wings on 8 September 1977, joining the Small Faces for a short time, until he formed his own band, the Dukes. When he hadn't turned up for rehearsals on two consecutive days, his brother Jack visited Jimmy's Maida Vale flat and found his body on the floor. An open verdict was recorded on his death, although the pathologist reported that he had traced cannabis, alcohol and morphine in his body, and despite some mysterious circumstances. The flat contained no evidence of drink or drugs, there was no money to be found and a security chain on the door had been broken. Jack was to comment: "I'm sure someone was in the flat after my brother died and I'd like to find out who he was." The mystery has never been solved.

Jimmy McCulloch: difficult and short-lived Wings' member

McCULLOUGH, HENRY Irish guitarist who was a member of Wings for almost two years. His career began with the Skyrocket Showband, one of the many 'showbands' popular in Ireland. He then joined rock group Jean & the Gents before becoming a member of Eire Apparent in 1967. The group began to play in England and were spotted at London's UFO Club by Chas Chandler, then manager of Jimi Hendrix. The group's road manager was Dave Robinson (later to launch the successful Stiff Records) and I was their PR. They played a number of gigs with Jimi Hendrix, but the group never achieved the success they deserved. Henry moved on to Sweeny's Men and then Joe Cocker's Grease Band. He was already friendly with Denny Laine, but it was Paul's road manager who informed him that Paul was holding auditions for a new lead guitarist. Henry auditioned on Tuesday, and was asked to return to audition again the following Thursday. Later Paul rang him to ask him to join the band, in time to contribute to Wings' first single, appropriately 'Give Ireland Back To The Irish' (cf).

Henry toured with Wings in Europe in 1972 and in the UK in 1973. He can also be heard on the 1973 album *Red Rose Speedway* (cf). However, at the end of that year, just before the recording of *Band on the Run,* he quit the band. In interview with DJ Paul Gambaccini, Paul commented: "Henry McCullough came to a head one day when I asked him to play something he didn't really fancy playing. We all got a bit choked about it, and he rang up later and said he was leaving. I said, 'Well, okay.' That's how it happened. You know with the kind of music we play, a guitarist has got to be a bit adaptable. It was just one of those things." Henry told the press he had quit because he and Paul didn't see eye to eye musically and that he considered Linda an amateur and wasn't too happy with her being in the band.

He later signed with George Harrison's record company, Dark Horse Records.

McDONALD, PHIL Recording engineer who worked with Paul on *Wings Over America* (cf) and *Back to the Egg* (cf). Phil was used to working with Paul, having been an engineer on *Abbey Road* (cf). He also engineered six George Harrison and two John Lennon albums.

McDONALD THOMPSON, STEWART Man accused in early 1980 of burgling Paul's Wirral home. He was charged at Birkenhead Magistrate's Court.

McDOUGAL, JOHN The man who'd previously owned Low Park Farm (cf), one of the Scottish farms which Paul bought. Paul later hired him to look after the farm as a caretaker.

McGIVERN, MAGGIE When Paul's long romance with Jane Asher (cf) came to an end in 1968, Paul often frequented the Revolution Club in Bruton Place, London. He took a shine to one of the waitresses there, Maggie McGivern, and the two of them went off for a holiday in Sardinia together. News of the couple on holiday appeared in the Sunday newspaper, the *People.*

McKENZIE, JOHN Scottish film director who was responsible for a series of

Henry McCullough: unhappy about Linda being in the band

critically acclaimed TV plays and movies from 1967 when he made his directorial debut with a BBC 1 Wednesday Play: *Voices in the Park*. His films include *One Brief Summer, Unman, Wittering & Zigo* and *The Long Good Friday* (which George Harrison had a hand in distributing). He was hired by Paul to direct the video film for the single 'Take It Away', based on a treatment written by Paul. The film took five days to shoot in June 1982 at EMI's Elstree Studios in Hertfordshire.

McQUICKLY, DIRK Dirk was the Paul figure in the Beatles TV spoof *The Rutles,* which was later released on a video cassette as *All You Need Is Cash.* Dirk was portrayed by Eric Idle. In the lampoon, when the Rutles split up he joins a group called the Punk Floyd.

MACCA Nickname by which Paul is known and one which is frequently used in the musical press. He was first given the nickname when he attended Liverpool Institute High School.

MACLINEAGE Title of the family tree which Mike McCartney (cf) drew for his *Thank U Very Much* book. The tree traces his family back to the 1840s, with James McCartney, upholsterer, on his father's side, and Michael McGergh on his mother's. Other professions are represented by a boilermaker, coroner, plumber, fishmonger, tobacco cutter, coal merchant and nursing sister.

McMILLAN, KEITH Videofilm director. He made the 'Ebony & Ivory' promotional video in which Paul and Stevie Wonder are featured on piano. The two stars were not filmed simultaneously. Keith filmed Paul in London and then flew to Los Angeles to complete the Stevie Wonder section, then merged the two on the completed film.

MAGNETO & TITANIUM MAN A track from *Venus and Mars* (cf). It was also issued as the flipside of the 'Venus & Mars'/'Rock Show' medley single issued in America in October 1975, and in Britain the following month,

and was included on *Wings Over America* (cf). The number was also in the repertoire of the Wings 1975/76 world tour. During the performance of it, cartoon characters were projected onto a screen on stage. Paul claimed it was inspired by Marvel Comics. He told Paul Gambaccini: "When we were on holiday in Jamaica, we'd go into the supermarket every Saturday, when they got a new stock of comics in. I didn't use to read comics from eleven onwards, I thought I'd grown out of them, but I came back to them a couple of years ago. The drawings are great. I think you'll find that in twenty years time some of the guys drawing them were little Picasso's. I think it's very clever how they do it. I love the names. I love the whole comic book thing."

MAGPIE Childrens' ITV series in Britain. Paul appeared in a special insert, 'A Day In The Life Of Mary Hopkin', which was filmed at the Apple offices and screened in 1968.

MAISIE Track on Laurence Juber's (cf) 1983 album *Standard Time* on which Paul plays bass guitar for the former Wings member.

MAITLAND SMITH, GEOFFREY Paul's accountant in the late sixties. In 1982, as chief executive of Sears Holdings, he expressed interest in buying Northern Songs for his company.

MAJOR McCARTNEY Character played by Paul in a cameo scene in *Magical Mystery Tour*. Costume advisers must have been absent that day as he was actually wearing the uniform of a colonel. Paul sits at a desk in an army recruitment office with two little Union Jacks decorating the wall behind him. The scene was in fact created for Victor Spinetti (cf) who plays the recruiting sergeant.

MAKE A WISH A British organisation seeking to help cheer up the lives of the more unfortunate members of society. In 1984 they arranged for Paul to make a personal visit to see Ely Coly, a 17-year-old girl suffering from a spinal disease.

Major McCartney – in a colonel's uniform!

MAKING MUSIC Book about the music industry, edited by George Martin (cf) and issued in Britain by Pan Books in 1983. In order to produce a "guide to writing, performing and recording," George invited a number of prominent members of the British music industry to contribute an article or interview on an aspect of the industry they were involved in. Paul contributed two pieces, the first on 'Songwriting', the second on 'Playing Bass.' The songwriting section was developed from a conversation George had with Paul and it provides insight into his songwriting process, taking the genesis of 'Ebony & Ivory' as an example. Paul relates how the number first arose: he was in Scotland, sitting at his piano, and he remembered a title he'd had in his head for some years after hearing Spike Milligan (cf) using the black and white notes on the piano as an analogy of harmonious race relations. The song developed from there, with Paul visualising it being performed with a black artist, his first choice being Stevie Wonder, the two of them sitting side by side at a piano. The arrangements were made and the recording took place at Montserrat (cf) with George Martin suggesting that Paul and Stevie do the number without additional musicians and singers.

Paul then describes his first songwriting inspirations with numbers such as 'I Lost My Little Girl' and 'When I'm Sixty Four'. ("Possibly the first song I ever wrote on the piano.") He then continued, describing his first meeting with John Lennon and their songwriting efforts together. (See *Twenty Flight Rock.)*

Another conversation with George Martin provided the basis for the two-page article 'Playing Bass'. Paul relates how he originally came to play bass. The first bass player in the band was Stu Sutcliffe. Paul played one of the three front-line guitars with John and George. His model was a cheap one, in contrast to the more expensive guitars of his colleagues and it broke during the group's trip to Hamburg. Stu left the band, so Paul took over on bass, borrowing Stu's guitar and eventually being allowed to change the strings around, as he was left-handed. Since the group were so poverty-stricken, they used to snip the piano wires from club pianos and use them on his bass guitar. He found them quite effective! Paul also mentioned during the conversation that the bass guitarists he admired included Louis Johnson, George Porter and Stanley Clarke (cf).

MAMUNIA Track from the 1973 Wings album *Band on the Run.* During his trip to Nigeria, Paul noticed a phrase on a plaque which inspired him to think up the theme for the number. The title was adapted from the name of a hotel in Marrakesh which Paul had stayed in.

MARNE, PATRICIA British graphologist. When preparing a book about London's Capital Radio in 1983, she analysed the handwriting of celebrities who had signed the guest book. Of Paul, she wrote: "Very fast, indicating fluency of thought. The rising lines show an ambitious nature and the strange end strokes shows a desire to keep the world at bay from one's private life."

MARSDEN, GERRY Leader of Gerry & the Pacemakers, the first British band ever to have three No.1 hits with their first three releases. Gerry's band was regarded as second only to the Beatles, but on the day that his 'How Do You Do It?' reached No.1, Gerry came out of Brian Epstein's Nems office in Liverpool and saw John and Paul chatting to Steve Day, leader of another Mersey band. "And how is Brian Epstein's number two group?" he asked them.

However, the friendship between Gerry and the Beatles was quite strong and when Gerry celebrated the twentieth anniversary of his recording career with a party at Stringfellows club in London in 1983, Paul, who was recording at the time, sent him a birthday cake. When Gerry gathered together a group of recording artists to make a charity record for the relatives of those killed in the Bradford City Disaster (a soccer club in which a fierce fire killed a number of spectators), he gave them the name 'The Crowd', and they re-recorded one of his No.1 hits 'You'll Never Walk Alone' (now a football anthem) which also reached No.1 after it's release on 20 May 1985 on BRAD 1. Paul was invited to participate and he recorded a 17-second message which appears on the flipside of the single, which is called 'Messages'. Gerry also recorded an album of Lennon & McCartney numbers which was released in England by K-Tel Records in 1986.

He was Paul's special guest on the TV special *James Paul McCartney* (cf).

MARTHA The most famous of Paul's pets. This Old English sheepdog gained immortality when Paul used her name in the song 'Martha My Dear'. Martha was born in 1966 and died of old age in the summer of 1982. The love song was recorded at London's Trident Studios in October 1968 and was featured on *The Beatles* white album.

MARTIN, ROSE Housekeeper whom Paul first employed in 1967. Her Christian name was the inspiration for the album title *Red Rose Speedway*.

Gerry Marsden, with his Pacemakers – second only to the Beatles

MARTIN, GEORGE The Beatles producer for eight years. Martin had joined the Parlophone label in 1952 and became label head in 1955. He remained with Parlophone until 1965 when he formed the Association of Independent Record Producers (AIR) with John Burgess, Peter Sullivan and Ron Richards. Although he'd officially left Parlophone, he continued to produce the Beatles right up to *Abbey Road* (cf).

During the sixties he also recorded Beatles material under his own right, contributing arrangements, and orchestral and instrumental tracks to the soundtracks of *A Hard Day's Night, Help!* and *Yellow Submarine.* He released a number of instrumental singles, and also two albums – *Off the Beatles Track,* August 1964, and *The Beatle Girls,* March 1967, the latter

George Martin has had a long and fruitful working relationship with Paul, from Abbey Road days to 'Broad Street'

featuring songs such as 'Eleanor Rigby' (cf) and 'Michelle' (cf).

Paul had also asked George to help him on the theme music for the film *The Family Way* (cf), in particular the track 'Love In The Open Air'. Although ten years were to pass between *Abbey Road* and *Tug of War* (cf), the album that Paul asked George to produce for him, Paul also called in George to help him when he composed the theme for the 1973 James Bond movie *Live and Let Die* (cf). As a result, George was asked to compose further background material for the soundtrack. The team was also reunited on the *Pipes of Peace* (cf) and *Give My Regards to Broad Street* (cf(3)) albums.

George has been the subject of a *This Is Your Life* programme, has had an autobiography *All You Need Is Ears* published, and also edited the book *Making Music* (cf) in which he interviewed Paul about songwriting and playing the bass guitar.

MARY HAD A LITTLE LAMB At the height of Beatlemania, people often said that there was so much adulation aimed at the Beatles that they could have a hit reciting passages from the Bible or singing nursery rhymes. Paul took them at their word with this number which is an adaptation of the familiar children's rhyme. It was issued in 1972, in Britain on Apple R5949 on 5 May, and in America on Apple 1851 on 29 May. It reached the position of No.6 in Britain and No.28 in the US. 'Little Woman Love' was the flip. Following the highly controversial single 'Give Ireland Back to The Irish (cf), the seemingly lightweight 'Mary Had A Little Lamb' incurred heavy flack from the music press and Paul was later to admit that "it wasn't a great record." In an interview he commented: "It was written for one of our kids, who's name is Mary, and I just realised if I sang that, she'd understand. That's it with us, that's what you might expect from us – just anything. The quote that sums up that song for me is I read Pete Townshend saying that his daughter had to have a copy. I like to keep in with the five-year-olds!"

MASSEY & COGGINS Liverpool firm of electrical engineers. Following the Beatles first trip to Hamburg in 1960, Paul, who had left school against the advice of his father, abandoning his idea of becoming a teacher, felt guilty about not getting a regular job and approached the Labour Exchange. Initially he worked temporarily for a parcels delivery service, being laid off after the Christmas rush. He was then sent to Massey & Coggins where he received a wage of £7. He admits he was not very good at the job which consisted of him winding electrical coils all day long. Whereas fellow labourers would complete between eight and fourteen coils per working week, Paul confessed he was lucky if he managed one and a half. One of his workmates called him 'Mantovani' because of his long hair, and his boredom with the job was such that after two months he didn't bother turning up one morning.

MASSEY, PAUL A news photographer who attempted to take photographs of Paul when he was on his way to the BBC to record *Desert Island Discs* (cf). Paul gave the eighteen-year-old photographer a fierce shove, which knocked him to the ground. Paul regretted the incident and apologised, saying: "I'm sorry I blew my top, mate. I knew there was only one way to stop you taking pictures and that was to lay into you."

MAYBE I'M AMAZED Highly praised as the outstanding track on Paul's first album in 1970. It resurfaced in 1976 on *Wings Over America* (cf). This later version was a live cut from their American tour and was issued as a single in 1977 in Britain on Parlophone R6017 on 4 February and in the US on Capitol 4385 on 7 February. Capitol, in fact, issued a promotional 12" record for American radio stations which included four different versions of the number. It reached No.27 in the British charts and No.11 in the American. The flipside was 'Soily'. Rod Stewart and the Faces recorded 'Maybe I'm Amazed' on *Long Player,* their 1971 album. Wings performed it on their European, world and both the British tours. It was also one of the numbers included in the TV spectacular *James Paul McCartney* (cf).

MELLOW YELLOW A major hit single for Donovan (cf) in February 1967. The Pye Records release featured Paul playing bass guitar.

THE MESS The 'B' side of 'My Love' on 23 March 1973. The number is a live recording from a performance at the Congresgebouw in Holland which took place on 21 August 1972 during Wings' European tour. The number was also featured on their British University tour in 1972, their British tour of 1973 and in the *James Paul McCartney* TV show (cf).

THE METERS Band hired by Paul to play at a party he organised for the Press in New Orleans in February 1975 during the recording of *Venus and Mars*. He rehired them the following month when he threw another party aboard the *Queen Mary*. The ship was docked at Long Beach in California and the occasion was the completion of the album. George Harrison was among the star-studded array of guests, as was Dean Martin, Bob Dylan, Ryan O'Neal, Cher, Carole King, Micky Dolenz and Michael Jackson (cf).

MICHELLE The number first surfaced on *Rubber Soul* on 3 December 1965. Numerous other versions were rushed out and both the Overlanders and David & Jonathan found themselves with a major hit, the former reaching the No.1 spot in Britain. It was included on the Beatles EP 'Nowhere Man', issued in July 1966, and on several albums, including *A Collection of Beatles Oldies (But Goldies)* in 1966, *The Beatles 1966-1970* in 1973, *Love Songs* in 1977, and *The Beatles Ballads* and *The Beatles Box* in 1980.

There were a staggering number of versions recorded by over 700 artists throughout the world. They included Booker T and the MG's, the Four Tops, Jan & Dean, Jack Jones, Johnny Mathis, Diana Ross and the Supremes, George Shearing, Sarah Vaughan and Andy Williams.

Michelle Howard (cf), whose father worked for the Beatles, claimed she'd been the inspiration behind the number. Paul comments: "I just fancied writing some French words and I had a friend whose wife taught French and we were sitting around and I just asked her, you know, what we could figure that was French. We got words that go together well. It was mainly because I always used to think the song always sounded like a French thing, and I can't speak French really, so we sorted out some actual words."

MIKE'S BROTHER Title of a painting of Paul by Irish-born artist Sam Walsh who has lived in Liverpool since 1960. Walsh, who was a friend of John Lennon's, now lives in the basement of the house in Gambier Terrace where John once rented a flat. He painted several pictures of Paul in the sixties, and *Mike's Brother* is his own way of saying that he was more familiar with Mike McCartney than with Paul. The painting was exhibited in the 'Art Of The Beatles' in 1984, is the property of Jim Cassles and is an oil on canvas close-up of Paul's face.

THE MIKE YARWOOD SHOW Paul and Wings appeared on this British TV show on Christmas Day 1977, performing 'Mull Of Kintyre' (cf). They also appeared in a comedy sketch with Yarwood, a leading impressionist, in a routine in which he acted as Dennis Healey, then Chancellor of the Exchequer.

MILLER, CARA Baby rescued by Paul following a car crash in October 1980. Paul was rehearsing with Wings in the manor house owned by Cara's father Martin, a publisher, in Tenterden, Kent. They heard the sounds of a crash and rushed out of the house to find that a car had crushed the fourteen-month-old Cara's pram and the family's 21-year-old Japanese au pair girl, Hisako Kawahara. The baby was unconscious and Wings' road manager drove her and her mother Judith to a nearby hospital. Paul remained behind to comfort Hisako while they waited for an ambulance. She died in hospital a few hours later.

MILLIGAN, SPIKE British comedian and former member of the Goons. In 1981 he asked if Paul and George Harrison could contribute to a fund to set up a sanctuary for otters in Gloucestershire. They chipped in with £800 each. Paul had once taken Jane Asher (cf) to see Spike in *Son of Oblomov* on 8 March 1964. Spike also inspired Paul to write 'Ebony & Ivory' (see *Making Music*).

MILLION MILES Track on the 1979 album *Back to the Egg* (cf) on which Paul plays concertina.

MINE FOR ME Song which Paul penned for Rod Stewart and the Faces, which was included on their 1974 Mercury album *Smiler*. Paul and Linda took the stage with Rod and the band to sing the number at the Odeon, Lewisham, on 18 November 1974.

MONEY, ZOOT Zoot (George Bruno) established himself in the London scene in 1964 with his Big Roll Band which had the hit single 'Big Time Operator' in 1966. The band became Dantalion's Chariot in 1967, but Zoot had no great success on the music scene so he became an actor and also appeared in a number of TV commercials. He worked with Paul on the *McGough & McGear* album and also worked with Mike McCartney (cf) in the group Grimms. In April 1977 he teamed up with Paul, Denny Laine (cf), and Vivian Stanshall to record with Mike McCartney. A number of tracks were cut at the sessions, but they remain unreleased.

In 1980 Paul suggested that Zoot did an album of MPL (cf) numbers. Zoot said: "I leapt at the chance. There was a list of songs as long as Oxford Street. I picked at those I'd fancied and Paul paid for the session. Also, Paul helped to design the sleeve." The album, *Mr Money*, was issued in Britain on Magic Moon Records Lune 1 on 25 September 1980, and a single 'The Two Of Us' c/w 'Ain't Nothin' Shakin' But The Bacon' was also issued, on 5 June 1981 on Magic Moon Records Mach 6.

MONROE, MARILYN Arguably Hollywood's most famous film star. Paul and Linda paid $5,000 for a life-size, full colour statue of Marilyn by a female artist from Holland. It now decorates their home in Scotland.

MONTSERRAT Caribbean island where George Martin (cf) built his AIR Studios in 1978, although it wasn't until Paul had recorded there that the stars began to flock to the place. Paul and Linda recorded *Tug of War* (cf) there in February 1981. Paul commented: "I wanted to work with George again. We hadn't worked together since Beatle days and it was something I had wanted to do for ages. I suppose I could have done that in London, but wouldn't you rather go to a paradise island if you had a choice?"

Paul arrived with Linda and his four children on 1 February and was soon followed by Ringo Starr, Carl Perkins (cf) and Stevie Wonder (cf), who were guesting on the album. Stevie was so impressed with Montserrat that he composed a number about the island and spent his last night there listening to a steel band at the only local club bar, the Agouti.

MONUMENTAL BULLRING Venue in Madrid, Spain, where the Beatles appeared on 2 July 1965 as part of their European tour. Paul introduced the group's numbers in Spanish to an audience of 10,000 people.

MOORE, ROGER While filming *Live and Let Die,* Roger kept a diary which was later published by Pan Books, entitled *Roger Moore as James Bond.* In it he writes: "Paul McCartney has written the song and I had lunch today with the man who is arranging the music, George Martin, who was responsible for so many of the Beatles' hits." He went on to predict that the record would top the charts three weeks after release. The highest position it reached was No.7.

MORSE MOOSE AND THE GREY GOOSE At six minutes and twenty-seven seconds, the longest track on *London Town*. During their recording sessions in the Virgin Islands (cf), Paul and Denny Laine (cf) were fooling around, Paul poking away at an electric piano and Denny thumping on a standard piano. They enjoyed the unusual sound, which Paul likened to morse code, and began to write a song around it which they completed in London.

MOSES, BRIAN English master at East Sussex School. On 6 June 1985, the 34-year-old teacher was one of two pickets outside the school as part of the selective strike the National Union of Teachers was staging over a 12.5 per cent pay claim. Paul arrived at the school with his six-year-old son James. On seeing the pickets, Paul was heard to say to his son: "Take a good look. They are striking teachers." Moses went over and handed him a leaflet concerning the claim. Paul said, "Did teachers go on strike when you were at school?", tore up the leaflet and left.

Moses commented: "I was taken aback by it all. When one of your heroes behaves like that it is upsetting. I did explain the teachers were sad and reluctant to have to take such action. But he didn't give me a chance to talk to him. I grew up with the Beatles music but this, sadly, has changed my opinion of Mr McCartney." He added: "He sat in his car reading it (the leaflet), then he made sure we were watching while he tore it up. I had always admired him for sending his children to State schools. I expected more support."

A spokesman for Paul commented: "Paul didn't disagree with the pay claim. But he felt their timing was unfair as pupils were sitting for exams."

MOTHER NATURE'S SON One of the songs Paul composed during his sojourn in India. It was recorded during the early hours of one morning in 1968 after John, George and Ringo had gone home to bed, so Paul recorded it playing acoustic guitar. Brass backing was added later and the number appeared on *The Beatles* white album.

MPL Abbreviation of McCartney Productions Limited, the company originally conceived by Paul in 1970 and launched a few years later in a small, two-roomed office in the West End of London, before moving into grander premises at No.1 Soho Square, as the company flourished. Owned jointly by Paul and Linda, MPL is involved in various activities ranging from film production to book publishing. The main bulk of the company's millions, however, comes from the vast musical publishing catalogue which Paul has been purchasing over the years. He has the rights to the music of major musicals ranging from *Grease* and *Annie* to *The Chorus Line,* has bought up existing companies such as Whale Music and the Edwin H Morris Music Company, and has also purchased the musical catalogues of songwriters and composers such as Scott Joplin, Ira Gershwin and Buddy Holly (cf). Managing Director of MPL is Steven Shrimpton (cf) and there are approximately a dozen full-time staff members working for the company.

MR TIBBS A white Appaloosa that Paul rides around High Park Farm (cf) in Scotland. (See also *Lucky Spot).*

MULL OF KINTYRE Britain's biggest-selling single ever, taking over the honours from 1963's 'She Loves You' until finally overtaken itself in 1984 by the Band Aid single 'Do They Know It's Christmas?' Originally issued as a double 'A' side with 'Girl's School' (cf) in Britain on Capitol R6018 on 11 November 1977, it swiftly became the most rapid-selling single in Britain, passing its millionth pressing a month later in December. On 23 December this millionth pressing was purchased by David Ackroyd who discovered a slip in the sleeve with a message from EMI informing him that he had won a Christmas hamper, to be presented by Denny Laine (cf). He also received a specially pressed Gold Disc. Denny had helped Paul with the song's composition in 1976; the title referred to a point on the southern tip of the Kintyre peninsula, near Paul's farm in Campbeltown. At the time of release, Wings comprised Paul, Linda and Denny, who made a promotional film at the Mull featuring the Campbeltown

Pipe Band, a 21-piece group of bag-pipers who also performed on the record.

In America the single was issued on Capitol 4504 on 14 November but failed to make anything resembling the impact that it had in Britain. In fact, the side promoted in America was 'Girls School', a number which Paul said referred to a "pornographic St Trinians." St Trinians was the famous anarchic girls' school created by cartoonist Ronald Searle and featured in several British comedy films. Paul also claimed to have received added inspiration from adverts in American newspapers for soft porn films with titles such as *School Mistress*. The number didn't make much impact and only reached No.33 in the American charts.

MUMBO Song which Paul co-wrote with Linda. It was the first track on the first Wings album, *Wild Life* (cf), issued in December 1971 and consising of a string of nonsense words. No doubt a lot of mumbo jumbo.

THE MUSIC LIVES ON Surprise addition to the London Weekend Television programme schedule for Friday 7 September 1984. Unadvertised, it was slipped on to the tail end of the evening's programmes at 12.40am (so, strictly speaking, Saturday morning), following *The Making of 'The Company of Wolves'*. It was, of course, Buddy Holly week (see *Holly, Buddy*) and the ten-minute short was produced by MPL Communications (cf) as a tribute to Buddy Holly.

It begins with a black-and-white film of Buddy Holly and the Crickets performing 'Oh, Boy'. His mother, Mrs Ella Holly, then relates how he thought his fame wouldn't last. A group of British Holly fans, dressed in colourful Teddy Boy costumes, then wax enthusiastic, followed by Scottish comedian Billy Connolly talking about the durability of Holly's music. A black-and-white film of couples jiving and jitterbugging to 'Brown-Eyed Handsome Man' is followed by Buddy's brother Travis showing off a guitar that Buddy bought in 1951, a second-hand instrument and one of

the first of many guitars. He mentions that he only taught Buddy to play a few chords. More archive film of a performance of 'Peggy Sue' is followed by Ella talking about his early career playing locally at high school and graduation dances, then going to Norman Petty's studio in Clovis.

Buddy Holly: MPL promotes his name with such ventures as the 'Music Lives On'

A still photograph of Buddy with the tune of 'Think It Over' in the background is followed by Ella mentioning that she wrote a song herself, which Buddy performed. The number was 'Maybe Baby'. The Crickets are seen performing it at one of Paul's Holly Week concerts.

Buddy's other brother Larry talks about the number 'That'll Be The Day' and how Buddy being flat broke, called New York to enquire about how the song was doing. He was told it was getting airplay and would sell a million, so he asked if he could have a cheque for $500.

Archive film of Buddy performing 'That'll Be The Day' is followed by his widow Maria Elena Holly mentioning that he'd been talking about expanding his career, producing other artists, seeking new talent, and recording with artists such as Paul Anka and Phil Everly.

Don Everly and Albert Lee are seen performing 'Bye Bye Love' at Paul's Holly concert.

There is a black-and-white wedding picture and Maria Elena mentions the songs 'It Doesn't Matter Any More', 'True Love Ways' and 'Raining In My Heart'.

Denny Laine then performs 'Raining In My Heart'.

Roy Orbison is interviewed and mentions that Buddy was a kindred soul and that they had a friendly rivalry.

Paul McCartney next appears performing 'It's So Easy To Fall In Love'. Then he performs 'Bo Diddley' with the Crickets (Sonny Curtis, Joe Maudlin, Jerry Allison), Don Everly and Denny Laine. Bo Diddley briefly utters the sentence 'Gold Bless Rock'n'Roll' and Maria Elena mentions that her favourite song was 'True Love Ways'. The number is played as a photo of Buddy appears on the screen and the credits roll.

MUST DO SOMETHING ABOUT IT Track from the 1976 *Wings at the Speed of Sound* (cf). Paul had decided to give each member of the group the opportunity to sing on the album and on this track drummer Joe English (cf) is the lead vocalist.

MY DARK HOUR Single issued by the Steve Miller Band and released in the US on 16 June 1969 on Capitol 2520 and in Britain on 18 July 1969 on Capitol CL 15604. It was recorded at AIR Studios in London on 3 February of that year. Paul played drums, bass guitar and sang backing vocals, and used his old pseudonym Paul Ramon (cf) for the session. The track was also included on the band's album *Brave New World*, also issued in 1969 in America in June, and in Britain in October.

MY LITTLE GIRL Sometimes called 'I Lost My Little Girl'. The first song that Paul ever wrote. It remains unrecorded.

MY LOVE Single issued on 23 March 1973, in Britain on Apple R5985, and in America on Apple 1861. It reached the No.1 spot in the US and No.7 in Britain. The flip was 'The Mess' (cf). 'My Love' was recorded during the preparation of *Red Rose Speedway* (cf) and is included on the album. It's also on *Wings Greatest* (cf). The song was included in the repertoire on Wings' 1972 tour of Europe, the British tour of 1973 and the world tour in 1975/76.

MY SWEET LADY JANE American fan magazine devoted to Jane Asher (cf). Editor Penny Lane has the largest collection of Jane Asher photographs in the world and the magazine covers all aspects of Jane's life and career, including the years of her romance with Paul.

NAME AND ADDRESS A track on *London Town*, recorded at Abbey Road Studios and featuring Paul on lead guitar. Jimmy McCulloch (cf) and Joe English (cf) had already left Wings at the time this track was recorded. Hank Marvin, guitarist with the Shadows, dropped in on the session, although he didn't play. The number was Paul's tribute to Elvis Presley.

NASHVILLE DIARY 1979 bootleg album (PRO 1234) containing tracks recorded by Wings during rehearsal sessions in Nashville in the summer of 1974. They include numbers such as 'My Love', 'One Hand Clapping', 'Hi Hi Hi' and 'Soily'.

THE NEW YORK PHILHARMONIC ORCHESTRA Paul hired this orchestra to perform on three tracks of *Ram*, which he recorded in New York in 1971, his first recording stint outside Britain. He personally conducted the orchestra on the tracks 'Uncle Albert/ Admiral Halsey', 'Long Haired Lady' and 'Back Seat Of My Car'.

NEWSFRONT American television show on which Paul appeared with John Lennon (cf) on 15 May 1968. This was during their special trip to America to promote Apple. In addition to discussing their new project they also touched on a number of political subjects. The interview was repeated a week later on 22 May.

THE NIGHT BEFORE A Paul song from the *Help!* album. In the film it was used during the Salisbury Plain sequence. It was also included on *Rock and Roll Music.*

NIGHT OWL Track featured on Carly Simon's *No Secrets,* released in 1972. The number was penned by her husband James Taylor, a former Apple artist, and both Paul and Linda provided backing vocals, together with Doris Troy and Bonnie Bramlett.

19 MAGAZINE British monthly publication whose March 1983 cover declared: "Paul McCartney's Stepsister Reveals What Life With A Beatle Was Really Like." It referred to a feature by Ruth McCartney (cf), ghosted by Tony Barrow, one of the Beatles' former publicists. "My Stepbrother Was A Beatle" was the headline, but the story depicted Paul as being more paternal than fraternal, especially after his own father died. Ruth recounted how Paul played the parental role when she introduced him to a boy she thought she might marry; how she came to London to attend the Wings launch, with new shoes and a new hair-do, only to be told by Paul that she should babysit instead; how an entire room at Cavendish Avenue was full of Linda's gowns; how Jim and Angie (her mother) had to sleep on a mattress in a garage at the Campeltown farm, and so on.

The article is quite a tender piece, with affectionate memories of Paul, unlike the series by her mother which Tony Barrow had ghosted in the *Sun.*

NINETEENTH CITY SCHOOL SCOUTS Boy scout troop which Paul and his brother Mike joined soon after they entered their teens. Their first camping trip with the scouts took them to North Wales. Their second, in July 1957, took them to Hathersons in Derbyshire. There was an accident during the trip in which Mike broke his arm.

NOCON, GENE Photographic printer who first began to print all of Linda's photographs in 1976. Her daughter Heather (cf) took up photographic printing after being introduced to Gene.

NO MORE LONELY NIGHTS Number from *Give My Regards to Broad Street* (cf (1)) which was issued in Britain on 24 September 1984 and entered the charts on 6 October where it was to reach the No.2 position, with a chart life of thirteen weeks. After its release, it was discovered that about 100,000 copies of the single said "Lonley" on the label. Paul insisted that all copies be returned to the pressing plant so that the spelling could be corrected. Obviously, copies of the single that slipped away with the misspelling have become collectors' items.

The song was written specially for the film, and was effectively the theme tune, being played throughout the movie. This was known as the 'ballad' version, as the song is played in two tempo's. Paul commented: "Twentieth Century Fox asked for an upbeat play-out as people leave the cinema, so I was happy to rearrange it in an up-tempo version as the play-out: that's more of a dance version."

Two pressings of this double-A side disc were issued which featured both versions of the number. There was the normal 7" single on Parlophone R6080 and a special 12" pressing on Parlophone 12R 6080. Then on 8 October the 12" pressing was issued as a picture disc in a special limited edition on Parlophone 12RP 6080. Writer Mark Lewisohn, in a special article in the January 1985 issue of *Beatles Monthly* entitled "It's All Too Much", bemoaned the fact that there were so many versions of this particular song. He pointed out that it would cost the collector, and in particular the completist, a small fortune to catch up with all the different editions of the same number. Mark reckoned that it would cost a collector £33.34 to buy the different *British* versions of the single, which included the 7" ballad version; a 7" special dance mix of the ballad version; a 12" extended version, over eight minutes long; the 12" picture disc; a 12" extended ballad version, with 'Silly Love Songs' and two versions of 'No More Lonely Nights'. This was in addition to the versions on the album, cassette and compact disc. Another 7" special dance mix was also included on the November 1984 compilation *Now That's What I Call Music 4*, issued by EMI/Virgin.

THE NOTE YOU NEVER WROTE This was a track from *Wings at the Speed of Sound*. Although the number was written by Paul, it was sung by Denny Laine.

NOTTINGHAM UNIVERSITY The venue for Wings' first-ever gig which took place at lunchtime on 9 February 1972 and was hurriedly arranged the previous day. Notices announcing: "Tonight! Guest group: Paul McCartney & Wings! Admission 50p" drew an audience of 700 students. It was Paul's first live gig in nearly six years and the group's share of the take was £30.

NO VALUES A track from *Give My Regards to Broad Street* (cf (1)). The song came to Paul in a dream. He'd been on holiday and was just waking up and he found he was still dreaming and was watching the Rolling Stones perform a number called 'No Values'. He remembered the chorus quite clearly when he woke up. He was sure that his own mind had created it in the dream. To make sure he checked that the Stones hadn't done a song of that title and when he found they hadn't, wrote the number and included it in the film and album.

NO WORDS Collaboration by Paul and Denny Laine. Denny had started off writing the song and Paul helped him to complete it. They shared writing credits when it appeared on the Wings 1973 album *Band on the Run* and performed the number during their British tour in 1979. Vocal harmony was provided by Paul, Linda and Denny.

NOW HEAR THIS SONG OF MINE One of the numbers written and recorded by both Linda and Paul in 1971 at the time of the *Ram* (cf) sessions. It was not included on the album and was never released as a single, although a thousand copies were pressed and circulated within the music industry to aid the promotion of *Ram*.

NOW IT'S PAUL McCARTNEY, STEVIE WONDER, ALICE COOPER, ELTON. Single by Clive Baldwin issued in America in 1975 on Mercury 73680. It was penned by I Levine and L Russell Brown and the flipside was 'Disco Rag'.

THE NURK TWINS Paul and his brother Mike first thought up this name when they were kids and used it when they entertained friends or family with a duet. In 1960 John and Paul made an appearance as a duo at a gig in Bending, Berkshire, and called themselves the Nurk Twins.

OB-LA-DI OB-LA-DA Lighthearted song inspired by reggae music. The number was originally intended to be a Beatles single, but John and George vetoed it. It was recorded by the Marmalade who had a No.1 hit with it and also by the Bedrocks who reached No.17 in the British charts. The number was featured on *The Beatles* white album and the compilation *Beatles 1967-1970*. Ironically, it was issued as a Beatles single in America years later on 8 November 1976 on Capitol 4347.

OCEAN, HUMPHREY Former member of Kilburn and the High Roads, who became a painter. He contributed to the inner sleeve of the *Wings at the Speed of Sound* (cf) album and Paul commissioned him to join the Wings tour of America and document it as "artist in residence". The result was a book, *The Ocean View* (cf). Humphrey was also commissioned by the Imperial Tobacco Portrait Award. Paul sat for him for a total of thirty hours in six separate sittings in his Sussex home. The painting was unveiled at the National Portrait Gallery, London on 2 February 1984. A gallery spokesman commented: "This is a painting that puts the singer in a very unusual light. He looks nothing like he does on the record sleeves – it's bound to cause a few surprises." Humphrey said: "I'm happy with it. I believe it shows Paul in a relaxed setting."

Humphrey Ocean's 'unusual' portrait

THE OCEAN VIEW Book published by MPL Communications (cf)/Plexus Publishing in 1982. It is a collection of paintings and drawings by Humphrey Ocean from the Wings American tour which took place between April and June 1976. The works were commissioned by Paul who wanted pictorial documentation of the tour. He explains in a Preface to the book that he was inspired by Captain Cook, who took an artist to record the discovery of Australia for posterity. As Humphrey actually managed to do the work during the tour, it is hard to see why six years should have passed before publication. There are sixty illustrations in the book ranging from brief sketches to completed paintings. A number of them are Hockneyesque, but they serve as a fresh visual record of the momentous tour. Humphrey also kept a diary and his entries are reproduced in eight pages of text. These also illuminate life on the road. The entry for Friday, 18 June, which was Paul's thirty-fourth birthday, reads: "The road-crew gave a birthday party with tortillas, enchiladas and a ten-piece Mexican band." Wings were in Tuscon, Arizona.

O'CONNOR, DES British singer, comedian and chat show host. Des appeared on the bill of Buddy Holly's (cf) last tour, two weeks before his tragic death, and Buddy made a present of his guitar to him. Paul, being one of Buddy Holly's staunchest fans, has been seeking to buy the guitar from Des, who says: "I won't sell unless I'm really hard up! I value it not only as a souvenir of a good friend but because it has memories of so many good times. Paul can borrow it if he likes – but only if he comes on my TV show and plays it!"

ODD SIX Bootleg double album, issued in America in 1982. Tracks include 'Girls' School'; 'Daytime Nightime Suffering'; 'Goodnight Tonight'; 'Coming Up'; 'The Mess'; 'Oh Woman, Oh Why'; 'Give Ireland Back To The Irish'; 'Mary Had A Little Lamb'; 'Little Woman Love'; 'C Moon'; 'I Lie Around'; 'Walking In The Park With Eloise'; Bridge On The River Suite'; 'Lunchbox & Odd Sox'; 'Country Dreamer'; 'Sally G'; 'Seaside Woman'; 'Wonderful Christmastime'; 'Rudolph The Red-Nosed Reggae'; 'Check My Machine'; 'Secret Friend'; and 'The Zoo Gang'.

OLAF Polar bear from Chipperfields Circus. The animal (eight-foot-high when standing) was hired to appear in a video with Paul to promote the 'Waterfalls' single. The video was made inside an aircraft hanger and one and a half tons of polystyrene were used as snow. It was eventually shown twice on Independent TV.

ON OUR WAY HOME Number penned by Paul which was recorded by the New York trio, Mortimer, in April 1969. Apple was going to release the single, but never did. The number eventually re-emerged, with a different title, 'Two Of Us', in the film *Let It Be* and was recorded by the Beatles for the album.

ON THE WINGS OF A NIGHTINGALE Everly Brothers single issued on 24 August 1984. Released on Mercury (Mer 170), the number was specially written for the duo by Paul and was produced by Dave Edmunds. It was also featured on *The Everly Brothers* issued on 5 October 1984.

THE ONE AND ONLY One of the numbers Paul wrote during a holiday in the Virgin Islands in 1964. It remains unreleased.

ONE HAND CLAPPING Film from McCartney Productions, directed by David Litchfield, of Wings rehearsing and recording in Nashville.

ONE LOVE Single by the legendary Bob Marley, issued posthumously by Island Records (IS 169) on 6 April 1984. It leapt high into the British charts and Paul made a fleeting appearance on the accompanying video. He is seen briefly clasping Don Leets, who directed the video, and his lips voice the words *one love*. The video was also included on the video compilation 'Legend', issued by Island Video in May 1984.

ONE OF THOSE DAYS IN ENGLAND Album by Roy Harper, released in Britain in February 1977. Paul guested as a backing vocalist.

OPEN EYE GALLERY Exhibition hall in Whitechapel, Liverpool, where photographs from Linda's two books, *Linda's Pictures* and *Photographs*, were exhibited in January 1983. There was a catalogue which took an editorial line towards the exhibition, pointing out that there were no photographs of George Harrison and introducing a point of view of their own: "You [Linda] seem to be portraying a very safe and comfortable world which is far removed from how life looks from here."

THE ORIENTAL NIGHTFISH An animated film by Ian Eames with music by Linda McCartney and Wings. It was first released in British cinemas in October 1978, on a bill with the feature film *Driver*.

ORIENTAL NIGHTFISH Bootleg album issued by Reading Railroad (HAR 169) in the States in 1978. Among the tracks is a demo disc of the title song and live recordings from Wings' tour of Europe in 1972. All five tracks on Side Two are taken from a concert in Hanover, Germany.

OUI MAGAZINE Glossy man's magazine which included an interview with Paul in its March 1982 issue.

OVER THE RAINBOW Evergreen tune immortalised in the film *The Wizard of Oz* by Judy Garland. Paul used to sing the number in the Beatles' early days, although he'd been inspired by the Gene Vincent version of the number rather than Garland's.

PAOLOZZI, EDUARDO Internationally renowned Scottish sculptor who helped secure Stuart Sutcliffe a place at an art school in Hamburg. Paul bought one of his works called *Solo* and used another on the cover of *Red Rose Speedway* (cf).

PAPERBACK WRITER Paul wrote this song, although John helped with one or two words in the lyrics. Some sources claim it was written in connection with John's two books, hence the mention of nonsense writer Edward Lear in the fourth line. A young man working for the *Daily Mail* wants to become a paperback writer. It is also suggested that Paul even worked out the man's name, a character called Ian Iachimore, which he devised because it sounded like his own name after it had been played backwards on a tape loop. The number was used quite successfully as the tune of a television book series in Britain called *Read All About It*.

The single was issued in Britain on R 5452 on 10 June 1966 and reached No.1 in the charts. The flipside was 'Rain'. It also reached No.1 in the States when it was issued on Capitol 5651 in May 1966. It was featured on several album compilations, including *A Collection of Oldies (But Goldies)*, *The Beatles 1967-1970*, the 1979 *Hey Jude* album and *The Beatle Box*.

PARISIAN ROCK Title of an item by Paul which was published in the 4 January 1962 issue of *Mersey Beat*, issue No.13. Paul would send me letters when he travelled around the country or abroad. I liked his style and humour so much that I decided to print some of them as pieces in their own right. This particular letter was sent to me from Paris where Paul had gone on the invitation of John, who had received some money from an aunt in Scotland and fancied a short holiday. I'd had it for some time before I realised it would fit nicely into one of the issues. I wrote a short introduction to the piece, and the entire item read as follows: "Unabridged, unexpurgated, uncensored, we now present a startling report on the rock and roll scene in Paris by the Beatles. This item has long lain in our files, collecting dust whilst we pondered over the thought: 'Dare we print it?' Due to Christmas feelings, we are a bit merry, so we brushed off the dust, and here it is.

"It was 10 o'clock, o'clock it was, when we were entering the Olympia in Paris to see the 'Johnny Halliday Rock Show'. The cheapest seats in 'les theatre' (French) were seven and sixpence, so we followed the woman with the torch (English).

"When Johnny Halliday came, everybody went wild — and loud was the cheering and many the dancing in the aisles, too. But the man said 'sit down', so we had to.

"The excitement rose, the audience rose to dance, like the many boys and girls dancing along the back rows. Also old men, which is stranger still, isn't it?

"Meanwhile, later the same week, we go to 'Les Rock Festival' held in a club in Montmartre with Danny et les Pirates and many more groups for your evening's entertainment. Topping the bill was Vince (Ron, my boy, Ron) Taylor, star of English screen and two I's [famous Soho coffee bar of the fifties].

"The atmosphere is like many a nightclub, but the teenagers stand round the dancing floor which you use as a stage. They jump on a woman with gold trousers and a hand microphone and then hit a man when he says 'go away'. A group follows and so do others, playing 'Apache' worse than many other bands. When the singer joins the band, the leather jacket fiends who are the audience join in dancing and banging tables with chairs.

"The singers have to go one better than the audience, so they lie on the floor, or jump on a passing drummer, or kiss a guitar, and then hit the man playing it. The crowd enjoy this and many stand on chairs to see the fun, and soon the audience are all singing and shouting like one man, but he didn't mind.

"Vince (Ron, Ron) Taylor finally appeared and joined the fun, and in the end he had so much fun that he had to rest. But in spite of this it had been a wonderful show, lovely show . . . lovely." (See also *A Little Bare.*)

PARKER, BERTRAM Headmaster of the Liverpool Institute (cf) at the time Wings performed their free concert for pupils and faculty at the Royal Court Theatre (cf), Liverpool. Mr Parker had been Paul's geography teacher when he attended the school in the fifties. Pupils had nicknamed him 'Blip' and during the Royal Court Concert, Paul was to announce from the stage: "Hello Blip — nice to see you."

PARNES, LARRY Major British rock impressario of the fifties who once booked the Silver Beatles to back Johnny Gentle on a tour of Scotland in 1960. In 1983 he filed a suit against Paul and the BBC over some comments Paul had made in 1982 on *Desert Island Discs* (cf). Paul had said that the group had never been paid for that particular tour.

PAUL Magazine published in America in 1964 by SMH Publications. It was part of a series of separate publications on each member of the Beatles.

PAUL IS DEAD An American student phoned DJ Russ Gibbs (cf) at the 'underground' Detroit radio station WKNR-FM on 12 October 1969 suggesting that if he listened to a number of Beatles songs he would discover that Paul had died. The implication was that Paul had been involved in a road accident on 9 November 1966.

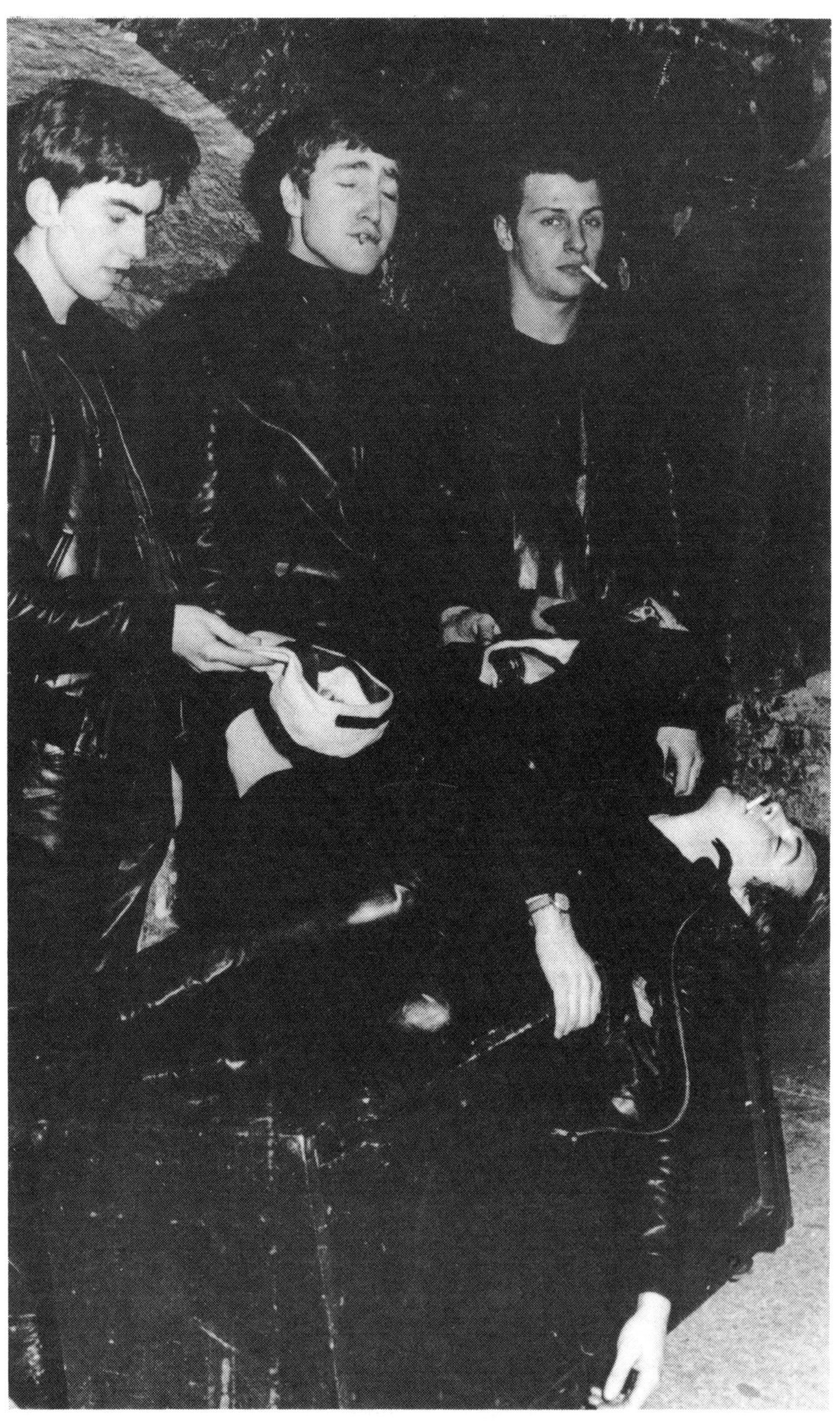

A Cavern photo predates the 'Paul Is Dead' campaign

One story said that the car crash was a fatal one and Paul's head had been severed from his body, another that there were two passengers in the car — one young and dark-haired who had been disfigured. It was said that Paul officially passed away on 10 November 1966 and had been replaced by a lookalike called William Campbell (cf). (See also *Shears, Billy*.)

A few days after the Gibbs radio discussion, the subject was taken up by the newspaper, the *Michigan Daily*, when *Abbey Road* was reviewed by Fred LaBour. He pointed out several 'Paul Is Dead' clues on the album cover (see *Abbey Road (1)* for details), and elsewhere. The cover of *Sgt Pepper* is said to depict the Beatles standing at a graveside near which have been placed Paul's bass guitar and a bunch of yellow flowers spelling 'Paul'. The raised hand above Paul's head is, apparently, an Indian death sign. The fact that he had his back to the camera in the backcover photo was taken as further proof of his demise. In fact, he was in America visiting Jane Asher (cf) at the time the photograph was taken, so Mal Evans donned the Sgt Pepper uniform and deputised.

The line referring to someone blowing their mind out in a car in 'A Day In The Life' (cf) was said to be evidence of Paul's car accident, but in fact referred to the death of the Beatles friend Tara Brown. At the end of 'Strawberry Fields Forever' it is suggested that John has introduced the words *Paul Is Dead*, but what he actually says is the nonsensical *cranberry sauce*.

On the centre spread of the sleeve Paul is pictured wearing a badge with the intials 'OPD' which the rumour-fans said stood for 'Officially Pronounced Dead'. However, Paul had been given the badge by a Canadian police officer and it stands for 'Ontario Police Department'.

Another raised hand (the Indian death sign again) is shown behind Paul on the *Yellow Submarine* sleeve and a similar sign is to be found in two photographs in the 24-page *Magical Mystery Tour* booklet. This also sports another photo of him without shoes (see *Abbey Road* (1)) and a shot of him sitting behind a desk on which there is a sign saying "I was". There is also a photograph of the Beatles wearing white suits with three of them sporting red carnations and Paul wearing a black one. The number 'Revolution 9' (cf) is said to contain the words *Turn me on, dead man, turn me on, dead man.*

Over the next few years, the 'clues' became ever more complex and obscure; American schoolteacher Joel Glazier has made this particular subject his own and regularly entertains audiences at Beatle conventions with his 'Paul Is Dead' slide shows. He also has an unpublished book on the subject entitled *Here's Another Clue For You.*

The rumours continued despite the fact that Paul told *Life* magazine: "Rumours of my death have been greatly exaggerated. However, if I was dead, i'm sure I'd be the last to know."

PAUL McCARTNEY Single by British singer/songwriter Tony Hazard, issued on the Bronze label.

PAUL McCARTNEY Book for the younger reader, published by Hamish Hamilton in Britain in 1983 in their

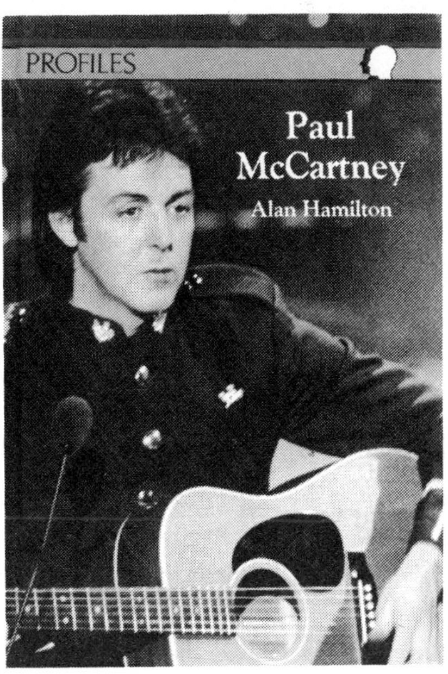

'Profiles' series. Describing the series the publishers write: "They aim above all to tell an interesting and enjoyable story, while providing sound factual information both about the figures profiled and their times." Alan Hamilton, a journalist for *The Times* wrote the text, a lightweight biography which skims over Paul's life and career. Two dozen illustrations by Karen Heywood, however, prove to be the most rewarding items in the book. A similar book, *John Lennon,* appeared in the same series in 1985.

PAUL McCARTNEY: A BIOGRAPHY IN WORDS AND MUSIC A slim (fifty-six pages), illustrated volume published in America in 1977 jointly by Sire Books/Chappell Music and penned by music journalist John Mendlesohn.

PAUL McCARTNEY AND WINGS A large-format hardbound book by Jeremy Pascall, published in Britain by

Two books, one story . .

Hamlyn in 1977, priced at £2.95. A sympathetic treatment of the Wings story, lavishly illustrated with seventy photographs, many of them in colour. The chapter titles cleverly use song titles. The material consists of: 'Yesterday', a recap of Paul's life and career with the Beatles; 'Long And Winding Road', his departure from

the Fab Four; 'Another Day', the formation of Wings; 'Wings Take Off', the story of Wings' initial successes; 'Band On The Run', details of the various personnel changes and 'Wings Across The World', their tours and career up until 1976. The entire style, layout and concept is similar to the Tony Jasper book of the same name (see next entry).

PAUL McCARTNEY AND WINGS Large pictorial record of Wings' career by Tony Jasper, published by Octopus Books in 1977, priced at £2.50. Very similar to the Jeremy Pascall book of the same name (see above), published at approximately the same time. Tony's book contains over a hundred photographs, most of them in colour, and was 45p cheaper. The chapters are: 'The Formation of Wings', the events which led up to Paul's decision to form the group; 'The Story Of Wings', details of the group's development; 'The Band (On The Run)', the various personnel changes; 'The World Tour, 1975-1976', the story of their world tour; 'Paul And Linda' – The Family Way', background to Paul's married life, and 'Behind The Albums', details of the album releases. There is also a 'Calendar of Events', a discography and a selection of quotes from Paul.

PAUL McCARTNEY: FROM LIVERPOOL TO BROAD STREET Two hour radio programme on Paul's career, syndicated in America to coincide with the *Broad Street* film.

PAUL McCARTNEY'S BEDSIDE MANNERS Title of the radio show on which Paul played singles and relayed messages to fans in August 1983. The programme was heard on the entire British Hospital Radio Network.

PAUL McCARTNEY – COMPOSER, ARTIST A book crediting Paul as author, published by Pavilion Books in 1981 in both hard and soft covers. In many ways this was a disappointment, because pre-publicity had led many people to think the book would be Paul's equivalent of George Harrison's *I, Me, Mine.* A book of Paul's songs on

which he had actively worked with the publishers should have resulted, it was felt, in something better than this. Personal comments from Paul on all the numbers, some incisive background as to how he came to write the songs, some replicas of the material (papers, tissues, menu cards) on which he originally penned his ideas and so on would have produced a publication which provided some insight on Paul as 'Composer/Artist'. In fact, what we are given is a hundred-word introduction, three photos by Linda, forty-seven doodles and forty-eight songs. Described as "an extra-special glimpse into McCartney's creative mind. . . revealed through songs and never-before-published drawings", it fails to deliver. The music and lyrics are as beautiful as ever – but they are available in many songbooks. This is, in fact, a glorified songbook. The spidery drawings don't even illustrate the actual songs they are placed alongside and the majority of them are merely sketches of faces, while the general standard of the drawings is uneven, to say the least.

Paul actually sent a special collector's edition of the book to the Artists For Animals group, which is an anti-vivisection organisation. The idea was for them to auction it and raise funds for their cause. It proved to be an embarrassing move because they had to send the book back. Their spokeswoman Viv Smith commented: "We don't criticise Paul. He's a compassionate guy who gives a lot of support to animal causes. But if we were to auction the book we would be accused of animal exploitation because it is bound in skin!"

PAUL McCARTNEY DEAD – THE GREAT HOAX US magazine issued in 1969 by Countrywide Publications Inc, which presented articles surrounding the Paul Is Dead (cf) controversy. Blurbs on the cover proclaimed: "Paul's Mysterious Double, Who Is He?"; "The Death Clues"; "The Beatle Death Curse" and "Why Did The Beatles Keep Paul's Death A Secret?" (see also *Beatles National Lampoon; Campbell, William; Gibbs, Russ;* and *Shears, Billy.*)

PAUL McCARTNEY – FREEZE FRAME Thirty-minute TV programme broadcast in some ITV areas in Britain late in the evening of 7 September 1984. Film of Paul and George Martin (cf) during the recording of *Tug of War* (cf) was followed by a conversation in which Paul discussed the album. The programme also included four complete Macca videos: 'Take It Away', 'Coming Up', 'Tug Of War' and 'Ebony & Ivory'.

PAUL McCARTNEY, IDOL LANE Title of a Robert Freeman photograph that was included in the 'Art Of The Beatles' exhibition in 1984. The picture presents a small figure of Paul at the extreme bottom of the print, against a white wall on top of which is perched the street sign: 'Idol Lane, EC3'.

PAUL McCARTNEY IN HIS OWN WORDS Another *Rolling Stone* inter-

view that formed the basis for a book, although this is no *Lennon Remembers.* Penned by American DJ Paul Gambaccini (cf), domiciled in England, the book is divided into seven sections. The first six were adapted from interviews Gambaccini conducted in November and December 1973, and the final part was written in the summer of 1975. The sections are entitled: 'McCartney The Lad: Butlins To Ham-

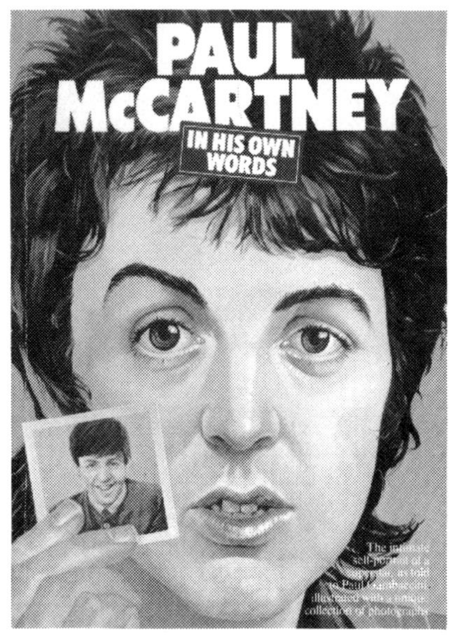

burg'; 'Beatles: Liverpool To The World'; 'The Rot Of Apple: Sue Me, Sue You'; 'Life With The Family: Mr & Mrs McCartney'; 'The Singer, The Songs & The Songwriter'; 'Wings In Flight: Band On The Run'; and 'Venus And Mars Are Alright'.

Published by Omnibus Press in 1976 (and, incidentally, launching their series of 'In His Own Words' books), the large-size publication has semi-stiff covers. An uncredited painting on the cover features a long-haired Paul holding a photograph of himself from the Beatles days in front of his face. There are over one hundred photographs (the page ten pic which is captioned 'on stage in Hamburg' was taken at Liverpool's Cavern Club!) which take up more space than the actual text. The interview is not as probing or as incisive as the one Jann Wenner conducted with John, but

Lennon was undergoing therapy at the time and was prepared to 'open up'. Paul answers a series of questions in a manner that makes for pleasant, though not engrossing, reading.

THE PAUL McCARTNEY JOB Name by which the Newhaven CID referred to the 1984 plot to kidnap Linda McCartney (cf). Detectives said they had uncovered a kidnap plot in which Linda was to be snatched in a military-style operation on a country lane near the Sussex farm. The kidnappers intended to hold her hostage in a woodland lair and demand £10 million ransom. Paul was reluctant to discuss the matter, commenting: "Any talk of a kidnap plot is bound to give ideas to all sorts of nutters."

THE PAUL McCARTNEY STORY Readable 1975 British paperback by George Tremlett, published by Futura Books and part of a series of almost two dozen pop biographies written by Tremlett. A freelance journalist, he was quick to see the value of the documentation of material on the Beatles and interviewed them on

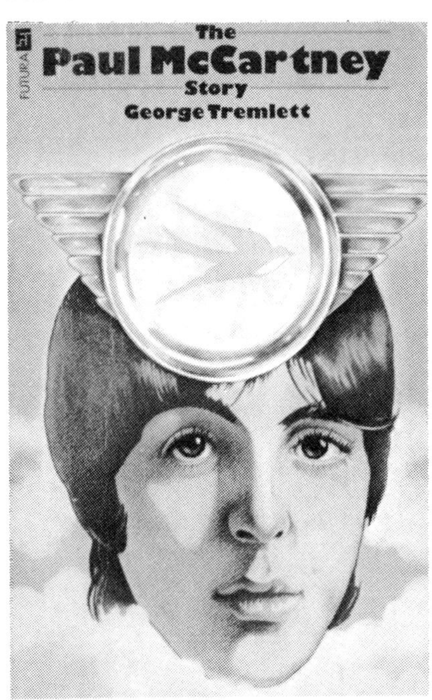

Yet another version

several occasions. The book is crammed with interesting anecdotes and observations. When citing examples of Paul's remarkable ability to remember people and the things they talked about, he mentioned a long interview he and his wife conducted with Paul and Linda: "We started talking about their farmhouse in Scotland and our cottage in Devon. . . My wife mentioned that she was looking for some Tiffany-style lampshades, and Linda had recently found some. About a year later we attended a Wings concert at Oxford, when there was a conference for journalists from all over the world afterwards – and McCartney suddenly called across to me: 'Have you been down to Devon recently?' A few minutes later Linda asked: 'Did your wife get those lampshades?'"

The book also contains a photo section and a large chronology of Paul's life and career.

PAUL McCARTNEY TALKS ABOUT HIS DEAR FRIEND JOHN LENNON Bootleg EP issued in a limited edition of 500 copies in Holland in 1984. The material is taken from an interview Paul did in Holland in which he discussed a range of subjects relating to John and his reaction to John's death.

PAUL McCARTNEY: THE DEFINITIVE BIOGRAPHY 80,000-word book by Chris Welch (cf), published in Britain by Proteus Books in September 1984. The book has a large picture section and Chris took almost two years to write the biography, which again has chapter headings utilising the titles of songs by Paul. It's a straightforward life story, culled from interviews Chris conducted with Paul and approximately a dozen other people. The early years are filled in quite briefly as the bulk of the book comprises the story of Paul's career from the formation of Wings

PAUL McCARTNEY: THE MAN, HIS MUSIC, HIS MOVIES American television special, screened in various States in the first quarter of 1983. The programme was half an hour in length and narration was by Tom Bosley. There

The last word?

were clips from various films and newsreels over the years in which Paul was featured, including the early Beatles movies and behind-the-scenes shots of the making of *Give My Regards to Broad Street (cf(1))*, in addition to clips from the film itself, including the ballroom scene. There was also an interview with Paul.

PAUL'S CHRISTMAS ALBUM A unique album which Paul made specially for his fellow Beatles as a Christmas treat in 1965. Only four copies of the record were pressed.

PEEBLES, ANDY Radio One disc jockey who conducted the final BBC interviews with John Lennon, which were published in book form as *The Lennon Tapes*. Andy interviewed Paul on 18 April 1982, when they discussed the new *Tug of War* (cf) album, track-by-track. The interview was also broadcast on the New York station WNEW-FM on 2 June.

PENINA Song written by Paul while he was on holiday in Portugal. 'Penina' was the name of the hotel at which he was staying. Singer Carlos Mendes heard Paul singing the number and liked it so much that Paul allowed him to have the song to record. That version was released in Portugal on 18 July 1969 on Parlophone QMSP 16459; The flipside was 'Wings of Revenge'. The following year a Dutch band Jotte Herre also recorded it. At the time, Paul had forgotten to inform Northern Songs about the number and the fact that he'd let someone record it without telling them about it.

PENNY LANE One of the most evocative songs of the sixties, Paul's tribute

to the local Liverpool landmark which immortalised the street in the same way that Abbey Road became famous due to the album. The street signs of both Penny Lane and Abbey Road began to disappear with frequency once souvenir hunters sought their trophies. Characters mentioned in the song – firemen, barbers, etc – became local celebrities and Penny Lane is now a fixture on the many Beatle-related tours in Liverpool. The song was issued as a double 'A' side in Britain with John's Liverpool tribute 'Strawberry Fields Forever' on Parlophone R5570 on 17 February 1967 and reached the No.2 position. In the US it was issued on Capitol 5810 on 13 February 1967 and reached No.1. 'Penny Lane' is to be found on the American albums *Magical Mystery Tour* and *The Beatles Rarities*. It was also included on the collection *The Beatles 1967-1970*. With the *Rarities* album, the version featuring a trumpet solo finish, only previously used on a limited promotional release, was available generally for the very first time. A variety of instruments was used on this version, including congas, piccolos, flutes, string bass and flugelhorn.

PERKINS, CARL One of the original American rock'n' roll legends, Carl was born on 9 April 1932 in Lake City, Tennessee. He signed with the legendary Sun Records, wrote and recorded the classic rocker 'Blue Seude Shoes' and a number of other rock'n'roll standards. A serious car accident in 1956, in which his brother and manager were killed, left him hospitalised for a year. His career suffered a number of setbacks and he compounded

Carl Perkins: wrote 'My Old Friend' in tribute to Paul

his problems by drinking too much. He rose from the doldrums when Chuck Berry invited him to tour with him in Britain in 1964 when he met the Beatles for the first time. He met and chatted with Paul at a party in London and his career, personal life and finances were boosted when the Beatles recorded three of his numbers: 'Matchbox', 'Honey Don't' and 'Everybody's Trying To Be My Baby'. With the royalties he was able to buy his parents a farm. Over the years he kept in touch with Paul, visiting him whenever he was in England. In 1981 Paul invited Carl to Montserrat (cf) to be one of his guests on *Tug of War* (cf). Carl was so delighted with the invitation that the night before he left for the island he sat down and composed a number 'My Old Friend', in tribute to Paul.

Paul composed the number 'Get It' for the two of them to record and during the sessions they had a jam in which they played a number of Perkins classics, including 'Honey Don't', 'Boppin' The Blues' and 'Lend Me Your Comb'. Paul recorded all the jam sessions, in addition to studio conversations for his personal collection. Carl played Paul the number 'My Old Friend' on the day he was to leave Montserrat. Paul was so moved that he asked Carl if he had to leave that day and persuaded him to stay and record the number. Carl was to say that the number mean't more to him than any other song he'd written, including 'Blue Suede Shoes'. On the track, Paul added backing vocals and played organ, rhythm guitar, drums and bass, but didn't use it on *Tug of War*. 'Get It' was featured on the album and was also issued as the flipside of the 'Tug of War' single.

PEOPLE MAGAZINE Major American glossy magazine. The 14 November 1983 issue features a cover photograph of Paul to illustrate an article on the richest people in show business. They claimed that Paul was worth from $400 to $550 million.

PESTALOZZI CHILDREN'S VILLAGE Home for orphaned youngsters in Sus-sex, close to Paul's home. The children come from all over the world and Paul gathered a number of them to sing with him on 'Pipes Of Peace'. For Christmas 1983 he sent them a special video of their session with him and he secretly made a generous donation to their fund.

PHILLIPS, MACKENZIE Daughter of John Phillips, former member of the Mamas and the Papas. When appearing on the *Tonight* show on US TV, Mackenzie related how, when she was five years old, her father took her to visit Mama Cass – and she slept in a hammock with Paul.

PIPES OF PEACE Album which followed Paul's *Tug of War (cf)*. Some tracks recorded for the latter were never included on it, and Paul thought: "What would be the opposite of tug of war? Peace pipes, pipes of peace and stuff." In fact, he composed a number called 'Tug Of Peace' for the album, and his feelings for the concept of an album about love and peace are evident in the quote by Indian poet Rabindranath Tagore, which he placed on the sleeve: "In love all of life's contradictions dissolve and disappear." He continued his collaboration with George Martin (cf) to produce this eleven-track album, although there was no detailed listing

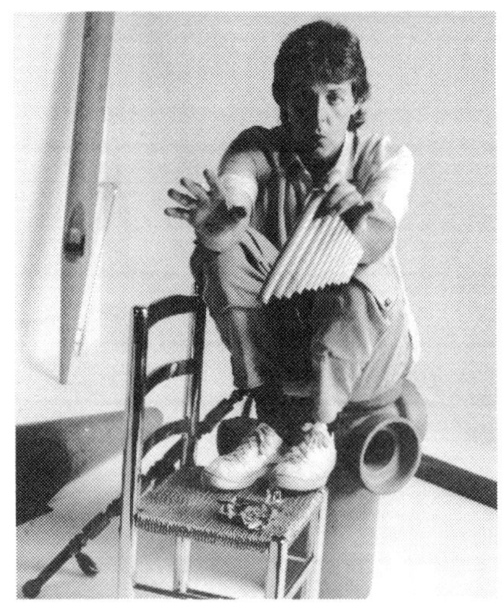

In appropriate Pan-like pose

of the musicians who participated, as there had been for *Tug of War*. Those participating included Ringo Starr, Michael Jackson (cf), Eric Stewart, Stanley Clarke (cf), Steve Gadd and Andy MacKay. The album was issued simultaneously in Britain and America on 31 October 1983, on Parlophone PCTC 1652301 and Columbia QC 39149 respectively. It reached No.4 in the UK and No.16 in the States. The title track provided Paul with a No.1 Christmas hit and a stunning video, and the album also contained two Mac and Jack (Paul and Michael) collaborations in 'Say Say Say' (cf) and 'The Man'. Paul co-wrote the instrumental 'Hey Hey' with bassist Stanley Clarke (cf) (the third musician on the track was Steve Gadd) and he pays tribute to Linda in another love song 'Through Our Love'. The other tracks on the album were: 'The Other Me', 'Keep Under Cover', 'So Bad', 'Sweetest Little Show' and 'Average Person'.

Paul's close collaboration with guest musicians was in keeping with the spirit of the album

PIAZZA SAN MARCO Famous Venetian square where Wings appeared before 30,000 people on 25 September 1976. The occasion was a UNESCO-organised series of major events to raise funds for the Venice restoration. Paul agreed to add the date to Wing's schedule and also generously offered to pay for the transport and equipment costs himself. UNESCO provided the hotel accommodation and organised the actual evening, erecting the scaffolding for the stage and preparing the seating. There was some irony in the event, the press pointing out that Wings did more to destroy the city than to restore it due to the fact that the heavy lorries containing their equipment cracked some paving stones in the ancient square. Paul commented: "I can't think of a more beautiful place to stage a concert." Seating had been arranged for 15,000 people, with some tickets costing £10. However, thousands more poured into the square, effectively doubling that number. Approximately £54,000 was raised by the concert which, after all expenses had been deducted, brought the fund a handsome donation of £25,000.

As the climax of the evening, seven lasers were used to provide a spectacular visual display as they alighted on the walls of the Cathedral at the far end of the square in the shape of a butterfly. (See also *UNESCO.*)

PICKLES, THELMA Former student at Liverpool College of Art. Whilst there she was one of John Lennon's early girlfriends and was privy to some of the John and Paul rehearsals in Menlove Avenue. Soon after the recording of 'Love Me Do' she began dating Paul. She later married Roger McGough, a Liverpool poet who was a member of Scaffold with Mike McGear (see *McCartney, Mike).*

PILCHARD Name of a play which Paul and John tried to write in their early days together. Paul later described it as: "a sort of precursor of *The Life of Brian*, about a working-class weirdo who was always upstairs praying. It was a down-market Second Coming. But we had to give it up because we couldn't actually work out how it went on, how you actually filled up all the pages."

THE PLASTIC MACS Ten different characters portrayed by Paul on the 'Coming Up' video.

PLAYGIRL Large-circulation American magazine, a female equivalent of *Playboy. Playgirl* features picture spreads of nude men, but Paul was fully clothed when he appeared on the cover of the June 1982 issue. There was an article inside reporting on Paul's life to date.

PLOMLEY'S PICK OF DESERT ISLAND DISCS Hardback book published by Weidenfeld & Nicolson in 1982 to coincide with the fortieth anniversary of the long-running BBC Radio programme *Desert Island Discs* (cf). It contains complete transcripts of interviews by Roy Plomley with forty-one celebrities who appeared on the programme over the years. The transcript of Paul's appearance on 30 January 1982 is included, together with a list of his record selections. Plomley tells of how, in 1963, he interviewed Brian Epstein and requested that the Beatles appear on *Desert Island Discs* with each member choosing two records. Epstein turned down the idea, suggesting it would be too difficult to control such a programme. Nineteen years later, Plomley was finally able to present a former member of the Beatles on his show.

POST CARD Mary Hopkin's (cf) debut album which Paul produced. He also designed the cover and wrote out the featured postcards on the sleeve which listed the songs on the album. Linda took the cover photograph. Paul plays guitar on the three tracks penned by Donovan – 'Lord Of The Reedy River', 'Happiness Runs (Pebble And The Man)' and 'Voyage To The Moon'. The album was issued in Britain on 21 February 1969 on Apple SAPCOR 5 and in America on 3 March 1969 on Apple ST 3351.

POWER CUT Written during the miners strike in Britain in 1972 when there

Paul as some of the Plastic Macs

were widespread power cuts. The number was included on *Red Rose Speedway (cf).*

PRINCE, TONY Disc jockey who recorded a special interview with Linda at Elstree Studios in March 1976. This was broadcast by Radio Luxembourg on *The Royal Rock Show* (because Tony was known as the 'Royal Ruler') on Saturday 20 March from 11pm to midnight.

Linda mentioned the new Wings album of the time *Wings at the Speed of Sound* (cf) and discussed the problems of travelling extensively on a two-month tour with her children, coping as a wife, mother and musician. She said she was pleased with the education that her children were receiving: "Heather is very worldly, just having gone with us everywhere we've gone." She mentioned that her children were just ordinary kids.

"They're not affected, posh or anything."

Discussing photography, she reiter-
ated that she was no relation to the
Eastman-Kodak family, and said that
she usually only carried one camera
around with her, always loaded. She
discussed her father and his profes-
sion in New York, pointing out that
Paul had wanted him to look after his
personal business affairs, but that
he'd never attempted to get involved
in managing the Beatles.

She discussed her diaries, in particular the Nashville diary and her diary of
Polaroid photographs, then mentioned her forthcoming book *Linda's
Pictures*. Tony then led her into details
of her background and how she became a photographer. She remembered seeing Paul for the first time at
the Bag O' Nails club in London and
their first dates, then discussed the
track about her on the new album,
'Cook Of The House'.

She told of her struggles to develop
her musical ability and the criticisms
she received in the early stages. Like
any normal couple they had their
"barnies", she said, and mentioned
the recent Scandinavian tour and the
trouble they'd had in finding drummers for Wings. For the future she
wanted Paul and herself to become
involved in some films and television
work and liked the idea of acting in
movies. She was asked about the superstars who were leaving England
because of the swingeing taxes introduced by Harold Wilson's government
and though she thought it was silly of
the Government to drive so many
people away, she maintained she and
Paul would remain in England: "because I don't believe money should
rule your life. I like England and Scotland." She mentioned that the people
in the music industry stimulated work
and brought a lot of money into
England, but with the new tax regula-
tions, a lot of this would be lost to
America. She admitted liking the English countryside – and the people:
"They're very sort of ordinary people,
rather than laid-back people. I'm normally a laid-back person myself."

On nights off Paul and Linda would
watch telly, have a good meal and put
their feet up, she said, and mentioned
that when they were at their farm in
Scotland: "We listen to music, watch
telly, paint a bit, draw a bit. Just talk.
Go out for a walk." They still discussed
the Beatles, she said, and had just
phoned John Lennon a few days previously; John and Paul were mates but
George and Ringo weren't seeing eye
to eye. Of her relationship with Yoko,
she commented: "Oh, I get on with
her great! Much to people's surprise. I
think she is really a nice, good person
. . . she's not pushy or anything."

PROFESSOR LONGHAIR Name used
by blues pianist Henry Roeland Byrd,
who led an R&B revival in New
Orleans in the seventies and was
known as the 'King of Rhumboogie'.
On 24 March 1975, Paul invited Professor Longhair to perform at a special
party he was hosting with Linda on
the *Queen Mary* at Long Beach in
California. Arrangements were made
to record his set and his manager
Allison Kaslow was to comment:
"Byrd had no idea who Paul McCartney was, he had never heard of the
Beatles. Even though he had been to
Europe and all across the country, his

*Professor Longhair: he'd never heard of
Paul or the Beatles*

world was right there on Rampart Street with his family." An album of the performance was issued in 1978 on Harvest (Capitol SW-11790) under the auspices of MPL Communications and sporting an album cover photograph taken by Linda. Professor Longhair died of a heart attack on 29 January 1980 at the age of 61. The album was rereleased in March 1986 by EMI Records on Stateside SSL 6004. (See also *The Meters.*)

PURE GOLD Track on Ringo's 1976 album *Ringo's Rotogravure* which Paul wrote. He and Linda also contributed backing vocals to the track.

PUTNAM, CURLY 'JUNIOR' Nashville ranchowner. When Paul was recording in Nashville in 1974, he rented Curly's farm for the family to live in while the sessions were taking place. The song 'Junior's Farm' (cf) was written in tribute to Curly's ranch.

QUEEN ELIZABETH HALL London music venue on the South Bank. Paul escorted Jane Asher (cf) there on 10 February 1968 to watch a performance of the Scaffold, the trio in which his brother Mike was a member (see *McCartney, Mike).*

RAM Paul's second solo album after leaving the Beatles, issued in 1971, in Britain on 21 May on Apple PAS 10003, where it was to reach the No.1 spot, and in the States on 17 May on Apple SMAS 3375, where it got to No.2. Paul recorded the album in New York between January and March.

Paul's second solo album and the picture that John Lennon was to satirise

The New York Philharmonic Orchestra (cf) was featured on the album, and Paul's backing musicians included Dave Spinozza and Hugh McCracken on guitars and Denny Seiwell (cf) on drums. Linda sang some backing vocals and her daughter Heather can be heard on backing vocals on 'Monkberry Moon Delight'. The cover featured a photograph of Paul holding a ram by the horns and John Lennon was later to satirise this picture when he included a postcard inside *Image* of himself holding a pig by the ears. The tracks on the album were: 'Too Many People'; '3 Legs'; 'Ram On'; 'Beat Boy'; 'Uncle Albert/Admiral Halsey'; 'Smile Away'; 'Heart Of The Country'; 'Monkberry Moon Delight'; 'Eat At Home'; 'Long Haired Lady'; 'Ram On' and 'The Back Seat Of My Car'.

RANSOME-KUTI, FELA Radical Nigerian musician and political dissenter, recently released from gaol. When Paul went to Lagos to record *Band on the Run* (cf) he went to listen to Ransome-Kuti and his band at his club. Paul very much enjoyed the music. Ransome-Kuti, however, made an unpleasant attack on Paul, accusing him of stealing from Nigerian musicians and of coming to Lagos with the intention of exploiting black music. Paul was to comment: "[He] accused us of stealing black African music. So I had to say, 'Do us a favour, Fela, we do okay. We're alright as it is. We sell a couple of records here and there. African music is very nice – but you're welcome to it!' He did have a great band, though." In fact, Paul was later to tell Paul Gambaccini: "They (the Nigerian musicians) are brilliant, it's incredible music down there. I think it will come to the fore. And I thought my visit would, if anything, help there, because it would draw attention to Lagos and people would say, 'Oh, by the way, what's the music down there like?' and I'd say it was unbelievable. It is unbelievable. When I heard Fela Ransome-Kuti for the first time, it made me cry, it was that good."

RAMON, PAUL Pseudonym Paul used when the Silver Beatles toured Scotland as backing band for Johnny Gentle (see *Parnes, Larry*). Paul couldn't remember why he chose that particular surname, but he thought it was rather glamorous. So much so, that he was to use it again, many years later, when he recorded a track with the Steve Miller Band, 'My Dark Hour' (cf), in 1969. The American punk rock band The Ramones are reputed to have taken their name from this alias of Paul's.

THE RECORD American music magazine, a sister publication to *Rolling Stone*. Paul was featured on the cover of the May 1982 issue.

RECORD MIRROR British musical weekly. The 24 April 1982 issue featured a colour cover of Paul, one of Linda's shots for the promotion of *Tug of War* (cf). The two-page feature interview was conducted by Ray Bonici. Paul discussed the criticism he received over his comment, "It's a drag," when John was killed. He explained that he hadn't been able to think of anything else because he'd been so stunned. Yoko had told him that the times when John had been slagging him off were periods when he was just taking the mickey and not meaning to be hurtful. Paul discussed his relationship with John over the years and mentioned that his own obituary had already been prepared for the *Times* by Hunter Davies. He also pointed out the stereotyped image people had formed: "John was the aggressive one, Paul was the PR one." The conversation went on to the release of *Tug of War;* how Paul didn't want the pressures of continuing with a group anymore; the recording sessions in Montserrat (cf) and how he like working with all the musicians: Stevie Wonder (cf), Carl Perkins (cf), Michael Jackson (cf), Stanley Clarke (cf), Ringo, Eric Stewart and Steve Gadd. He discussed the fact that some people had regarded him as a dictator and had the general image of him as a PR man.

RED ROSE SPEEDWAY Album credited to Paul McCartney and Wings, and issued on Apple PCTC 251 on 3 May 1973 in Britain, where it reached

Title inspired by housekeeper, photograph by Robert Ellis

No.4 in the charts. In the US it was issued on Apple SMAL 3409 on 30 April 1973 and reached No.1. The original album was going to be a double one, but Paul was persuaded to abandon that idea. The album's title was inspired by the McCartney's housekeeper Rose, and Paul is featured on the cover with a rose in his mouth and a gleaming Harley Davidson motorcycle in the background. The gatefold sleeve featured lyrics to the songs and included a 12-page booklet with photographs of Wings on the road and drawings and paintings by noted artists, Alan Jones and Eduardo Paolozzi (cf). There were twelve tracks on the album: 'Big Barn Red'; 'My Love'; 'Get On The Right Thing'; 'One More Kiss'; 'Little Lamb Dragonfly'; 'Single Pigeon'; 'When The Night'; 'Loup (1st Indian On The Moon)'; 'Medley'; 'Hold Me Tight'; 'Lazy Dynamite'; 'Hands Of Love' and 'Power Cut'.

REMBRANDT Name of the house which Paul bought for his father in July 1964 for £8,750. Situated in Baskervyle Road, Heswall, Cheshire, overlooking the River Dee estuary and fifteen miles from Liverpool, the five-bedroomed detached house even had its own wine cellar. A further £8,000 was spent on central heating, furnishing and decorations. The removal of furniture from Forthlin Road (cf) took place at midnight to escape the fans who gathered outside the house during the day.

REPLICA STUDIOS Paul obviously had great affection for EMI's No.2 Studios at Abbey Road, where so many Beatles and Wings records had been made; he decided to build an exact replica in the basement of MPL's (cf) London offices, hence the name Replica Studios. The studios were completed in 1978, ready for *Back to the Egg* (cf), part of which was recorded at Replica. Paul had attempted to book time at EMI's No.2 studio and found it was full up, which is why he was inspired to build Replica Studios as a standby.

RETURN OF THE SAINT Projected film. In 1977 producer Anthony Spinner offered Paul the role of a rock star who is kidnapped. Paul was interested provided he could compose the music and also direct, but plans fell through and the film was never made.

REVOLUTION 9 Number penned by John and featured on the *White Album* in November 1968. It is over eight minutes long and is experimental. John used thirty tape loops to provide the unusual effect. He was to comment: "All the things were made with loops, I had about thirty loops going. I fed them into one basic track and one loop, chopping it and making it go backwards and things like that to get the sound effects." The avant-garde number, which was mastered solely by John, was to become associated with the many 'clues' put forward to prove that Paul was dead. In this instance, fans claimed that when the track was played backwards, the words "Turn me on, dead man, turn me on, dead man" could be heard – in their eyes yet another nail in Paul's coffin. (See *Paul Is Dead.)*

RHONE, DOROTHY According to all reports, Paul's first serious girlfriend. Paul did, of course, have many girlfriends in Liverpool and was particularly partial to blondes, but Dot was the girl he dated for several years, from the end of the fifties until late in 1962. Mike McCartney (cf) in his book *Thank U Very Much* states that Dot was Paul's first real sweetheart. He has a photograph of Paul holding her in his arms in the background of the Forthlin Road (cf) house and she's pictured again, with her arms around Paul's neck, in a photo taken at Rory Storm's house. Once the Beatles began to do the rounds in Liverpool and Hamburg, she became friends with another regular Beatle girlfriend, Cynthia Powell. Dot was seventeen at the time. In her book *A Twist Of Lennon,* Cynthia mentions Dot on a number of occasions. She says that Dot lived with her parents and worked at a dispensing chemist's shop on the outskirts of Liverpool. Of their first meeting, Cynthia says: "Dot was lovely, seventeen years old, slim, short blonde hair (not out of a bottle), and the most attractive pixie face you have ever seen. Dot was such a gentle soul, she spoke almost in a whisper, blushed frequently and idolised Paul."

When the Beatles set off for their Top Ten Club season in Hamburg in April 1961, they invited Cynthia and Dot to follow them over. Cynthia took time off from Liverpool Art College as it was the Easter Holiday, but Dot had some difficulty in getting her parent's permission for her first trip outside Britain. The couple set off for their holiday fortnight from Liverpool's Lime Street Station, travelling by boat train via the Hook of Holland. When they arrived at Hamburg station, they were met by a scruffy-looking reception committee, exhausted by the long hours of playing and the Hamburg night life. Cynthia was to stay with Astrid Kirchherr at her home in Eims Butteler Strasse and Dot joined Paul on a barge on the river, where Paul had been staying with Tony Sheridan. The 'houseboat' was owned by Rosa, the lavatory attendant at the Top Ten Club, who had become an almost maternal figure to the boys, having previously worked in Bruno Koschmeider's clubs where she had dispensed supplies of Preludin to the band. (See *Drugs.)*

Several months after that trip, Cynthia was living in a tiny room in a Liverpool house. When the room next to hers became vacant, she persuaded Dot, who had now become her close friend, to move into it. It was in this boarding-house that Cynthia discovered she was pregnant; Dot, too, was

Gigging at the Cavern – watched no doubt by girlfriend Dorothy Rhone

in for a dramatic shock. She had just washed her hair and had put it into rollers and was "dressed in a tatty old sweater and a pair of her mother's bloomers" when Paul arrived, took her into her room and told her that their affair was over. Dot was heartbroken, packed her bags and went back to her parent's home in Childwall.

Whatever happened to her? In February 1984, in a special Beatles edition of the *Sunday Times* magazine, Sandra Hedges threw some light on the subject. She mentioned that Dot had bought black leather gear during her trip to Hamburg: "The girl who hunched her black leather-clad shoulders and hurried away in black calf-height boots from catcalls of 'cowgirl' from Scouse youths unaccustomed to the sight of such 'gear'. She was very much in love with Paul and he, in his turn, would jealously guard her (to her chagrin) by placing her amid the group while playing." Sandra went on to say that within a year of her split with Paul, Dot emigrated to Canada and later married. According to Sandra, "Dot with her husband and elder daughter Astrid were Rolls-Royced some years later to meet up with Paul when Wings played at Spring Gardens in Toronto. When she met Paul again the ghost was laid."

Sandra also mentioned that Dot was the inspiration for Paul's song 'PS I Love You'.

There is a final chapter to the story. In September 1984, Dot placed six items for sale in the auction at Sotheby's in London. They included her personal memorabilia from the Hamburg days, mainly photographs, including one of her and Paul sitting among a group of tourists on a river cruiser in Hamburg.

RICE, TIM Co-writer of *Jesus Christ: Superstar* who also became a radio and television celebrity, panellist and interviewer. In 1980 he interviewed

Paul for the Independent Television network and the occasion was screened by Thames Television on 4 August and by Granada TV on 27 October. It was also featured on a number of TV channels around the world.

Sir Ralph Richardson: 'Broad Street' was his last film

RICHARDSON, SIR RALPH A well-loved and much-respected British actor who was born in Cheltenham in 1903. He made his first major appearance on the London stage in 1926 in *Yellow Sands* and developed into one of Britain's leading film and theatre actors, receiving much acclaim for his many roles with the Old Vic Company. His film career stretched from the thirties to the eighties and included scores of movies ranging from *The Shape of Things to Come* to *The Heiress* and *Dr Zhivago*.

Paul's film *Give My Regards to Broad Street* (cf) was Sir Ralph's last, as he died a few months after filming was completed. Discussing how he first approached him, Paul commented: "I've found out over the years that the best people in any field are the most approachable, so I wasn't nervous. I was a bit nervous about *acting* with him, but he was such a wonderful actor, he made me look better. He did it all *for* me."

Director Peter Webb (cf) was to add: "Ralph's is a small role but so is that of the wizard in *The Wizard of Oz*. It's crucial. In the scenes they play together, Old Jim, in a sense, is Paul's inner voice telling him to have faith and continue the quest. Ralph quickly caught on to this element in the story, and it enabled him to develop the role as only a great actor can. He loved the part with its simple straightforward dialogue capable of being given subtle nuances. It was the kind of dialogue he liked."

Discussing how he felt about appearing with Sir Ralph, Paul said: "I was frightened to do it, because he's a big, famous, old British actor, and that's intimidating because a person's image does walk ahead of them. He made it easy. He had a twinkle in his eye all the time. I thought my script might not be to his liking, and I said, 'Look, this isn't Shakespeare or Chekov, so we can change it if you like.'" Sir Ralph wouldn't have any of that, and he complimented Paul's script by saying "Thank you, dear boy, not a comma out of place."

Sir Ralph's appearance is only brief. Paul, worried that his friend Harry has disappeared with the master tapes of his new recordings, knocks on Old Jim's door. Jim lives above a pub and opens the door, his pet monkey in his hands. He welcomes Paul into his room which is full of old *Picture Post*

Sir Ralph and Paul relax off-set

magazines, a wireless set, a room still decorated in the style of the forties. When asked by Paul, Jim mentions that he'd seen Harry the previous evening in the pub – and he did have a large blue box with him. Old Jim advises: "You're always running around. If you didn't run around so much you might get a better view of the world, you know." After a short chat Paul leaves, saying: "Thanks all the same, Jim, I've got to be off." With a twinkle in his eye, Jim replies: "You've been off for years."

Linda was able to take a photographic session with the actor and has a good set of shots of Paul and Sir Ralph together.

RICKENBACKER American guitar. Paul bought a Sunburst Rickenbacker 4000 stereo bass guitar in America in 1965. It was a specially built model for left-handers. Paul used it mainly on recording sessions and didn't play it on stage until the Wings' tours. The Dutch artists known collectively as the Fool painted a colourful design on the guitar. Paul also used the instrument in *Magical Mystery Tour,* on the *Our World* television show and in the promotional video 'Hello Goodbye', recorded at the Saville Theatre. Paul later had the Fool design removed.

RITZ HOTEL Famous London hotel, situated in Piccadilly. Paul and Linda held their wedding reception there on 12 March 1969. (See also *McCartney, Linda.*)

ROCK AND OTHER FOUR LETTER WORDS Book in which Linda McCartney's first photographs of Paul were published.

ROBBINS, KATE Paul's cousin, who has become a recording artist in her own right and has occasionally guested as a backing vocalist on some of Paul's records. Paul took a hand early in her career and produced her recording 'Tomorrow', the song from the musical *Annie (cf),* which was part of his own MPL (cf) publishing catalogue. The single was released in Britain on Anchor ANC 1054 on 30 June 1978, but was unsuccessful. Her big-

Kate Robbins and friend

gest hit was 'More Than In Love', a song featured on the television soap opera *Crossroads* (cf), which brought her to a No.2 position in the British charts when the single was issued on RCA in May 1981.

THE ROCKESTRA A rock orchestra created by Paul. Originally used for two numbers on *Back to the Egg* (cf), 'The Rockestra Theme' and 'So Glad To See You'. Paul invited a host of noted rock musicians to join Wings and their brass section at Abbey Road Studios on 3 October 1978 to make the recordings. The line-up of musicians was: Pete Townshend, Dave Gilmour (of Pink Floyd), Hank Marvin (of the Shadows), Laurence Juber (cf) and Denny Laine (cf) on guitars; Ronnie Lane (fomerly with the Small Faces), John Paul Jones (of Led Zeppelin) (cf) and Bruce Thomas (of Elvis Costello's Attractions) on bass; Tony Ashton (of Ashton, Gardener & Dyke), Gary Brooker (of Procol Harum) and Linda McCartney on keyboards; John Bonham (of Led Zeppelin), Kenny Jones (of the Small Faces) and Steve Holly (cf) on drums; Morris Pert, Speedy Acquaye and Tony Carr on percussion; and Thaddeus Richard, Tony Dorsey (cf), Howie Casey (cf) and Steve Howard on brass. During the sessions a special film of the occasion was taken for posterity, intended for showing as a telelvision item.

The Rockestra was to be gathered together for one special surprise live appearance. Paul had been contacted by Kurt Waldheim of the United Nations regarding the tragedy in Kampuchea, where millions of people were starving. As a result, The Concerts For The People Of Kampuchea were organised at the Hammersmith Odeon, London, in December 1979. Paul and Wings appeared on the bill on 29 December, with Elvis Costello & the Attractions and Dave Edmunds and Nick Lowe in Rockpile. At the end of the Wings set the Rockestra took the stage. Musicians included Pete Townshend, John Bonham, John Paul Jones, Kenny Jones, Bruce Thomas, Rockpile and Robert Plant. They performed 'The Rockestra Theme', 'Lucille', with Paul on lead vocals, 'Let It Be' on which Pete Townshend had an exceptional solo spot and 'Rockestra Theme' again. The concerts were filmed for television and were screened on 4 January 1981. There was also an album issued on Atlantic K 60153 on 3 April 1981 which featured Paul, Wings and the Rockestra.

ROCKSHOW Paul's first feature length film produced for the cinema. 102 minutes in length, it featured the Wings concert at the Kings Dome, Seattle, on 10 June 1976. An audience of 67,000 people watched the concert. Some numbers were edited in from film of other locations on the tour.

Altogether there were twenty-three numbers in the film, a further six having been edited out of the finished print. Songs included 'Venus and Mars', 'Yesterday', Band On The Run', 'Let Me Roll It', 'The Long And Winding Road', 'Maybe I'm Amazed', 'Jet' and 'Bluebird'. The film was made by Paul's company MPL (cf) and edited by Robin Clark and Paul Stein. The amplification system used during the film was capable of generating 15,000 watts. The movie was premièred at New York's Ziegfeld Theatre on 26 November 1980, but the European Charity Première at the Dominion Theatre, Tottenham Court Road, London, was the star-studded event. It took place on 8 April 1981 and was graced by the Earl and Countess of Snowdon. The charity première was in aid of the Snowdon Award

Scheme for Physically Handicapped Students and was attended by a host of stars including comedian Billy Connolly, musicians Mike Oldfield, Steve Harley, Phil Lynott, Eric Stewart and Gary Glitter, and luminaries from the world of politics, fashion and theatre. The movie was distributed in Britain by Miracle International and in America by Mirimax Films. *Rockshow* is now available on videocassette in Dolby stereo sound on Thorn EMI VHS TVD 90 03342.

ROCK STARS IN THEIR UNDERPANTS Publication by Virgin Books, issued in Britain in 1981. Trendy blonde Paula Yates, who was writing for *Record Mirror* at the time, had come up with the idea of photographing famous rock stars in their underpants. Virgin gave her a Polaroid camera and sent her out on the assignment. She caught Paul in the middle of making his promotional video for 'Coming Up', but to oblige, he stuck a pair of underpants over his trousers and Paula was able to catch the spectacle for posterity!

Caught in his underwear for 'Rock Stars in Their Underpants'

RODDENBURY, GENE Producer and creator of *Star Trek* and several other television sci-fi shows. In 1976, Paul got together with Roddenbury to work on a science fiction musical film starring Wings. It was intended as a vehicle in which the group could show their acting as well as their musical talents and an announcement about the project was given to the press in November of that year. Unfortunately, nothing came of it. (See also *Asimov, Isaac*.)

RODERICK, EDDIE A Liverpool city councillor who, in January 1984, following press coverage of Paul's drug charge in Barbados (see *Drugs*), wanted the offer that had been made to Paul of the Freedom of the City to be withdrawn. Roderick said: "He has brought shame on the city." His request fell on deaf ears and Paul received the honour on 28 November 1984 in a ceremony held before the première of *Give My Regards to Broad Street*.

ROYAL COURT THEATRE Liverpool theatre which saw the launch of Wings' 1979 UK tour with a free concert on 23 November with new group members Laurence Juber (cf) and Steve Holly (cf). The theatre had been threatened with closure due to financial problems earlier that year and Paul had donated £5,000 to the venue. At the city council a motion by Conservative members to thank Paul for his generosity was voted down by Labour councillors. One of them was Roy Stoddard and he ungraciously commented: "I don't see why Paul McCartney should be singled out for special praise. The Beatles could have given a million and not missed it. They made their millions and we have not seen them since."

The free concert was held in honour of Paul's former school, the Liverpool Institute (cf). Pupils and staff were invited and Paul was to say: "It's my way of saying 'Thank you' for some very happy years. Everyone seems to knock their schooldays but for me they have fond memories." Wings also played to full houses at the Royal Court for the next three days.

Backstage at the Royal Court with Liverpool friend Joe Flannery

THE ROYAL IRIS Famous Liverpool ferry boat which was available for dances and parties and proved to be a popular showboat on the Mersey. When Paul made his appearance in Liverpool with Wings in November 1979 (see *Royal Court Theatre*), he took the group for a thirty-minute cruise on the boat at a cost of £150. He was to comment that the Beatles "played in the salon of the Royal Iris for a fiver each – and we weren't asked back!"

RUDE STUDIOS Name Paul gave to the studios he had built on his farm in Scotland. It was here, in 1975, that he produced and recorded *Holly Days*. He later changed the name to Spirit of Ranachan Studios.

RUPERT AND THE FROG SONG Full title: 'Paul McCartney's Rupert And The Frog Song', a video cassette issued by Virgin Video in Britain on 14 November 1985 on VVC 109 (VHS and Beta). The 15-minute animation of the Rupert story is the main item on the 25-minute video, which also features the short films 'Seaside Woman' (cf) and 'The Oriental Nightfish' (cf). The video became the No.1 hit that Christmas and Britain's best-selling music video up till then.

RUPERT BEAR One of the most famous British comic strip characters, originally created in 1932. He is a white bear who walks upright and wears a red cardigan, checked yellow trousers with scarf to match and white boots. He lives in Bear Cottage on Nutwood Common with his parents, Mr and Mrs Bear.

Rupert Bear annuals regularly sell in the region of 175,000 copies per year and the strip has been running in the *Daily Express* newspaper for decades. Paul used to read *Rupert Bear* annuals as a child and rediscovered the character when he started reading the stories to Heather. Paul says that he thinks of Rupert as a twelve-year-old boy and in 1969 commented: "I've bought up the film rights for Rupert Bear, the cartoon character from the *Daily Express.* As a kid I loved that strip – I've still got all the old Rupert annuals at home."

He originally began to develop the idea of an eight-minute featurette of Rupert with animator Oscar Grillo (cf) and actually penned about eleven songs for a projected full-length animated movie. In 1980 he recorded 'We All Stand Together' at AIR Studios. George Martin (cf) produced the

Paul bought the film rights of his favourite comic strip character as far back as the late sixties

sessions on 31 October and 3 November. Paul was backed by 38-piece orchestra, the St Paul's Choir and the Kings Singers. He completed a script himself called *Rupert & the Frog Chorus* and worked with Geoff Dunbar (cf), an award-winning British designer who actually animated the final project. This turned into a 13½-minute film, which Geoff also directed. In the story Rupert leaves Bear Cottage one morning and sets off into the countryside, saying 'Hello' to some of his friends on the way. He discovers a waterfall, finds a secret passage and witnesses a huge gathering of frogs. He is enchanted as they begin to sing and their King and Queen arise out of a cascade. The magical moment is upset by two mischievous black cats and a large owl. The congregation scatters but they are unharmed by the interlopers. Rupert returns home to tell his mother of the adventure.

The cartoon was a great success when it was included on the bill with *Give My Regards to Broad Street,* and Paul's single 'We All Stand Together' was a chart hit.

In the programme *The Rupert Bear Story,* first broadcast on channel 4 TV in Britain on 8 December 1982, Paul described his nostalgic feelings for Rupert. Hosted by Terry Jones, the programme paid tribute to Alfred Bestall, the artist who drew Rupert's adventures from 1935-1965. Other people in the documentary included Sir Hugh Casson, President of the Royal Academy; Dr John Rae, headmaster of Westminster School; artist Anthony Green; and architect Richard Rogers.

RUSSELL, WILLIE Award-winning Liverpool playwright whose first major stage play *John, George, Paul, Ringo . . . and Bert* won the *Evening Standard* Award as Comedy of the Year. He also received an award for *Blood Brothers* and penned several television plays based in Liverpool. Paul commissioned him to write a film script for a movie tentatively titled *Band on the Run.* Willie completed the project, but the film was never made.

SAINT PAUL Another American single inspired by the 'Paul Is Dead' (cf) rumours. Recorded by Terry Knight and issued in 1969 on Capitol 2506 with 'Legend of William and Mary' on the flip. (See also *Brother Paul.*)

ST JOAN Play by George Bernard Shaw. Paul appeared as a Monk in a school production of the work.

ST JOHN'S One of the American Virgin Islands (cf) where Paul and Wings went to record in the summer of 1977. While moored there they were fined. Paul explained: "... It's a National Park. One of the rules is you must not play amplified music. I think they meant trannies. But we had a whole thing going. You could hear it for miles. We got fined fifteen dollars."

ST SWITHIN'S Roman Catholic church in the Gillmoss area of West Derby in Liverpool. Paul's father James was married to his mother Mary at this church on 15 April 1941. At the time Paul's dad, who was a cotton salesman, was 39, and had been living at 58 Fieldton Road, West Derby. (See also *McCartney, Jim* and *McCartney, Mary (1).*)

SATURDAY NIGHT LIVE American TV show on the NBC network. Paul and Linda were guests on the programme in May 1980.

SAY SAY SAY Song both penned and recorded by Paul and Michael Jackson (cf), during the same sessions which produced 'The Man'. The track was used on *Pipes of Peace* (cf) but was also issued as a single in Britain on Parlophone R6062 on 3 October 1983 with 'Ode To A Koala Bear', a McCartney number, on the flipside. The number went to No.3 in Britain and to No.4 in the US when it was issued there on 10 October on Columbia 44-04169. A 12" pressing had a seven-minute version of the 'Say Say Say' instrumental on the flipside, in addition to 'Ode To A Koala Bear'. The American John 'Jellybean' Benitez had been called in to remix both the vocal and instrumental 'Say Say Say' and made longer versions. He ex-

Mac and Jack in harmony

tended the vocal version from four minutes to five minutes and forty seconds.

SAVAGE, BILL An entrant in the 1984 London Marathon. He did the run in aid of Hemel Hempstead General Hospital and Paul was said to have been one of his sponsors – for £2 per mile.

SCHWARTZ, FRANCIE Pennsylvania-born, New York City-educated brunette who arrived in Britain in 1968 seeking backers for a film script she had written. She took it along to the Apple office in Wigmore Street and Paul noticed her in the reception lounge. They chatted for a while and he said he could make herself useful in the Apple offices. She gave Paul her address in London and he came to see her one Monday morning. She was to comment: "He settled right into a chair with me on his lap. The kisses started. . . and later we visited friends in the country and ran barefoot in the rain."

The brief affair had begun while Paul was still courting Jane Asher (cf), but she was away on tour. According to stories of the time, Francie had become a regular visitor to Paul's Cavendish Avenue house when, about three weeks into the arrangement, Jane turned up. Her tour of the provinces with the Old Vic, had ended ahead of schedule. Margot Stevens, one of the Apple Scruffs (the group of fans who hung around the Beatles' homes, offices and recording studios),

spotted Jane arriving in her car and pressed the Entryphone, warning Paul of her arrival. He didn't believe her. Jane, who had her own key, entered the house and found Francie dressed only in Paul's dressing gown. She left. Later that evening her mother arrived in an estate car and took away some of Jane's belongings.

Soon after, the fling with Francie was over and she wrote a piece about the romance in the *News of the World,* saying: "He (Paul) hadn't formally ended his friendship with Jane Asher, so at first I was a secret." She returned to America where she sold a story of the affair to *Rolling Stone* magazine entitle 'Memories of an Apple Girl'. She then wrote a book called *Body Count* for *Rolling Stone* publishers, Straight Arrow, concerning her various love affairs. She devoted a full chapter to her short affair with Paul, whom she described as: 'a little Medici prince pampered and paid on a satin pillow at a very early age.'

SCOTT, JIMMY Jamaican-born friend of Paul's who often used the expression "ob-la-di, ob-la-da, life goes on, bra," which Paul made into a song.

SEASIDE WOMAN Number written by Linda McCartney following a trip to Jamaica. She recorded it with backing from Wings members and Paul produced the session. It was decided to use the name Suzi and the Red Stripes in reference to the local Jamaican beer. However, the single, although recorded in 1973, wasn't issued until 1977 when it was released in America on 31 May 1977 on Epic 3-50403. Flipside was another joint McCartney composition, 'Side To Seaside'. In Britain, it wasn't released until August 1979 on A&M AMS 7461. The following year, a 34-minute animated film based on the song and made by Oscar Grillo (cf) was entered in the Cannes Film Festival. It won first prize in the Short Film Competition, and due to this success, A&M reissued the single on 18 July 1980 on A&M AMS 7548.

THE SECOND COMING OF SUZANNE Film script by Michael Barry, son of actor Gene Barry. Mickie Most at one time considered filming the story, which concerned Christ's return to Earth in contemporary times – as a woman! One of the plum roles was that of a pop star – and Mickie wanted Paul for the role. The film was never made.

SEIWELL, DENNY The first member of Wings to be recruited by Paul and Linda, Denny was born in Leighton, Pennsylvania, and his father had once been a drummer. At the age of seven Denny began to play snare in the local Boy's Orchestra and was later to join the army as a bandsman. In the sixties, on leaving the army, he moved to Chicago where he played jazz with various outfits before moving on to New York, where he also played in jazz clubs and did a lot of session work. When Paul was in New York to record his album *Ram (cf),* he auditioned drummers in a rather seedy basement. Denny was to comment: "A lot of the boys were really put out at being asked to audition. Paul just asked me to play, he didn't have a guitar, so I just sat and played. He had a certain look in his eye. He was looking for more than a drummer. He was looking for a certain attitude, too. I just played." He got the job and recorded the *Ram* sessions between January and March 1971. Paul then asked him if he would be interested in joining a band with him and Denny agreed. Together with his French wife Monique, he left New York to move into Paul's farm to await the Wings formation. He and Monique were later to buy a house in London and a farm in Scotland, just like Paul and Linda. Some say the official formation of Wings took place on 3 August 1971 during the *Wild Life* (cf) sessions; others put it a month later when Stella was born, saying that Paul actually thought of the name 'Wings' (cf) at this time.

Denny recorded two Wings albums, *Wild Life* and *Red Rose Speedway* (cf) and drummed on the singles 'Mary Had A Little Lamb', 'Hi Hi Hi' and 'Give Ireland Back To The Irish'. He toured with the band in Britain and Europe in 1972 and 1973. His reasons for leaving the group are not clear. When he phoned Paul to tell him he was quitting three hours before the band were due to fly out to Lagos, Nigeria, to record *Band on the Run* he gave his reason as the fact that he did not want to go to Africa. He quit on 30 August 1974, five days after Henry McCullough (cf). McCullough said he was unhappy with the band because he felt Linda didn't belong in it. Seiwell is also said to have been unhappy about Linda's involvement.

SEVEN QUEENS OF ENGLAND Book which Paul received as a prize for an essay he'd written in 1953. The essay was about pot-holing. The book was written by Geoffrey Trease and published by Heinemann. Paul still has it.

SFX Now defunct British audio cassette magazine which included an interview with Paul in its issue dated 17 April and 1 May 1982.

SGT PEPPER'S LONELY HEARTS CLUB BAND American movie, based on *Sgt Pepper* and screened in 1978. The film starred Peter Frampton and the Bee Gees. The Robert Stigwood Organisation, who produced the film, originally offered Paul the leading role of Billy Shears (cf), but he turned it down.

SHEARS, BILLY A mythical character created for *Sgt Pepper* on which Ringo took the part. The character was fleshed out by the many wild stories in the 'Paul Is Dead' (cf) campaign of 1969. One American 'underground' paper, *Rat Subterranean News,* ran a full page story written by Lee Merrick and proclaiming that Billy Shears had become a substitute for the dead Paul McCartney. The story was published on 29 October 1969 and had supposedly been rushed by cable from London the day before publication.

Merrick began his 'exposé' with the words "Paul McCartney is dead." He then mentioned that he'd become very friendly with the Apple crowd during the previous six months and had seen the Beatles and 'Paul' around the offices. He went to a party with several Apple friends during the course of which he was given the story. He wrote: "Billy Shears was a young London rock musician who did short gigs in London nightclubs and occasional tours, waiting for the chance to make it big." At the beginning of the sixties Billy was on the Continent, presumably in Hamburg, when, "In 1962 Shears played on the same nightclub bill as Paul McCartney. In fact, he was a dead ringer for Paul. Of course, you could tell the difference if they stood side by side. Billy had a somewhat oversized beak-shaped nose. But in photographs or at a distance, they were absolutely indistinguishable."

The article goes on to relate how the two kept in touch as friends. Then: "In November 1966, Paul McCartney was involved in an auto accident — a fatal accident. John, George and Ringo first wanted to stage a gigantic funeral in memory of Paul, but super-sharp manager, Brian Epstein, feared that Paul's death would destroy the Beatles mystique and managed almost entirely to suppress the news. Epstein's calculating mind had already devised a scheme for keeping the Beatles intact — at least for the public. With a minor nose job, Billy Shears would make a perfect replacement for Paul. Though hesitant at first, Shears soon accepted Epstein's offer. What musician could resist the opportunity to step into the shoes of one of *the* superstars of the rock world."

Merrick then goes on to say that because they knew the ruse wouldn't last, the Beatles began to scatter 'clues' on their albums. (See *Abbey Road (1)* and *Gibbs, Russ.)*

He continues: "Even though I knew that my friend, who asked to remain unnamed, had known and worked with the Beatles from the early days in the fifties, history seemed almost too fantastic to believe. And certainly people who did not know him would have no reason to believe that Billy took Paul's place three years ago. So, for the next few days, I searched for evidence to absolutely confirm the story.

"My search ended in the quiet Chelsea section of London where I talked with Philip Shears, father of the new Paul McCartney. At first Mr Shears hesitated to discuss the matter. He had kept his lips sealed for three long years in the pleasant, middle-class home his son had bought for him. But after I repeated the story my Apple friend told me, the elderly Mr Shears relented and confirmed the facts. 'Mum and me always knew that it couldn't stay secret for ever. The Beatles are a bunch of wonderful lads and have made a whole new world for us.' But, he added, 'It's high time our Billy received the credit he deserves'. (See also *Campbell, William.*)

SHE'S A WOMAN Paul penned this rocker literally on the spot during a recording session in October 1964, and it was issued as the flipside of 'I Feel Fine' in November. The Beatles performed the song on their Christmas show in 1964 and on their subsequent tours. The number was included on the American album *Beatles '65* and on *Beatles at the Hollywood Bowl* and *Beatles Rarities.*

SHE'S LEAVING HOME A track from *Sgt Pepper* which was also included on the *Love Songs* and *The Beatles Ballads* compilation. It's a poignant song which George Martin (cf) admitted made him cry when he heard it. Paul commented: "It's a much younger girl than 'Eleanor Rigby', but the same sort of loneliness. That was a *Daily Mirror* story again: this girl left home and her father said: 'We gave her everything, I don't know why she left home.' But he didn't give her that much, not what she wanted when she left home."

SHRIMPTON, STEVEN MD of MPL (cf) and Paul's right-hand man, who joined the company in January 1980. Stephen was born in Melbourne, Australia, and joined EMI Australia in 1969 as national marketing and sales manager, eventually rising to the post of managing director in April 1974. He got to know Paul when he was in charge of all the Wings product in Australia. Stephen intended to return to Australia after the filming of *Give My Regards to Broad Street* (cf) — in which Australian actor Bryan Brown (cf) portrayed a character based on him – but Paul talked him into remaining with the company.

SOUTH BANK SHOW Arts programme on London Weekend Television, hosted by Melvyn Bragg. Paul made his first appearance on the show on its debut screening on 14 January 1978 when he was subjected to a detailed interview which spotlighted his songwriting career. Another special edition of the show on 14 October 1984 was devoted to *Give My Regards to Broad Street* (cf(1)) and featured filmed interviews with Paul and George Martin (cf) during the making of the movie and behind-the-scenes coverage of the recording of the songs.

SPEEDY PROMPT DELIVERY SERVICE Liverpool firm where Paul worked for a fortnight in December 1960 on his return from the first Hamburg trip. His father had suggested he find himself a job so he went to the local office of the Labour Exchange and was given a job with the firm, which he called SPD, spending his time as second man on the back of a lorry delivering parcels, mainly in the area of the Liverpool docks. Paul told Hunter Davies in *The Beatles: The Authorised Biography*: "I used to sit on the back of the lorry and helped to carry parcels. I was so buggered sometimes. I fell asleep on the lorry when we went to places like Chester. I was with them about two weeks and felt very worldly, having a job and a few quid in me pocket. But I got laid off. The Christmas period was over and there wasn't so much work."

SPIES LIKE US Dan Aykroyd/Chevy Chase spy spoof feature film. Paul's eponymous song is only heard on the closing sequences of the movie, but the single was released in Britain on Parlophone R6118 on 18 November. The 'B' side was the Wings recording of 'My Carnival', previously unreleased although recorded in New Orleans as far back as 1975. There was also a three-track 12" single issued on 2 December on 12R 6118 which contained 'Spies Like Us (Party Mix)',

'Spies Like Us (Alternative Mix)' and 'My Carnival'. A 7" picture disc on RP 6118 was also issued. The record proved to be a Top Ten chart entry in the States (Capitol B-5436), although it only reached No.13 in the British charts. A promotional video included footage from the movie and shots of Paul in various disguises at Abbey Road Studios. Dan Aykroyd and Chevy Chase also appeared in the Abbey Road sequence of Paul's video.

Paul played all the instruments on 'Spies Like Us', with the exception of the synthesiser, which was played by Eddie Rayner. The backing vocals were by Linda, Kate Robbins (cf), Ruby James and Eric Stewart (cf). Musicians on 'My Carnival' were Paul, Linda, Denny Laine (cf), Jimmy McCulloch (cf), Joe English (cf), George Porter and Benny Spellman.

SPINETTI, VICTOR British comic/actor who appeared in more Beatles movies than anyone apart from the Beatles themselves. Victor became a close friend of the group and appeared in a small cameo role in Paul's video of 'London Town'. The two of them took part in the 'recruiting scene' in *Magical Mystery Tour*. Victor had been asked to become a member of the actual tour party but he was appearing in a play at the time. However, he managed to get enough time off to appear in this scene, in which the character he plays is based on his role in the film *Oh, What a Lovely War!* Paul McCartney (cf), Victor the Army Recruiting Sergeant.

SPIN IT ON Song written by Paul which was issued as the 'B' side of 'Old Siam Sir' in Britain on 1 June 1979 and as the flipside of 'Getting Closer' (cf) in America on 5 June. A few days later it appeared as the fourth track on *Back to the Egg* (cf). It was included on the *Back to the Egg* TV special and Wings performed the number as part of their repertoire on their 1979 British tour.

THE STARS ORGANISATION FOR SPASTICS Charity which held an auction of drawings and paintings by celebrities on 20 October 1982. Paul

'Spies Like Us': Paul fittingly appeared in disguise in the video for the film's title song

contributed a drawing called 'A House And A Little Man In A Top Hat'.

STARDUST Evergreen number by the late Hoagy Carmichael. Paul arranged the number for Ringo for his 1970 album *Sentimental Journey.*

STARDUST MEMORIES Collection of interviews by Ray Connolly, published in 1983 by Pavilion Books. There are two interviews with Paul, the first from a meeting which took place in February 1968. At the time, according to Roy, Paul was the only Beatle "who lives in London . . . the social Beatle . . . the one who goes to the most fashionable clubs . . . who gets the most invitations to parties, and who accepts the most."

There is a detailed description of the St John's Wood house and Paul discusses his reaction to the critical attack on *Magical Mystery Tour*: "It was like getting a bash in the face." He said he'd always felt guilty about acting big-time with Ringo when the drummer first joined the group, that the group could have turned into "four Hitlers", but went in the direction of helping people by forming Apple, a business concern "rather like a Western Communism."

The second interview took place in April 1970. It mainly concerned the storm which broke out after Paul announced he was leaving the Beatles. He'd been silent about it all for a year, but decided to clear the air and took Linda along with him when he met Ray in a Soho restaurant. He felt that Klein was wrong to think that his desire to have Lee Eastman (Linda's father) look after the Beatles affairs was pure nepotism – he genuinely thought the lawyer would be the right man for the job. Then Paul takes great pains to detail the entire background leading to the split. He mentions that he found it difficult to write when Yoko was around, that he'd tried writing with John again, but it hadn't worked. "I told him on the phone the other day that at the beginning of last year I was annoyed with him. I was jealous because of Yoko, and afraid about the break-up of a great musical partnership. It's taken me a year to realise that they were in love. Just like Linda and me."

STEVENS, JOE American photographer whom Paul hired in 1972 to document the Wings tour of Europe. The New Yorker had been living in London working for various 'underground' publications. Due to difficulties with obtaining a work permit for him, he was nicknamed Captain Snaps and a company called Women's Tango Lessons Ltd was formed to collect the profits from the sale of the photographs, which were then to be divided between Paul, Linda and Stevens. Captain Snaps once mentioned how Paul did not want to hear any talk of the Beatles at the time, saying: "I think he'd been almost brain-damaged for a while from having been Paul of the Beatles."

STEWART, ERIC Guitarist from Manchester, originally with sixties hit band the Mindbenders, and later with 10cc. Eric played on some tracks of *Tug of War* and was then asked to play on the *Pipes of Peace* sessions. He was also featured on *Give My Regards to Broad Street (cf(3))* and appeared in the film. In an interview with the Dutch fanzine *Beatles Unlimited,* Eric discussed how he was first asked to play on the *Tug of War* sessions: "I meet Paul fairly often and we've known each other ever since way back when he was with the Beatles and I was with the Mindbenders. We used to play in the Cavern together . . . we used to play the same kind of music, American R&B, and we're both from the North, we have the same accent, the same sense of humour. . . After I had a car accident a while back, Paul phoned me up to see if I was all right. I said I was, but in fact I was still rather messed up and still had to use drugs and all that. But Paul asked me if I felt like playing on his new LP so I said 'Great!'" When he was a member of 10cc Eric played on Mike McGear's solo album *McGear* on the tracks 'The Man Who Found God On The Moon' and 'Givin' Grease A Ride'. Paul produced the album and that was when Eric and he renewed their acquaintance.

Eric Stewart joins Ringo, Barbara and Paul

STINE, JOE Musician who appeared as Paul in *Beatlefever*, an American musical touring show, similar to *Beatlemania*. Dave Boxley portrayed George, Johnny Prophet was Ringo and Steve Burton played John.

STOCKTON WOOD ROAD PRIMARY SCHOOL A large, primary school, built in the Speke area of Liverpool after the war. It was close to where Paul and his younger brother lived at the time and was the first primary school they attended. Within a short time it had taken on so many pupils that, at over 1,500, it had the largest primary school enrolment in Britain. Paul and Michael moved on to the Joseph Williams Primary (cf) school because of the overcrowding.

STOP AND SMELL THE ROSES Ringo Starr's November 1981 album, issued on the RCA label. Ringo was originally going to call the album *Can't Fight Lightning,* the title of a song that he'd written with his wife Barbara Bach. Ringo played guitar and Paul played drums on it. However, a dispute with CBS, who were originally to issue the album on the Portrait label in the States, put paid to this. Ringo made his deal with RCA, and dropped 'Can't Fight Lightning' as a track and as the album title. Paul produced the album and wrote three numbers for it. 'Private Property', 'Attention' and 'Sure To Fall (In Love With You)'. Paul joined the recording sessions in July 1980 at the Superbear Studios in Nice, France. In addition to Paul and Ringo, Linda, Laurence Juber (cf) and Howie Casey (cf) were present at the sessions. Howie's sax was heard on 'Private Property' and 'Attention'. Lloyd Green contributed the pedal steel guitar work on 'Sure To Fall'.

STOPPARD, TOM Leading British playwright whom Paul once asked to write a film script for him. "Tom was interested," said Paul, "but he got bogged down with all that Solidarity stuff. I think he was doing *Squaring the Circle,* and I couldn't really ring him up and say: 'Get a move on, Stoppard'. I mean, he's an artist!"

STRANG, AMANDA British girl who suffered from blackouts due to various allergies. When Linda McCartney read that Amanda's house had been burgled in the summer of 1983, she contacted her and offered to replace the stolen goods, which included tapes and a video recorder.

STREISAND, BARBRA American singer and actress. Paul met her in the canteen at Elstree Studios. He was filming *Broad Street,* she was editing *Yentl.* He went over to her and introduced himself and they had a chat. "Nice girl" is how he described her.

SUITABLE FOR FRAMING A 1982 bootleg album of tracks by Wings. Side One includes: 'I'll Give You A Ring'; 'Rainclouds'; 'Maisie'; 'I Would Only Smile'; 'Take It Away'; 'Send Me The Heart' and 'Ebony & Ivory'. Side Two includes: 'Waterspout'; 'Hi Hi Hi'; 'Waterfalls'; 'Arrow Through Me'; 'Winter Rose'; 'Love Awake'; 'Weep For Love' and 'Complain To The Queen'.

SUNDAY BEATLE Special supplement of the *Sunday Mirror* in Sydney, Australia. In June 1963 it ran a special competition to link up with Paul's twenty-second birthday, in conjunction with the Sydney *Daily Mirror,* and offered the "chance of a lifetime". Under the headline "You . . . Could Go To Paul's Birthday Party", the competition announced that a selection of girls between the ages of sixteen and twenty-two could win the opportunity of attending Paul's birthday party on Thursday, 18 June at the Sheraton Hotel, Sydney. Initially, the girls had to submit a fifty-word essay on the theme: "Why I Would Like To Be A Guest At A Beatle's Birthday Party." There were 10,000 entries and the finalists had to attend an interview at the hotel before a panel of judges who included Derek Taylor, Dave Allen, the Irish comedian, Hugh Bingham, editor of the *Sunday Mirror,* and Leicester Warburton and Blanch d'Alpuget, also from the *Mirror.*

There were seventeen winners and fifteen runners-up. The latter were invited to meet the Beatles after their

Paul wrote three numbers for Ringo's 'Stop and Smell the Roses'

concert on the Friday evening.

The girls invited to Paul's Thursday bash were: Glennys Smith; Jenny Lamb; Sandra Linklater; Caroline Styles; Ines Truse; Evelyn Mac; Patricia Thompson; Christine Buetter; Claire Hogben; Caroline Keirs; Carmel Stratton; Anne-Marie Alexander; Marcia McAmeny; Delphine Dockerill; Jannette Carroll; Nancy Haddow and Sandra Stevenson.

Jannette Carroll, who was only sixteen at the time, commented: "As we were leaving Paul shook all our hands and by this time I was even braver so I said, 'I'm not used to shaking boys' hands on their birthday' and offered him my cheek. He very gently took my chin, turned my face around and gave me a beautiful kiss right on the lips. I know it sounds corny, but for about two weeks I washed every part of my face but my lips."

The party took place around midnight, after their show was over, and as the Beatles entered the room, Paul was heard to say: "Ee, it's a proper do, isn't it?" (See also *Yates, Kerry*).

SUPERBEAR STUDIOS Recording studios situated 2,700 feet up a mountain, close to Nice on the French Riviera. In July 1980, Paul and Linda took a trip to the studios to join Ringo Starr and record tracks for his forthcoming album. Paul produced four of the tracks. Other musicians present were Lloyd Green on steel guitar, Laurence Juber (cf) on guitar, Howie Casey (cf) on sax and Sheila Casey and Linda on backing vocals. The engineer was Peter Henderson.

TALES FROM THE SADDLE Book compiled by singer Alvin Stardust and published by Stanley Paul in 1984. Proceeds of the book were donated to Save The Children Fund, and HRH Princess Ann wrote the Foreword. Alvin gathered anecdotes from many celebrities, including Paul and Linda. Linda related how, during the first Wings tour of the States, they'd rented a house in Dallas. They'd decided to buy an Appaloosa, the original American pony. On the way to Fort Worth one day they spotted one which they felt they just had to buy

and made enquiries at the ranch. They were told it had just been reserved for some children. When the kids heard that Paul and Linda had set their hearts on the horse, they let them buy it and chose another instead. The kids and their parents were invited to some Wings shows and the horse is now happily ensconsed in England (see *Lucky Spot).*

TALK OF THE TOWN Major variety showcase in London's West End. It was finally closed in the early eighties, to be re-opened as the Hippodrome in late 1983 by club-owner Peter Stringfellow. As the Talk of the Town, the venue booked many top American acts during the sixties and Paul visited the venue in 1968 to watch a performance by the Supremes.

TELL ME WHAT YOU SEE Composition by Paul for the *Help!* film and used on the film soundtrack. The number was also included on the American *Beatles VI* and on *Love Songs.*

THINGS WE SAID TODAY Paul was on holiday in the Bahamas with Jane Asher (cf), Ringo and Maureen in 1964, when he wrote this song. It was featured in the film *A Hard Day's Night,* on the flipside of the single of that name and on the soundtrack album and film EP. It was included in the *Beatles Box* collection, the American album *Something New*, and a live version is to be found on *Hollywood Bowl.*

THATCHER, MARGARET First female Prime Minister of the UK and leader of the Conservative Party. Paul and Linda's opinions over the years seem to suggest the couple favour Socialism. During the 1981 industrial dispute over nurses' salaries, Paul actually sent a telegram to Margaret Thatcher in November. It read: "What the miners did for Ted Heath, the nurses will do for you." This referred to the fact that the Conservative Government under Heath had been brought down by the miner's strike in 1972. Paul's prediction didn't come true. In 1984 Paul and Linda met Mrs Thatcher and said:

"When we were talking to Mrs Thatcher, we said how in a lot of council houses the plumbing was bad, the paint and ceilings were cracking. Why don't they take people on the dole, who want to work, and give them jobs repairing council homes? Maggie Thatcher said: 'Oh, the Unions wouldn't allow me to do that.'"

THINGUMYBOB Comedy series, starring the late Stanley Holloway, produced by London Weekend Television and first networked in Britain on 2 August 1968. Paul penned its theme tune, which was performed by the Black Dyke Mills Band (cf).

THOMAS, CHRIS British record producer who had recorded various acts, including the Sex Pistols and Badfinger. Thomas was originally an assistant engineer to George Martin (cf) and Paul hired him to co-produce *Back to the Egg* (cf) with him. 'Daytime Nightime Suffering', the flipside of 'Goodnight Tonight', was also co-produced by Paul and Chris.

THRILLER Multi-million-selling LP by Michael Jackson (cf), issued in Britain on Epic Records (EPC 85930) on 5 November 1982. It included 'The Girl Is Mine' (cf), which was co-written by Michael and Paul and on which Paul sings and plays.

THRILLINGTON An orchestral version of *Ram,* issued on Regal Zonophone EMC 3175 on 29 April 1977. Attributed to Percy 'Thrills' Thrillington, an orchestra leader, the material was arranged and conducted by Richard Hewson. The cover design by Hipgnosis (cf) features artwork by Jeff Cummins depicting a ram in evening suit playing a violin, sitting in front of a music stand. The back cover shows a view of a recording session in a studio; a figure with a ram's head is discussing the music with the seated musicians, and Paul's head is reflected in the glass pane of the studio window. This picture is based on an actual photograph taken during the *Ram* sessions, when the standing figure was Paul.

The album was an MPL (cf) production with the credit: "Produced by Percy 'Thrills' Thrillington", so we must assume that Percy is a pseudonym for Paul. The little biographical blurb below the photo reads: "Percy 'Thrills' Thrillington was born in Coventry Cathedral in 1939. As a young man his travels took him to Baton Rouge USA, where he studied music for five years on the trot. Moving later to Los Angeles he gained expertise in the marketing, conducting and arranging fields. Eventually the path led to London where his long ambition to form his own orchestra was finally realised. On this record Percy takes the themes from Paul McCartney's *Ram* with the help of some of London's best musicians, forces them into orchestral versions that bear the unmistakable imprint – the mark of . . . "

THUMBIN' A RIDE Old Coasters number that Paul found on the flipside of one of their singles he had in his collection. He liked it so much that in 1969 he produced a version with Jackie Lomax singing. George Harrison and Billy Preston were among the backing musicians. In between recording sessions, Paul managed to squeeze in his marriage to Linda (see *McCartney, Linda).*

TILL THERE WAS YOU Song written by Meredith Willson for the Broadway musical *The Music Man,* which starred Robert Preston and was also filmed. Paul particularly liked the number after hearing Peggy Lee's version, and it was included in early Beatles acts. Paul sang the song during the Beatles' Decca audition and it has resurfaced on various albums of Decca tapes, including *The Complete Silver Beatles*. He also performed it on stage at the Star Club, Hamburg, and it became one of the many that Adrian Barber recorded live at that venue. This live version was to appear almost twenty years later on various albums of the Star Club performances. The official studio version was recorded for *With the Beatles,* issued in Britain in November 1963, and also appeared on the *Meet the Beatles* collection, released in America in January 1964.

In the early days one of Paul's favourite songs was 'Till There Was You'

TIMON Merseyside singer and one of the artists to record for Apple in its early days. However, the numbers he recorded were never released because George Harrison didn't like them. On one track, called 'Something New Everyday', produced by Peter Asher, Paul plays piano.

TITCHENER, LIONEL President of the Tattoo Club of Great Britain. Titchener, who has a shop in Oxford Street, London, told the newspapers that Paul visited him at his shop to discuss the making of a film about tattooing. Titchener suggested that he attended the annual tattooists' convention in Ramsgate and commented: "Paul said he would and we agreed he could bring a full film crew. Among the events he will shoot are our male and female tattoo beauty contests. I don't know whether Paul or his wife have any tattoos. Who knows, they might come away from the convention with some?"

THE TONIGHT SHOW Famous American chat show, hosted by Johnny Carson (cf). When Paul appeared on it on 23 October 1984 he attracted the biggest studio audience applications ever for the show. He was appearing during the US promotion his film *Give My Regards to Broad Street (cf(1))*. Paul had previously appeared on the programme on 15 May 1968 when the host was Joe Garragiola. On that occasion he was discussing the Beatles' plans for the Apple Corps organisation.

TOMORROW Song from the musical *Annie (cf)*. Paul, who owns the publishing rights to all the *Annie* numbers, produced a record of his cousin Kate Robbins (cf) singing the song. It was issued in Britain on Anchor Records in 1978.

THE TOURS Paul's first post-Beatles tour took place in 1972 from 9-23 February when the fledgling Wings first took flight on a short tour of British Universities, beginning at Nottingham and ending at Oxford. Wings members at the time were Paul, Linda, Denny Laine (cf), Henry McCullough (cf) and Denny Seiwell (cf). They played a number of gigs with Brinsley Schwarz, using that band's equipment. The numbers they played on this initial tour were 'Lucille'; 'Give Ireland Back To The Irish'; 'Blue Moon Of Kentucky'; 'Seaside Woman'; 'Help Me Darling'; 'Some People Never Know'; 'The Mess'; 'Bip Bop'; 'Say Darling'; 'Smile Away'; 'My Love'; 'Henry's Blues'; 'Wild Life' and 'Long Tall Sally'.

In July 1972 they embarked on a European tour, which ran from 24 August and took in France, Germany, Switzerland, Finland, Denmark, Sweden, Holland and Belgium. The numbers performed were: 'Bip Bop'; 'Smile Away'; '1982'; 'I Would Only Smile'; 'Give Ireland Back To The Irish'; 'Blue Moon Of Kentucky'; 'The Mess'; 'Best Friends'; 'Soilie'; 'I'm Your Singer'; 'Seaside Woman'; 'Henry's Blues'; 'Say You Don't Mind'; 'Wild Life'; 'Mary Had A Little Lamb'; 'My Love'; 'Maybe I'm Amazed'; 'Hi Hi Hi' and 'Long Tall Sally'.

Their first gig of 1973 was a charity performance at the Hard Rock Café (cf) in London on 18 March just before their British tour which commenced on 11 May and finished on 10 July. The numbers performed on this tour were: 'Soilie'; 'Big Barn Bed'; 'When The Night'; 'Wild Life'; 'Seaside Woman'; 'Little Woman Love'; 'C Moon'; 'Live And Let Die'; 'Maybe I'm Amazed'; 'My Love'; 'Go Now'; 'Say You Don't Mind'; 'The Mess' and 'Long Tall Sally'. There were originally two concerts set for the Hammersmith Odeon, but a third had to be added due to the huge demand for tickets.

The band's third British tour took place in 1974 between 9-23 September. Numbers performed were: 'Venus and Mars'; 'Rock Show'; 'Jet'; 'Let Me Roll It'; 'Spirits Of Ancient Egypt'; 'C Moon'; 'Maybe I'm Amazed'; 'Lady Madonna'; 'Long And Winding Road'; 'Medicine Jar'; 'Picasso's Last Words'; 'Richard Corey'; 'Bluebird'; 'I've Just Seen A Face'; 'Blackbird'; 'Yesterday'; 'You Gave Me The Answer'; 'Magneto And Titanium Man'; 'Go Now'; 'Letting Go'; 'Live And Let Die'; 'Call Me Back Again'; 'My Love'; 'Listen To What The Man Said'; 'Band On The Run'; 'Hi Hi Hi' and 'Soilie'. Later that year, the group toured Australia from 1-14 November.

In 1975 they performed the first of their short Euro-minitours (part of the mammoth '75/'76 world tour), appearing in Denmark, Germany, Holland and France between 20-26 March. The numbers performed were: 'Venus and Mars'; 'Rock Show'; 'Jet'; 'Let Me Roll It'; 'Spirits Of Ancient Egypt'; 'Medicine Jar'; 'Maybe I'm Amazed'; 'Call Me Back Again'; 'Lady Madonna'; 'The Long And Winding Road'; 'Live And Let Die'; 'Picasso's Last Words'; 'Richard Corey'; 'Bluebird'; 'I've Just Seen A Face'; 'Blackbird'; 'Yesterday'; 'You Gave Me The Answer'; 'Magneto And Titanium Man'; 'My Love'; 'Listen To What The Man Said'; 'Let 'Em In'; 'Time To Hide'; 'Silly Love Songs'; 'Beware My Love'; 'Letting Go'; 'Band On The Run'; 'Hi Hi Hi' and 'Soilie'.

This was the basic repertoire also used on the lengthy American section of the world tour, which began on 3 May and ended on 23 June 1976. Later that year, between 19-27 September they appeared in Austria, Yugoslavia, Italy and Germany, culminating with three major concerts in London at the Empire Pool, Wembley.

Wings toured Britain once more, in 1979, but their touring days were virtually over. In 1980 their Japanese dates were cancelled and soon afterwards they disbanded.

TREE TOP HOTEL Famous hotel in Nairobi where Paul enjoyed a holiday in 1966.

TRIVIA QUIZ Special 25-question quiz concerning Paul, published in the 28 January 1984 issue of Britain's *Record Mirror*. Topped with a photograph of Paul and Mike McCartney, the half-page compilation presented some interesting, though fairly simple, questions concerning Paul.

TRENTHAM GARDENS Venue in Stoke, England, where Wings appeared on 5 July 1973. On the same evening the group attended the premiere of *Live and Let Die* (cf) at the Odeon, Leicester Square, London.

TUG OF WAR (1) Title track of the 1982 album, which was released as a

Paul invited several guest musicians to play on this UK and US chart-toppping album

single with 'Get It' as the flip. Musicians backing Paul on the track included Denny Laine (cf) and Eric Stewart (cf) on electric guitars and Campbell Maloney on military snares. The single was issued in Britain on Parlophone R6057 on 20 September 1982, but made no impression on the charts. It was issued in America on 14 September 1982 on Columbia 38-03235, but only managed to reach the No.55 position.

TUG OF WAR (2) Paul's follow-up to *McCartney II (cf)*, released on 26 April 1982 in Britain on Parlophone PCTC 259, and in the States on Columbia TC 37462. It topped the charts in both countries. Part of the album was recorded on the island of Montserrat (cf), where George Martin (cf) has a studio; George co-produced part of the album with the aid of engineer Geoff Emerick. Paul invited a number of guest musicians to play on *Tug of War;* the artists performing on each track are as follows:

'Take It Away': Paul on piano, bass, acoustic guitar, vocals: Steve Gadd and Ringo Starr on drums; George Martin on electric piano; and Paul, Linda and Eric Stewart (cf) on backing vocals.

'Somebody Who Cares': Paul on acoustic and Spanish guitars and vocals; Stanley Clarke (cf) on bass; Steve Gadd on drums and percussion; Denny Laine (cf) on guitar and synthesiser; Adrian Brett on pan pipes; and Paul, Linda and Eric Stewart on backing vocals.

'What's That You're Doing?': Paul

on bass, drums, electric guitar and vocals; Stevie Wonder (cf) on synthesisers and vocals; and Paul, Linda and Eric Stewart on backing vocals.

'Here Today': Paul on guitar and vocals; Jack Rothstein and Bernard Partridge on violins; Ian Jewel on viola; and Keith Harvey on cello.

'Ballroom Dancing': Paul on piano, drums, bass, electric guitar, percussion and vocals; Denny Laine on electric guitar; Jack Brymer on clarinet gliss; and Paul, Linda and Eric Stewart on backing vocals.

'The Pound Is Sinking': Paul on acoustic guitar, electric guitar, synthesisers and vocal; Stanley Clarke on bass; Denny Laine on acoustic guitar; and Paul, Linda and Eric Stewart on backing vocals.

'Wanderlust': Paul on piano, bass, acoustic guitars and vocal; Adrian Sheppard on drums and percussion; Denny Laine on bass; Paul, Linda and Eric Stewart on backing vocals; and further music from the Philip Jones Brass Ensemble.

'Get It': Paul on acoustic guitar, percussion, vocals, synthesisers and bass; and Carl Perkins (cf) on electric guitar and vocals.

'Be What You See': Paul on guitar and vocoder.

'Dress Me Up As A Robber': Paul on vocals, guitars and bass; Dave Mattacks on drums and percussion; Denny Laine on synthesiser and electric guitar; George Martin on electric piano; backing vocals by Paul and Linda.

'Ebony & Ivory': Paul on bass, guitar, synthesisers, vocals, vocoder, percussion; backing vocals by Paul and Stevie.

Paul considered 'Wanderlust' his favourite track on the album. 'Here Today' (cf) had been written in tribute to John Lennon.

TUNISIA Paul visited this North African country for a short holiday in January l965, in the two weeks' break between the end of the Beatles' Christmas show at Hammersmith and the commencement of the filming of *A Hard Day's Night*.

TURNER, JACK Barber from St Leonard's-On-Sea who, in July 1981, gave Paul a short-back-and-sides. Paul wandered into his shop, waited in turn behind five customers, then told Jack he hadn't gone to a top salon because: "I don't want that. I want a traditional hairdresser. I don't want fuss and bother." Linda sat down with son James in her lap and the four-year-old boy had his hair cut, too.

TURPENTINE When Paul made his decision to form a band of his own in 1971, the name he originally came up with was Turpentine. An elderly fan was horrified and talked him out of it. Paul thought again and came up with Wings (see also *The Dazzlers*).

TWENTY FLIGHT ROCK Number popularised by the late Eddie Cochran and the first song to unite Paul and John. When they first met at Woolton Parish Church, following an introduction by a mutual friend Ivan Vaughan (cf), Paul impressed John by his ability not only to play the piece, but to write down all the lyrics from memory. Recollecting the incident to Hunter Davies for *The Authorised Biography*, Paul commented: "I showed them (the Quarrymen) how to play 'Twenty Flight Rock' and told them all the words. They didn't know it. Then I did 'Be-Bop-A-Lula', which they didn't know properly either. Then I did my Little Richard bit, went through me whole repertoire in fact. I remember this beery old man getting nearer and breathing down me neck as I was playing. 'What's this old drunk doing' I thought. Then he said 'Twenty Flight Rock' was one of his favourites. So I knew he was a connoisseur." John also talked to Davies about the number and said: "I was very impressed by Paul playing 'Twenty Flight Rock'. He could obviously play the guitar. I half thought to myself — he's as good as me. I'd been kingpin up to then. Now, I thought, if I take him on, what will happen? It went through my head that I'd have to keep him in line, if I let him join. But he was good, so he was worth having."

TWICE IN A LIFETIME 1985 American film starring Ann-Margret and Gene Hackman. Paul sang the title song.

TWIGGY Born Lesley Hornby in London in September 1949, Twiggy was to become one of the leading models of the Swinging Sixties. In her autobiography *Twiggy,* she mentions that the first record she ever bought was 'Please Please Me' and that she went to see the Beatles at Finsbury Park Astoria in 1963.

Once she was established as a model she sought to expand her career by becoming an actress. She and her manager, Justin De Villeneuve, thought that William Faulkner's *The Hanging Tree* would make a good film project for her and decided to approach the Beatles for backing. They met John and Paul in the cutting room of *Magical Mystery Tour.*

Twiggy said: "For me it was like meeting God. Paul was the one who was my hero; he was the one I'd stuck pictures of all over my desk at school and on my bedroom wall. At thirteen it was him I'd screamed my head off for at the Finsbury Park Astoria. I was so excited to be meeting him at last, but trying to be cool. And he was lovely, just as I'd imagined, and he was the one I became most friends with. The Beatles did like the film idea, but we never managed to get it together."

However, Paul suggested they contact Ken Russell, and Twiggy was later to star in his film of *The Boyfriend.*

Twiggy also wrote: "I've stayed good friends with Paul and Linda McCartney. When Linda first came over here she didn't know anyone, and I felt quite sorry for her and I'd take her shopping. We became quite close."

In 1967, Twiggy toured America on behalf of Yardley's cosmetics. The Master of Ceremonies on her tour was Terry Knight, whom Twiggy thought was a talented singer and guitarist. "When we came back to England, it was just the time when Paul McCartney was looking for someone to produce, and we'd earned a lot of money from the tour so we paid Terry's air fare for him and we thought to bring him over to Paul would be a nice break for him. But when he arrived here, imagine it, Paul and Linda had gone off to their Scottish hideaway and Paul had forgotten all about the meeting. So poor Terry had to wait around a few days, and then he had to get his flight back and that was the end of it." Terry became a multi-millionaire within two years. He took over management of Grand Funk Railroad and later sent Twiggy back the cheque for the air flight.

In 1968 there were plans for Twiggy to tour Russia and Granada Television intended making a documentary film of the trip. Unforunately it fell through. Twiggy wrote: "Paul actually wrote a song for that trip to Russia that didn't come off – and it was 'Back In The USSR' (cf), which went on the Beatles white album. Justin was in Mr Chow's with Paul one night having dinner, and he said, 'Hey, what about that song you were going to do for us when we were going to Russia?', and immediately Paul started singing it at the top of his voice."

Twiggy also mentioned the time she was watching *Opportunity Knocks* on television one night and noticed Mary Hopkin (cf) singing 'Turn Turn Turn'. Twiggy knew that Paul was looking for artists to promote. She wrote: ". . . it just happened that that weekend we went to see Paul at his Dad's house in Liverpool. He mentioned that he was looking for people to record and I said, 'Did you see that girl on *Opportunity Knocks?*' and Angie, his step-mum, said she'd seen it too, and we all hoped Mary would win or we wouldn't see her the next week. So we all sat down and wrote cards for her, with our names – we got about twenty people rallied together to vote for her. She won easily, Paul watched the show, agreed she was wonderful and rang her up immediately. She didn't believe it was him on the 'phone! But he sent a chauffeured car down to Wales for her, and then got together to make her name."

After making *The Boyfriend,* Twiggy sought further roles, and a film called *Gotta Sing, Gotta Dance* was planned. The name was inspired by the Gene Kelly song from *Singing in the Rain* and the story was to be set on a cruise liner in the thirties. But the film was never made. Paul wrote the

Paul wrote two numbers for Twiggy, neither of which she recorded

title song for the film, which he never actually recorded. However, as the film project had been abandoned Paul later used 'Gotta Sing, Gotta Dance' as the main dance spectacular in the *James Paul McCartney* TV special (cf).

TWO OF US See *On Our Way Home.*

TYPHOO TEA Famous brand of tea available in England. When John and Paul used to play truant and spend time in Paul's house during his father's absence, the two of them devised an ingenious 'smoke'. Since Paul's Dad didn't leave any tobacco lying around the house, they used his empty pipes and filled them up with Typhoo Tea, which they then proceeded to smoke.

UDO, SEIJURO Japanese promoter who organised the Wings tour of Japan in 1980, a task which had taken him over two years. When the tour had to be cancelled due to Paul's arrest on drugs charge, Udo accused Paul of betraying him, claiming that the cancellation had cost him £200,000. Paul compensated him for the full amount. (See also *Drugs.*)

ULLMAN, TRACEY Talented British actress who also forged a successful career for herself as a hit recording artist. Her versatility was first noticed by critics when she did comic character impersonations in the BBC TV series, *Three of a Kind.* She made her film debut in *Give My Regards to Broad Street* (cf (1)). Paul made a guest appearance in her video to promote her record 'They Don't Know', which reached No.2 in the British charts in October 1983. She said: "Hey, Paul, I've been in your film, now you be in mine." And he agreed. Commenting on her role in *Broad Street,* she says: "I have to cry right the way through the film and generally look dreadful. McCartney's character has to comfort me all the while and because he was a childhood hero of mine that was very nice."

UNCLE ALBERT/ADMIRAL HALSEY A track from *Ram,* complete with back-ing from the New York Philharmonic Orchestra. The number was also included on the *Wings Greatest* (cf) compilation and was used in the *James Paul McCartney* television special (cf). It was issued in America as a single on Apple 1837 on 2 August 1971, with 'Too Many People' as the flip. It reached the No.1 position for a week and earned Paul a Grammy award for Best Arrangement/ Accompanying Vocalist. The single was re-released in the States on 4 December 1980 in the series Columbia Hall of Fame 13-33408, with 'Jet' (cf) as the flip. The song was inspired by one of Paul's late uncles who had a reputation for hitting the bottle – and also being a bible puncher!

UNESCO The United Nations Education and Cultural Organisation promoted a World Week for Venice in 1976 to focus global attention on the plight of the historic city and to raise funds for its restoration (it had been badly damaged by subsidence). UNESCO wanted a major name, someone who would appeal to all ages to highlight the week, during the course of which such international celebrities as Peter Ustinov, Ravi Shankar and Mort Shulman were also performing. They chose Wings. Mr Leon Davisco, the publicity director of UNESCO said: "We wanted a group which was not only one of the most important in the world, but an act that would appeal to people of all ages. I think Wings are a very good group, and when we approached Paul McCartney we were delighted when he agreed to perform." (See also *Piazza San Marco.*)

UNRELEASED SONGS 'My Carnival', issued as the flip of 'Spies Like Us' (cf) in 1986, on Parlophone R6118, was an example of a recorded Paul McCartney number that remained unissued for many years, in this case eleven. Apart from those tracks earmarked for *Cold Cuts* (cf), an album project and possible vehicle for many of the unreleased recordings, Paul has recorded several other numbers that have never been released. 'I Lost My Little Girl' was recorded as far back as 1962 (and a second version followed in

1964). Also in 1962 Paul sang on the track 'Keep Looking That Way' and recorded 'I'll Be On My Way' at another studio session. Demonstration discs made by Paul for other artists include 'I'll Keep You Satisfied' and 'It's For You' in 1963, 'Woman' in 1964, 'Step Inside Love' and 'Goodbye' in 1968 and 'Penina' in 1970. Songs recorded for Beatles albums, but not used include: 'I Forgot To Remember To Forget' and 'Lucille' in 1962 for *Please Please Me;* 'Leave My Kitten Alone' and 'Always And Only' for *Beatles For Sale;* 'If You've Got Troubles' in 1965 for *Rubber Soul;* 'Annie' in 1967 for *Sgt Pepper.* Although Paul sang 'Gotta Sing, Gotta Dance', the number he wrote for Twiggy (cf), on the *James Paul McCartney* (cf) TV show, it has never been issued on record.

VAL Surname unknown. In a 1964 interview, Paul's brother Mike said that Val was the first girl that Paul ever liked. He was at a tender age at the time and began to notice Val on the school bus, staring at her long hair. "Then one night word came along the grapevine that Val liked him," said Mike. "You should have seen the way he went on! He was completely knocked out! He took Val out once or twice — to the cinema, visiting friends, that sort of thing. Then the whole affair suddenly fizzled out."

VAUGHAN, IVAN A boy from the Woolton area of Liverpool. He lived in Vale Street, along with Peter Shotton and Nigel Whalley and the three of them became part of a small gang, together with John Lennon who lived close by. When he was six years old, Ivan went to Dovedale Primary School, as did John; in 1952 he moved to the Liverpool Institute (cf) where he was in the same class as Paul. Ivan played tea-chest bass occasionally in the Quarrymen, alternating with Len Garry. One day he asked Paul if he'd like to come along and watch the group at a church fête. Paul wasn't particularly struck on the idea, but Ivan said that it would be a great place to pick up girls, so Paul cycled along to the event that afternoon. The date was 6 July 1957 and when Paul arrived at St Peter's Church Garden Fête, Ivan took him into the Church Hall and introduced him to John. (See also *'Twenty Flight Rock'.)*

Ivan kept in touch with his friends, particularly Paul, over the succeeding years. He became a teacher and studied Education Psychiatry. When Apple was launched, the Beatles suggested that Ivan and his schoolteacher wife head the Apple School. Ivan was given an advance payment of £10,000 but it was decided that the idea was premature and the scheme was dropped. Ivan's wife helped Paul with the French section of 'Michelle' (cf).

Tragically, during the seventies, Ivan contracted a horrific ailment, Parkinson's Disease, for which there is no known cure. Ivan refused to accept the situation, bravely battling against the disease by using himself as a guinea pig for new drugs, mercilessly knocking his limbs against solid objects when they refused to respond. Jonathan Miller heard of his remarkable and courageous struggle and produced a documentary, simply called *Ivan,* which was transmitted on BBC 2 TV on 3 December 1984 as part of the *Horizon* series. Paul had granted the use of his song 'Blackbird' to be played at the beginning and end of the programme, free of charge, and an associate commented: "Paul was devastated by what has happened to Ivan. They have known each other since they were kids. Ivan was the lad who introduced Paul to John. He used to play tea-chest bass in John's skiffle group the Quarrymen. He went to America with them in the sixties." Paul invited Ivan to spend Christmas 1984 with the McCartney's at their home in Sussex.

Of the documentary, which centred on a day in his life, Ivan commented: "I decided to make my illness my hobby. Not as something useful. Not to help thousands. Just selfishly, to find out all I could about it and its implications. I wanted to explore it, to play with it, and even to laugh about it."

VEGETABLES Track on the Beach Boys album *Smile Smile,* issued on 18

September 1967 in the US and in Britain on 20 November. Paul had dropped in on a Beach Boys recording session on 10 April of that year and was invited to participate the next day. He produced the band performing the number 'Vegetables'. He also played bass guitar on 'On Top Of Old Smokey', but this track was never released.

VEGETARIANISM Paul first became a vegetarian following an incident at his farm in Scotland. The family was sitting down to a Sunday dinner of roast lamb when Paul looked out of the window and spotted a small lamb outside. "It really brought it home that we could probably do without this" he said. "Linda is a crazy animal lover, we have lots of pets, and as a kid I used to run around with my Observer book of birds in my pocket.

"So from then on we stuck to eating things where nothing had to loose a life. One Christmas, Linda even managed to make a kind of macaroni turkey: you could cut it into slices just like the real thing.

"I know it sounds a bit corny, but we really value being vegetarians, and it doesn't seem too daft because our place is a nut house anyway!"

George Harrison is also a vegetarian.

VENUS AND MARS The title is supposed to refer to how people relate to star signs, but critics assumed it referred to Paul and Linda. The album was the first McCartney LP to carry the MPL (cf) logo and was the first re-

Critics assumed the title referred to Paul and Linda's relationship

corded product by an ex-Beatle not to be issued on Apple. It was released in Britain on Capitol PCTC 254 on 30 May 1975 and reached the No.1 position in the charts. In America it came out on Capitol SMAS 11419 on 27 May 1975, and, also reached the No.1 spot.

Some tracks were recorded at Abbey Road Studios with Geoff Britton (cf) on drums, namely — 'Love In Song', 'Letting Go' and 'Medicine Jar'. The band then flew separately to New Orleans, moved into the Latin Quarter and recorded further tracks at the Sea Saint Studios. Geoff had been feeling that both Denny Laine (cf) and Jimmy McCulloch (cf) had been voicing their dislike of him to Paul. His fears seem to have been borne out, as Paul and Linda came to his room and told him he was no longer a member of the group. He was to comment, in a interview with Chris Welch (cf): "When I first joined I was promised royalities and we talked in telephone numbers. Then it became session fees and bonuses. But it was a waste to have let such a golden opportunity become such a bad experience. Maybe I should have given Jimmy McCulloch and Denny Laine the pasting they both deserved. Maybe Jimmy wouldn't be dead now and we'd all still be in Wings." He was replaced by Joe English (cf) and the sessions, which spread from January to April, moved on to the Wally Heider Studios in Los Angeles. When the album was completed there was a celebratory party held on the *Queen Mary* in Long Beach Harbour with guests who included Michael Jackson (cf), Joni Mitchell, Bob Dylan, Cher, Tatum O'Neil, Davy Jones and George Harrison.

The tracks on the album were: 'Venus And Mars'; 'Rock Show'; 'Love In Song'; 'You Gave Me The Answer'; 'Magneto And Titanium Man'; 'Letting Go'; 'Venus And Mars Reprise'; 'Spirits Of Ancient Egypt'; 'Medicine Jar'; 'Call Me Back Again'; 'Listen To What The Man Said'; 'Treat Her Gently'; 'Lonely Old People' and 'Crossroads Theme'.

VERMOUTH, APOLLO C Paul's pseudonym for 'I'm The Urban Space-

man' which he produced for the Bonzo Dog Doo Dah Band (cf) in March 1968. The single was issued in Britain on Liberty in October and in America on Imperial in December. The song was penned by Neil Innes and when the track was included on the album *Urban Spaceman* the following year, Paul was credited by his real name.

VIDEO VIEWER British video magazine which featured Paul on the cover of its January 1983 issue. An "exclusive interview" was trailered on the cover, but the two-page article by Patrick Newley is basically a piece about the history of the Beatles with reviews of *The Complete Beatles* and *Rockshow (cf)*. There are four brief quotes from Paul, the lengthiest taken from the October 1982 issue of *Woman's Own* magazine.

VIRGIN ISLANDS Group of islands in the West Indies where the second set of sessions for *London Town* (cf) were recorded, on a yacht. Denny Laine (cf) had the idea after seeing Rod Stewart record on a yacht moored off the California coast. Paul chartered the *Fair Carol*, and engaged the engineers from Record Plant, who'd arranged the Stewart sessions, to convert her into a floating recording studio complete with a 24-track machine. Accommodation for the twenty-strong party was provided on the *El Toro*, where Paul, Linda and family stayed, and on the *Samala* and the *Wanderlust*, where Wings, their families and the recording crew stayed. Other bits of necessary equipment were also stowed on these boats. All four yachts were moored in a bay off the island of St John's (cf).

The sessions lasted from 1-31 May, during which time nine tracks were recorded, seven of which were used on the album. Work tended to start at nightfall, as there were naturally too many distractions during the day — sunbathing, swimming and sightseeing! Everybody had a wonderful time, but as Paul was later to tell Rosie Horide of *Beatles Monthly*, there were problems. "The Virgin Islands were really great. The thing was that it's a big problem getting a studio on a

An 'exclusive interview' that could only boast four quotes from Paul

boat like that just for a whim. Okay, it's a great idea – and a lot of people would like to record on a boat, I'm sure. But the great problem was that we might get out there and find that the salt water had gone for the machines or that the machines just didn't work."

VOORMAN, KLAUS Son of a Berlin doctor who, in 1960, drifted into the Kaiser Keller club in Hamburg after hearing an exciting sound. The group on stage was Rory Storm and the Hurricanes, but Klaus was more impressed with the next band to appear – the Beatles. He then brought his girlfriend Astrid Kirchherr and fellow student Jurgen Vollmer to see the group. Klaus became a very close friend of the Beatles and, like Paul, decided to take up playing the bass guitar. He moved to England and formed a band with two Liverpool musicians: Paddy Chambers, former member of Faron's Flamingos and the Big Three, and Gibson Kemp, who'd replaced Ringo Starr in the Hurricanes and later married Klaus' former girlfriend Astrid. The group was called Paddy, Klaus & Gibson and they were initially managed by Tony Stratton-Smith, then by Brian Epstein.

Klaus designed the cover of the *Revolver* album, for which he won a Grammy, and married actress Christine Hargreaves who was then a regular in the soap opera *Coronation Street* (cf). He joined Manfred Mann and over the years became associated with the individual members of the Beatles on various recording projects, including the Plastic Ono Band, with whom he appeared in Toronto, Canada, in 1969.

When Paul instigated the legal action that heralded the end of the Beatles as a business partnership, John and George considered replacing Paul with Klaus. The *Daily Mirror* ran a story by Don Short on 20 March 1971 headlined "The New Beatles" in which the subheading read: "John, George, Ringo. . . Now Comes Klaus." An Apple spokesman commented: "Paul refuses to return to the group, so what are they to do?" The name they were to adopt was said to be the Ladders.

The group never came into existence. Klaus recorded sessions for solo projects with John, George and Ringo and in the eighties returned to live in Hamburg where he became a recording manager for PolyGram.

WALDORF, STEVEN Young assistant film-maker who was ambushed by police in London in January 1983. He'd been mistaken for a wanted gunman and was shot five times. Whilst recovering at St Stephen's Hospital, Fulham, he received a bouquet of flowers and the message: "We are thinking of you and we send all our love. Linda and Paul McCartney." Stephen commented: "I did a video for Paul McCartney some time ago and we've remained friends through work."

WALKING IN THE PARK WITH ELOISE Number originally written by Paul's father James in the early fifties. While Wings were recording in Nashville during June and July 1974, Chet Atkins, who was working on the sessions, suggested that Paul record it. It was issued on EMI 2220 on 18 October 1974 with 'Bridge Over The River

Peter and Gordon: they recorded 'Woman' by a certain 'Bernard Webb'

Suite' as the flip. When Paul made his appearance on *Desert Island Discs* (cf) he said that the record was one of his all-time favourites, so EMI re-released it on 3 March 1982.

WALKING MAN 1974 James Taylor album, issued by Warners. Paul provided backing vocals on the tracks 'Rock'n'Roll Is Music Now' and 'Let It All Fall Down'.

WALLY HEIDER STUDIOS Recording studios in Los Angeles where part of *Venus and Mars* was recorded. Other tracks had already been recorded at several other studios in London, New Orleans and Nashville.

WALTON HOSPITAL Situated at 107 Rice Lane, Liverpool 9. Paul was born here on June 18 1942 in a private ward, the first child of Mary and James McCartney (cf). Paul's mother had once been a nursing sister in the hospital's maternity unit.

WATERFALLS Name of Paul's Kent residence. It is also the title of a track that first appeared on *McCartney II* (cf) in May 1980. It was then issued as a single, in Britain on 14 June on Parlophone R6037 where it went to No.7 in the charts, and in America on 22 July on Columbia 1-11335 where it struggled to reach No.106. The picture sleeve on both sides of the Atlantic was a painting of a waterfall by Christian Broutin, the back cover featuring a photograph of Paul by Linda. The flipside of the single was 'Check My Machine'.

WATER WINGS Working title for the album that became *London Town* (cf), which was partly recorded on board a yacht.

WEBB, BERNARD Pseudonym used by Paul when he wrote the number 'Woman' (cf(1)) for Peter & Gordon. Bernard Webb was credited as songwriter on the actual record, but when it entered the charts, a few weeks later, eventually reaching No.21, Paul, admitted that he'd written it but wanted to see if he could enter the charts without using the magical Lennon & McCartney name. Webb was said to be an aspiring songwriter and a student in Paris. Paul also used the pseudonym A. Smith in connection with the single.

WEBB, PETER Director of *Give My Regards to Broad Street (cf(1))*. David Puttnam suggested to Paul that he should contact Peter, who had only previously directed television commercials. Commenting on *Broad Street*, Peter said: "I liked the Runyonesque feel and it's irony, which I understand. It's a totally imaginary story. What I've attempted to do is to make a film that is as original as the music within it, and as inventive. There's a mystical element in McCartney's music. The movie has a dreamlike quality. It's strength is its simplicity."

Webb had won several awards for his television commercials, which included ones for John Courage Ale, Ovaltine and Hovis. The Yorkshire-born director said: "I had worked with Paul six months earlier on a different project, and I knew that there wouldn't be any problem. Paul has a good visual sense and a quick grasp of cinematic construction. There is none of that star stuff about him; he respects professionalism. We never had any real arguments, but there were naturally some disagreements. I lost some and I won some as you would with anyone. Musically, I relied on him heavily, but even there he was flexible. One song we were doing fell a little short of what we wanted dramatically, and I told him. He went home that weekend and wrote me another chorus."

WE CAN WORK IT OUT It has been suggested that Jane Asher (cf) was once again Paul's inspiration when he wrote this song. And John once again helped him with the song's middle section. The number had the distinction of being the Beatles very first double 'A' side, with 'Day Tripper', and was issued in Britain on 3 December 1965 on Parlophone R5389, leaping straight to the top of the charts. In America it came out on 6 December 1965, where it sold a million and also topped the charts. It was included on *A Collection of Oldies (But Goldies), The Beatles 1962-1966, The Beatles Box, 20 Greatest Hits* and the American album *Yesterday And Today*. This is also a number which has been recorded by dozens of different artists, including Dionne Warwick, George Burns, Petula Clark, Deep Purple, Humble Pie, Johnny Mathis, Melanie, Johnny Nash, Sam & Dave and Caterine Valente. Stevie Wonder had the most successful version in 1971, when his single reached No.9 in the States and No.22 in Britain. The Beatles performed the song on their British tour in 1965.

WEE WILLIE HARRIS British rock-'n'roll performer of the late sixties. Paul liked the madcap singer, and in a *Sunday Times* interview, during which he discussed autograph hunters, mentioned how he had sought Willie's autograph. "I don't think fans are humbling themselves, I queued up at the Liverpool Empire for Wee Willie Harris's autograph. I wanted to do it. I don't think I was stupid."

WEISSMAN, MITCH American actor/singer who bore a marked resemblance to Paul and portrayed him in both stage and film versions of *Beatlemania*, which had originally opened on Broadway before going on the road to countries such as Japan and South America. Mitch had previously been a graphic artist at an advertising agency in New York before he took the part of Paul for a five-year period. The other actors who portrayed Paul during *Beatlemania's* long run included Joey Curatolo, Lenie Colacino, Tony Kishman, Don Linares and Alan LeBoeuf.

WELCH, CHRIS Author of *Paul McCartney: The Definitive Biography* (cf). Chris worked on *Melody Maker* for many years before turning freelance and concentrating on writing books about the music scene. "I think I would have enjoyed (the book) more if I could have been able to deal directly with Paul," Chris told me, "but the messages I kept getting back were – he didn't like books about

himself. I'm sure he'll write his own one day." During his time with *Melody Maker,* Chris interviewed Paul on a number of occasions and travelled on the coach with Wings to Bristol, Bath and Manchester during their 1976 tour. He also interviewed Paul at Abbey Road studios during the recording of *Back to the Egg* (cf), and Paul, Linda and family came to see him at the *MM* offices for a further interview.

WE LOVE YOU Single by the Rolling Stones that was issued in Britain on Decca F12654 on 18 August 1967, and in America on London 905 ten days later. Paul and John provide backing vocals.

WE'RE ALL PAUL BEARERS Another American 'Paul Is Dead' (cf) novelty disc issued in 1969 on Viking 1004 by Zacharias and the Tree People. It featured 'We're All Paul Bearers Pt II' on the flip. (See also *Brother Paul* and *Saint Paul*.)

WHAT DO WE REALLY KNOW? Number from Mike McCartney's 1974 album *McGear* which was produced by Paul. Paul also wrote it and can be heard singing alongside Mike.

WHAT LITTLE OLD MAN? Title Paul originally suggested for the Beatles' film. This was in reference to the Wilfred Brambell character, John McCartney, Paul's screen grandfather, who was referred to in an early sentence in the film as "What little old man?" The group settled on *A Hard Day's Night.*

WHAT'S THAT YOU'RE DOING Song Paul co-wrote with Stevie Wonder (cf). It took place during the recording sessions for the 1982 *Tug of War* (cf) album and was included on it; Stevie was one of the artists who'd agreed to contribute backing vocals. They wrote the song during a joint jam session. Stevie and Paul both sang lead vocals on the finished version, which was over six minutes long.

WHEN I'M SIXTY FOUR It's been said that Paul first began writing this num-

'When I'm Sixty-Four', completed in 1966, has remained one of the most popular Beatles songs with other artists

ber when he was sixteen. He is said to have completed it in 1966, as a tribute to his Dad who reached sixty-four in July of that year. The number was recorded in December and was issued on *Sgt Pepper* in 1967. It proved to be quite a popular singalong number and has been recorded by over forty different artists including Keith Moon, Kenny Ball & His Jazzmen, Bernard Cribbins, Georgie Fame and Frankie Howerd.

WHERE DID THE RINGO? This was the title suggested by Paul for the Beatles' second film, until they decided on *Help!*

WHY DON'T WE DO IT IN THE ROAD? Song written by Paul and included on *The Beatles* white album. Paul is the sole musician on the track, playing every instrument himself, including guitar, piano, bass and drums. He is also the vocalist and some passages have been double-tracked.

WILD HONEY PIE John, George and Ringo weren't around when Paul re-corded this brief number at Abbey Road studios on 20 August 1968. Paul sang, played guitar and bass drum and also double-tracked; at only 53 seconds in length, it is the shortest cut on *The Beatles* white album. Paul had originally penned the song in India but had never really intended record-ing it. However, both Jane Asher (cf) and Patti Harrison liked it and encour-aged him to record it. He commented: "This was just a fragment of an instru-mental which we weren't sure about, but Patti liked it very much so we decided to leave it on the album."

WILD LIFE First Wings album. It was issued in Britain on Apple PCS 7142 on 3 December 1971 where it reached the position of No. 11 in the charts. In America it came out on Apple SW 3386 on 7 December, reached No. 10 in the charts and achieved Gold Disc status. Paul had written the material for the album with Linda, then de-cided to form a group that they could take on the road and selected Denny Laine and Denny Seiwell as the basis of the four-piece Wings. The entire album was recorded in the studios in a three-day period during August 1971, which left the group open to criticism for the haste in which it was recorded. The only song which Paul and Linda didn't pen was 'Love Is Strange', which had provided the Everly Brothers with a hit in 1965. The tracks on the album were 'Mumbo', 'Bip Bop', 'Love Is Strange', 'Wild Life', 'Some People Never Know', 'I Am Your Singer', 'Tomorrow' and 'Dear Friend'.

WILD PRAIRIE MAID Number recorded by Linda McCartney and Wings during a session in Paris in 1974; they used the pseudonym Suzi and the Red Stripes again (see *Seaside Woman*). The song remains unreleased.

WILLIAMS, ANGELA Widow who, in 1964, married Paul's father Jim. Jim proposed on the couple's third meeting and Angela was initially hesitant as she had a five-year-old daughter, Ruth (see *McCartney, Ruth),* and Jim was more than twenty years her senior. After their marriage they lived in Rembrandt (cf), the house on the Wirral which Paul had bought. Following Jim's death, Angie attempted to make a living for herself by setting up a pop group agency in Liverpool, but Paul was angry at her use of the family name. In 1981 she moved south with her daughter and reverted to the surname Williams.

That same year she told her 'story' in a series of articles ghosted by Tony Barrow, the Beatles former PR. The articles appeared in the *Sun* and were highly critical of Paul and his attitude towards her, causing further estrangement between them.

WINCHELL, WALTER American columnist, writer of one of the most widely read syndicated columns in America. In 1964 he printed an erroneous story claiming that Paul and Jane Asher had married in secret. He had to print a retraction.

WINGS After leaving the Beatles, Paul toyed with the idea of forming his own group; the dream took substance on 3 August 1971 when Wings was officially formed with Paul, Linda on keyboards, Denny Seiwell (cf) on drums and Denny Laine (cf) on guitar. It was said that Paul came up with the name while praying for the safe birth of his forthcoming child, Stella, who was born in September of that year. His thoughts bent on the baby, he thought of the phrase 'Wings of an angel' and decided to call the band Wings. The group's first album *Wild Life* (cf) was issued on 15 November 1971, and they played their first gig together at Nottingham University on 9 February 1972 at the start of a short British University tour.

The first Wings single was the controversial 'Give Ireland Back To The Irish' (cf), issued on 19 February, followed by 'Mary Had A Little Lamb' (cf) on 6 May. The group were now five strong as guitarist Henry McCullough (cf) had joined them in January and they began a European tour on 9 July. 'Hi Hi Hi' (cf) was their next single, issued on 2 December, another controversial record and banned by the BBC.

In 1973 they issued 'My Love' (cf) on 24 March, followed by their second album *Red Rose Speedway* (cf). The group became part of the James Bond story when they recorded 'Live And Let Die' (cf), the title song of the new James Bond movie, which they issued on 1 June. Paul had made plans for Wings to fly to Nigeria to record *Band on the Run* (cf) in Lagos. Shortly before they were due to leave, Henry McCullough left the band on 25 August and Denny Seiwell followed on 30 August, the day they were flying out. Despite the setbacks, Paul, Linda and Denny Laine went to Lagos. On 20 October the single 'Helen Wheels' (cf) was issued and *Band on the Run* came out on 30 November.

1974 began with the release of 'Jet' on 8 February; guitarist Jimmy McCulloch (cf) and drummer Geoff Britton (cf) joined in the spring, and the group began recording in Nashville. The 'Band On The Run' single was issued on 28 June and 'Junior's Farm' (cf) on 25 October.

On 30 May 1975 *Venus and Mars* was issued. By this time, Joe English (cf) had replaced Britton as drummer with the band. This line-up began a

Ex-Beatle spreads new Wings

world tour which commenced at the Gaumont, Southampton, and continued late into the following year.

Wings at the Speed of Sound (cf) was issued on 26 March 1976, shortly before the American leg of their tour which began at Fort Worth on 3 May. 'Silly Love Songs' was issued on 30 April, followed by 'Let 'Em In' (cf) on 23 July. The first Wings' live album, which was also a triple, *Wings Over America* (cf), was issued on 10 December, the tour having finished with three concerts at the Empire Pool, Wembley.

1977 saw the release of a later version of 'Maybe I'm Amazed' (cf) on 4 February, and their biggest-selling single 'Mull Of Kintyre' on 11 November. Jimmy McCulloch left the group in September; they continued as a four-piece until Joe English departed in December; then they were three. In 1978 year they released the singles 'With A Little Luck' (cf) on 23 March, 'I've Had Enough' (cf) on 16 June and 'London Town' on 15 September and the albums *London Town* (cf) on 31 March and *Wings Greatest* (cf) on 1 December.

Their 23 March 1979 single 'Goodnight Tonight' introduced the new members of the band – guitarist Laurence Juber (cf) and drummer Steve Holly (cf). Their other releases that year were 'Old Siam Sir' on 1 June, *Back to the Egg* (cf) on 8 June and 'Getting Closer' (cf) on 10 August, the latter proving to be Wings' last single release. The group's planned tour of Japan in January 1980 was cancelled because of Paul's drug bust (see *Drugs)*, and Denny Laine left the band in April complaining they weren't touring. Paul commented: "He just decided he wanted to go his own way, saying he wanted to go on tour." Wings was more or less finished as a band. With John Lennon's murder, Paul no longer felt like going on tour and he was to say: "I hate the pressures of a group. With so many changes in the line up it distracted from the music. I got bored with the whole thing."

WINGS AT THE SPEED OF SOUND First issued in 1976, in Britain on Parlophone PAS 10010 on 26 March and in America on 25 March on Capitol SW 11525. It got to No. 1 in both the UK and US charts. Tracks on the album were: 'Let 'Em In', 'The Note You Never Wrote', 'She's My Baby', 'Beware My Love', 'Wino Junko', 'Silly Love Songs', 'Cook Of The House', 'Time To Hide', 'Must Do Something About It', 'San Ferry Anne' and 'Warm And Beautiful'. Each member of Wings was given the opportunity to take lead vocals: Denny Laine was lead vocalist on 'The Note You Never Wrote' and 'Time To Hide', Jimmy McCulloch sang his own composition 'Wino Junko', Linda sang 'Cook Of The House' and Joe English was lead vocalist on 'Must Do Something About It'.

WINGS FUN CLUB Fan club which was launched in the early seventies and continues today despite the demise of the group Wings. For the enrolment fee (£4 in 1986), a member receives an introductory package, including a membership card, a set of postcards, two posters, some back issues of *Club Sandwich* and a year's subscription to the magazine. There are also numerous club offers available to members, including a range of merchandise such as books, track suits, calendars, photographs, sheet music, magazines and T-shirts. The address is: Wings Fun Club, PO Box 4UP, London W1 4UP.

WINGS GREATEST Album compilation released during a period when Wings was undergoing personnel changes, which were to bring in two new members, Laurence Juber (cf) and Steve Holly (cf). It was issued in Britain on Parlophone PCTC 256 on 1 December 1978, reaching No.3 in the charts, and in America on Capitol SOO 11905 on 22 November 1978, where it only reached the position of No.29. The art-deco figurine on the album cover belonged to Linda and was flown to Switzerland where it was photographed amid the snow by photographer Angus Forbes. The figure was also used on a poster included with the album and is seen on the mantelpiece on the sleeve of *Back to the Egg (cf).* The 12 tracks on *Wings*

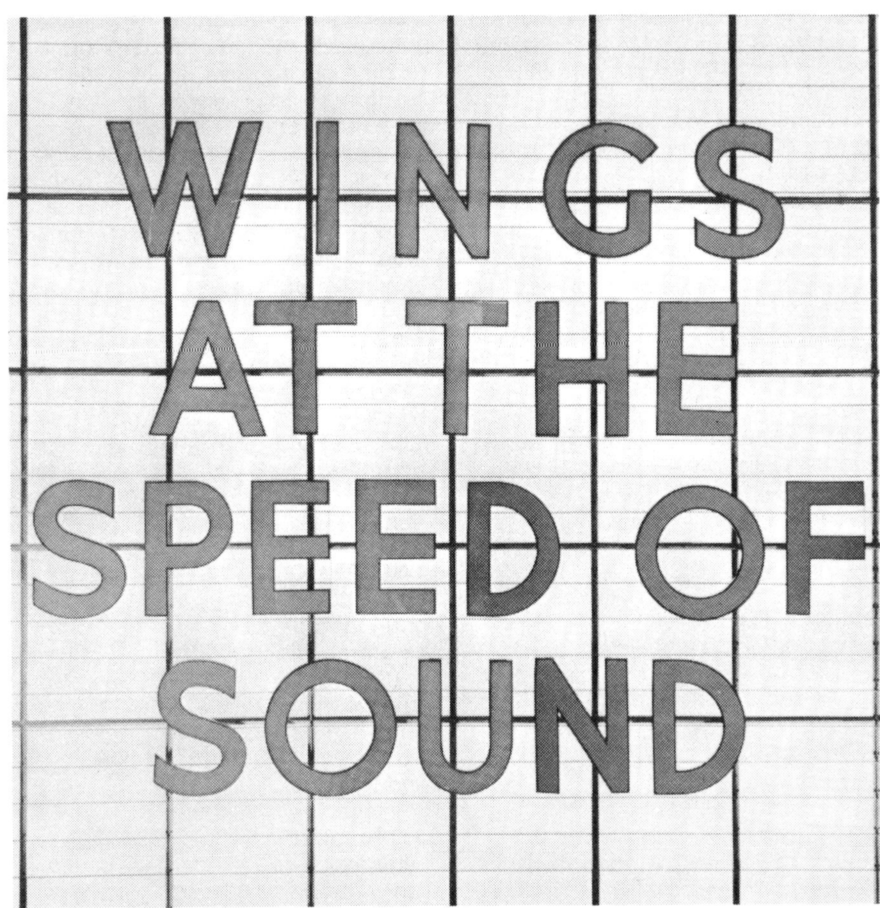

Paul shared out lead vocals to other members of the band on this 1976 album

Greatest were not all strictly from Wings releases as some had been taken from Paul's solo projects. The tracks were: 'Another Day', 'Silly Love Songs', 'Live And Let Die', 'Junior's Farm', 'With A Little Luck', 'Band On The Run', 'Uncle Albert/Admiral Halsey', 'Hi Hi Hi', 'Let 'Em In', 'My Love', 'Jet' and 'Mull Of Kintyre'.

WINGS JAPAN TOUR 1980 Japanese tour programme for the tour which never took place. The fifty-two page publication was packed with full colour photographs.

WINGS OVER AMERICA Thirty-track triple album of numbers recorded during the American tour of 1976. Issued in Britain on Parlophone PCSP 720 on 10 December 1976 it reached No.8 in the charts. It was issued in America the next day, on Capitol SWCO 11593 and reached No.1. The tracks were: 'Venus and Mars'; 'Rock Show'; 'Let Me Roll It'; 'Spirits of Ancient Egypt'; 'Medicine Jar'; 'Maybe I'm Amazed'; 'Call Me Back'; 'Lady Madonna'; 'The Long and Winding Road'; 'Live And Let Die'; 'Picasso's Last Words'; 'Richard Cory'; 'Bluebird'; 'I've Just Seen A Face'; 'Blackbird'; 'Yesterday'; 'You Gave Me The Answer'; 'Magneto And Titanium Man'; 'Go Now'; 'My Love'; 'Listen To What The Man Said'; 'Let 'Em In'; 'Time To Hide'; 'Silly Love Songs'; 'Beware My Love'; 'Letting Go'; 'Band On The Run'; 'Hi Hi Hi' and 'Soily'.

WINGS OVER ATLANTA Bootleg album issued in the States in 1978 on

Melvin Records (MM03). It contains nine numbers from Wings' second show at the Omni, Atlanta, on 19 May 1976.

WINGS OVER MERSEYSIDE Eight-page supplement in *Liverpool Echo* in November 1979 to celebrate Wings' appearance in Liverpool at the Royal Court Theatre (cf).

WINGS OVER SWITZERLAND: LIVE IN MONTREAUX 1972 Bootleg double-album of the appearance at Montreaux on 22 July 1972. It features twenty numbers: 'Bip Bop'; 'Smile Away'; 'Mumbo'; 'Give Ireland Back To The Irish'; '1882'; 'I Would Only Smile'; 'Blue Moon Of Kentucky'; 'The Mess'; 'Best Friend'; 'Soily'; 'I Am Your Singer'; 'Say You Don't Mind'; 'Henry

Blues'; 'Seaside Woman'; 'Wild Life'; 'My Love'; 'Mary Had A Little Lamb'; 'Maybe I'm Amazed'; 'Hi Hi Hi' and 'Long Tall Sally'.

WINGS OVER THE WORLD A 90-minute TV film of Wings' 1976 tour made by Jack Priestley, who also worked on *The Last Waltz*. It included interviews with the McCartney family at home, and scenes from Scotland, Australia and America. Subtitled *Paul McCartney Sings His Greatest Hits*, it included the numbers 'The Long And Winding Road'; 'Yesterday', 'Maybe I'm Amazed'; 'Silly Love Songs'; 'Let 'Em In'; 'Band On The Run' and 'Live And Let Die'. It was originally screened in America as a CBS TV special at 11.30pm on 16 March 1978 and repeated on 6 April 1979. A shorter

Linda's art-deco statuette was flown to Switzerland specially for this cover pic

Triple album of Wings' huge American tour

version, at 75 minutes, was screened in Britain on BBC2 on Sunday 8 April 1978.

WINGS PIN-UP AND STORY POSTER British poster magazine, published in the spring of 1977, which features eight large colour photographs of the group and a large centre-page poster of Wings, taken in 1975. There is also a colour pic of Paul on stage from 1973, a series of black-and-white shots and a full-page article.

WINGS STAR MONTHLY British colour magazine for Wings fans, published in the late seventies.

WITH A LITTLE HELP FROM MY FRIENDS Paul wrote this in March 1967 in his Cavendish Avenue work-room and received a bit of help from John with the lyrics. He'd used the working title 'Bad Finger Boogie' and was later to suggest Badfinger as a name for the Iveys. The song was included on *Sgt Pepper* and lead vocals were sung by Ringo. Paul commented: "Ringo's got a great sentimental thing. He likes soul music and always has, though we didn't see that scene for a long while 'til he showed us. I suppose that's why we write those sort of songs for him, with sentimental things in them, like 'With A Little Help From My Friends'." Joe Cocker was to have a No.1 hit with the song in 1968; Young Idea had only reached No.29 in the charts with their version in July 1967. The number was included on *The Beatles 1966-1970* album and Ringo sang it on his *Ringo*

TV special in 1978. There have been approximately one hundred cover versions by a variety of artists including Barbra Streisand, Count Basie, Peter Frampton, Herb Alpert and Ike & Tina Turner.

WITH A LITTLE LUCK A song which Paul wrote in Scotland, originally began recording during a Wings trip to the Virgin Islands in 1977, and completed at a recording session in London. It was first issued in America on Capitol 4559 on 20 March 1978 and rose to the No.1 position. It didn't fare so spectacularly in Britain when it was issued on Parlophone R6019 on 23 March, although it climbed to the No.7 position. The flipside in both Britain and America was 'Backwards Traveller/Cuff Link'. The number was also featured on *London Town* (cf), released later the same month, and on *Wings Greatest (cf),* issued on 1 December 1978.

WOMEN AND PHOTOGRAPHY Exhibition sponsored by Nikon, which opened in Zurich, Switzerland on 30 August 1980. The show, which ran until 9 October, featured the work of thirty-one female photographers. Linda's contributions included her shots of Paul from the filming of 'Coming Up'.

WOMAN (1) Number which Paul wrote for Peter & Gordon. It was the 'A' side of their single, issued in America in January 1966, and in Britain the following month. The flipside was 'Wrong From The Start'. The number was also the first track on the duo's album of the same name, issued in March of that year. Paul used the pseudonym Bernard Webb (cf) when he wrote the song because he was interested to see if a number of his could be successful without using the McCartney name. 'Woman' reached No.14 in the American charts and No.18 in Britain.

WOMAN (2) Sixteen-track album by Paul's brother Mike. It was issued in Britain on Island ILPS 9191 on 21 April 1972. Mike produced it himself and co-wrote most of the songs with Ro-

ger McGough. The cover of the album features a photograph of Mary McCartney (cf), Paul's and Mike's mother.

WONDER, STEVIE I was with the Beatles when they heard Stevie Wonder for the first time in 1963. It was at the Orrell Park Ballroom in Liverpool after an Undertakers gig, and John Schroeder, who released Tamla Motown records in Britain on the Oriole American label, played us Little Stevie Wonder's 'Fingertips' over the PA system.

On the backcover of Paul's *Red Rose Speedway (cf)* album is the braille message to Stevie: "We love you."

When Paul gathered together some famous guests artists to record on the island of Montserrat (cf), Stevie accepted his invitation to record 'Ebony & Ivory' (cf). Paul had wanted to do the number with a black artist and Stevie was his first choice. They recorded the song the day after Stevie arrived on the island with Paul playing piano and bass, Stevie on drums and synthesiser, and both of them sharing

Stevie Wonder, Paul's first choice for 'Ebony & Ivory'

the vocals. Paul was to say: "I'm a hero for life with the locals for taking Stevie to the island. They were quite interested in me, but not very excited. But Stevie Wonder! It was pandemonium. He is like a god to them." As a thank-you to Paul, Stevie penned a song about the island.

Stevie was born blind at birth in Saginaw, Michigan, on 13 May 1950. He was twelve years old when he signed with Motown and his single 'Fingertips' topped the US charts. Over the years he has become one of the most respected musicians in the world and has had numerous hit records.

WONDERFUL CHRISTMASTIME Christmas single, originally recorded in July 1969, issued in Britain on Parlophone R6029 on 16 November 1979 and in America on Columbia 1-11162 on 20 November. It failed to make a dent in the American charts, although it reached the position of No.7 in Britain. The flipside was Paul's interpretation of the famous Christmas song, 'Rudolph The Red-Nosed Reindeer' and was recorded by him in 1976. Paul performed the number on stage during the Wings British tour of 1979 when artificial snow added to the effect. Imprinted on the record itself are two messages. On 'Wonderful Christmastime' there are the words: "To lift a glass . . . Xmas '79"; and on the flip: "Love from Rudi! Xmas '79."

WOOD, RAYMOND A film double for Paul, who appeared in the 'Pipes Of Peace' video and *Broad Street*. In 1984, following the announcement that Paul's blood test proved that he was not Bettina Hueber's (cf) father, her mother Erika claimed that a double had stood in for the blood test. Raymond commented: "I have not been involved in any funny business about a blood test."

WRIGHT, MAGGIE Actress who played Maggie The Lovely Starlet, Paul's girlfriend in *Magical Mystery Tour*.

YOUNG PRINTER OF THE YEAR Annual award organised by the photographic company Ilford. Heather McCartney (cf) won the award in 1980 and was presented with it at a special lunch on 19 November at London's Hilton Hotel. She was given the award for the printing of 'Waterfall', a picture she had taken of drummer Steve Gadd and his wife Carol standing under a waterfall on the island of Montserrat (cf) early in 1980.

YATES, KERRY Australian journalist whose meeting with Paul benfited her career. Glenn A Baker relates the event in his book *The Beatles Down Under*. Kerry was seventeen years old and was working for *Woman's Weekly* when the Beatles arrived in Sydney in June 1963. She was among the large group of reporters and photographers waiting in a corridor in the Sheraton Hotel, hoping to get a story on Paul as he was celebrating his twenty-second birthday. Paul decided to have a few words with the press, but as soon as he saw Kerry he went straight to her and invited her to his room for an interview. Kerry commented: "I had long blonde hair and a pink sweater and I must have stood out from all the grey and brown suits because Paul made a beeline right for me and invited me up to his room. He let my photographer take shots of him surrounded by his presents and the next week we ran one of them in colour on the front cover with my 'exclusive' story inside. For years I've been asked what I had to do to get that scoop, which really did help my career. I know that everyone wants to know but I'm not saying if I did or if I didn't." (See also *Sunday Beatle).*

YESTERDAY Arguably Paul's most famous song, it first appeared on *Help!* in August 1965 and was the title track of a 1966 EP. It resurfaced later in 1966 on *A Collection of Beatles Oldies (But Goldies)* and on the 1973 album *The Beatles 1962-1966*. It was finally released as a single in Britain on 8 March 1976 on Apple R6013 with 'I Should Have Known Better' on the flip. It was included on the 1977 *Love Songs* album and on the 1980 album *The Beatles Ballads* and *The Beatles Box*. In America it was issued as a single on Capitol 5498 on 13 September 1965 with 'Act Naturally' as the flip. Another American release was on the 1966 album *Yesterday and Today*.

For such a classic love ballad, it had a very unromantic working title — 'Scrambled Eggs' is what Paul called the number for the first few days of the song's gestation period. He'd woken up one morning with the tune in his head and immediately began to put it down on the piano. When it came time to record the number, it turned out to be something of a solo job as his vocals were only accompanied by a guitar and string quartet (John, George and Ringo were not present on the track). Paul commented: "First of all, I was just playing it through for everyone, saying: 'How do you like this song?' I played it just on my acoustic and sang it and the rest of the Beatles said, 'That's it, love it.' So George Martin and I got together and sort of cooked up this idea. I wanted just a small string accompaniment and he said, 'Well, how about your actual string quartet?' I said 'Great, it sounds great.' We sat down at the piano and cooked that one up. I was so proud of it, I felt it was an original tune, it didn't copy off anything and it was a big tune, it was all there and nothing repeated. I got made fun of because of it a bit. I remember George saying, 'Blimey, he's always talking about 'Yesterday', you'd think he was Beethoven or somebody.' But it's the one, I reckon that it's the most complete thing I've

Billy J Kramer — he turned down 'Yesterday', one of the most-recorded songs of all time

ever written."

Paul has been quoted as saying that 'Yesterday' is his favourite self-penned number and he has continued to use it in his solo years, performing it on both the Wings' world tour in 1975/76 and the British tour in 1977. It's also included on *Wings Over America* (cf).

At one time Paul offered it to singer Chris Farlowe. He also offered it to Billy J.Kramer. Both artists turned the song down. Kramer had approached Paul in Blackpool and asked him if he had a song suitable to record. Paul played him 'Yesterday', but Billy said the song wasn't what he was looking for. As it turned out, it became one of the most recorded songs of all time and within seven years of release there were 1,186 separate versions of the number on record. A million-seller within ten days of release in the States, it received the 1966 Ivor Novello Award (cf) in Britain as the Outstanding Song of the Year and in America it was the most performed pop song for eight consecutive years, from 1965-1973. Among the artists who have recorded 'Yesterday' on disc are Cilla Black, Pat Boone, Nat King Cole, Perry Como, Marianne Faithfull, Tom Jones, Otis Redding, Smokey Robinson and the Miracles, and Frank Sinatra.

YESTERDAYS WITH A GUITAR Painting of Paul by David Oxtoby which was featured in the 1984 'Art Of The Beatles' exhibition. In his book *Oxtoby's Rockers,* David commented on the painting: "It is a combination drawing of Paul with my yesterdays. The background contains drawings based on the works of many of my friends while the badges scattered across Paul's chest have names of other friends. The drawing was born out of a conversation with David Hockney who told me he was working on a series of etchings based on a poem inspired by a Picasso painting. I figured one thing missing from that sequence was a drawing."

YOU GAVE ME THE ANSWER Track on *Venus And Mars (cf)*. It was also used as the flip of the 'Letting Go' (cf) single and was included on *Wings Over America (cf)*. Paul performed the number on stage during the Wings' world tour of 1975/76 and often dedicated this particular number to actor/dancer Fred Astaire.

YOU NEVER GIVE ME YOUR MONEY Number penned by Paul for the Beatles 1969 album *Abbey Road* (cf). The theme was inspired by the financial problems of Apple.

YOU'RE SIXTEEN Number written by Robert and Richard Sherman that had given Johnny Burnette a million-seller in 1960 and Ringo Starr a multi-million seller in February 1974. It was also included on the *Ringo* album. The track included a kazoo passage by Paul. Paul had been played the tapes of the album by producer Richard Perry and he felt that it needed something extra. He played the kazoo, a small mouth instrument which can produce a tinny sound that people used to imitate with a comb wrapped in paper, but which in this instance sounded almost like a saxophone.

YOU'VE GOT TO HIDE YOUR LOVE AWAY Number written by John Lennon and featured on *Help!* It provided the Silkie, a Brian Epstein-managed group, with a chart hit on the Fontana label. John and Paul produced the single and Paul played guitar on it.

ZENITH The first guitar Paul owned and one which he still possesses. He'd been presented with a trumpet by his father, but wasn't too keen on the instrument because he couldn't play it and sing at the same time, so he swopped the trumpet for a Zenith guitar. Initially, he had difficulty playing it, until he realised that a left-handed player had to reverse the strings, which he did. (See also *Rickenbacker.*)

THE ZOO GANG British television series starring Lili Palmer which was first screened in 1974. Paul penned the title song for the series and recorded it with Wings. It was issued as the flipside to 'Band On The Run' in June 1974.

Index